D1740536

Liminality of the Japanese Empire

 **Perspectives on the Global Past**

Anand A. Yang and Kieko Matteson
SERIES EDITORS

Liminality of the Japanese Empire

Border Crossings from Okinawa to Colonial Taiwan

Hiroko Matsuda

University of Hawai'i Press
Honolulu

Printed in the United States of America

24 23 22 21 20 19 6 5 4 3 2 1

Library of Congress Cataloging-in-Publication Data

Names: Matsuda, Hiroko, author.
Title: Liminality of the Japanese empire : border crossings from Okinawa to colonial Taiwan / Hiroko Matsuda.
Other titles: Perspectives on the global past.
Description: Honolulu : University of Hawaii Press, [2019] | Series: Perspectives on the global past | Includes bibliographical references and index.
Identifiers: LCCN 2018021985 | ISBN 9780824867560 (cloth ; alk. paper)
Subjects: LCSH: Ryukywuans—Taiwan—History—19th century. | Ryukyuans—Taiwan—History—20th century. | Ryukyu Islands—Emigration and immigration. | Taiwan—Emigration and immigration.
Classification: LCC DS799.43.R98 M38 2019 | DDC 305.8956—dc23
LC record available at https://lccn.loc.gov/2018021985

Cover art: A man against the background of Taiwan Island. Photo by Motohashi Seiichi

University of Hawai'i Press books are printed on acid-free paper and meet the guidelines for permanence and durability of the Council on Library Resources.

Contents

Illustrations, Maps, and Tables

Figures

Maps

Tables

Acknowledgments

This project became a book over the course of many years. I would like to first thank the interviewees for sharing their life stories with me. I am grateful for the cooperation of the members of Okinawa Taiwan-kai (Taiwan Association in Okinawa) and Shōwachō-kai (Association for Former Residents of Showa District). Regrettably, I cannot express my gratitude to those who have passed away in recent years.

I began this project at the Australian National University graduate school and gratefully acknowledge the enormous support of Jindy Pettman, Helen Keane, and Rosanne Kennedy during the first stage of my doctoral program. I am greatly indebted to Tessa Morris-Suzuki, Tamara Jacka, and Li Narangoa for their insightful guidance and warm encouragement while I was writing my dissertation. Thanks are also due to the students in the gender, sexuality, and culture program and the Research School of Pacific and Asian Studies for providing inspiration and warm friendship.

During my fieldwork on the islands of Okinawa Prefecture, numerous local historians, intellectuals, and librarians helped me come to grips with the issues involved in my research. The librarians of Ishigaki Municipal Library, Okinawa Prefectural Library, and Okinawa Prefectural Archives offered generous assistance over the course of this project. I am especially indebted to Miki Takeshi, Tokunō Toshimi, and Īda Yasuhiko for kindly offering valuable resources and information. While I was continuing my studies in Taiwan after completing my doctorate, Lu Kikuno and her family made Taipei my second home. I would like to particularly thank You Yunxia, Chen Shuan, Yan Xinru, Andy Wang, Yamamoto Kazuyuki, Huang Chih-huei, Pien Feng-kwei, Takenaka Nobuko, and Dominic Yang for helping me learn about Taiwanese history. Chang Lung-chih offered me much support when I was affiliated with the Institute of Taiwan History, Academia Sinica. As I learned what it means to produce a "national history" there, I am especially grateful for the hospitality and friendship of the members of its Cultural History Group.

Asia Research Institute at the National University of Singapore provided me with generous support and assistance as a postdoctoral fellow.

Friendly conversations and discussions with scholars in the various fields of Asian studies broadened my horizons. Special appreciation is due for the constant intellectual stimulation and helpful cooperation offered by Chua Beng-huat, Allen Chun, Wasana Wongsurawat, Michelle Miller, Liew Khai Khiun, Cho Younghan, and Ronit Ricci.

Additionally, I am extremely grateful for several opportunities to participate in joint research projects in Japan. I owe a large debt of gratitude to Araragi Shinzō for his generous support and encouragement. Participation in his research group provided many opportunities to meet scholars working on different forms of international migration. I also profited immensely from discussions with research group members. It was my privilege to work with Noiri Naomi, Matsuda Yoshitaka, Mizuta Kenji, and Kuninaga Michiko and coedit a Japanese book on relations between Yaeyama and Taiwan for a general audience. I cannot thank them enough for sharing their thoughts on the histories of Okinawa and Taiwan. Participation in Fujiwara Ken'ichi's research group on the history of Okinawan teachers also enabled me to consider my research from a different angle.

This book would not have materialized without the assistance of many scholars, editors, and anonymous reviewers. Edith Kaneshiro, Romit Dasgupta, Azuma Eiichirō, and Anand Yang have given me insightful advice on compiling and publishing my research in a scholarly book. Two anonymous reviewers offered excellent suggestions for improving the manuscript. Sharon Loo and Laura Iwasaki have been of great help in polishing my English-language writing and editing the manuscript. I have been extremely fortunate to have a chance to work with Masako Ikeda, my editor at University of Hawai'i Press, who kindly assisted in the preparation of this manuscript.

Financial support from JSPS KAKENHI Grant Numbers 10J02933 and 25885110 allowed me to work on this project while moving across several cities and countries. Over the years, so many people have contributed to the making of this book that I cannot possibly thank them all. However, I must particularly thank the following people for their valuable scholarly comments and special words of encouragement at different stages of this project: Sasaki Motoe, Hosihina Hironobu, Timothy Tsu, Ōta Atsushi, Lee Hyunjung, Īјima Mariko, Mori Akiko, Nagura Kyōko, Kobayashi Hiroshi, and Doi Tomoyoshi. My current colleagues at Kobe Gakuin University deserve a special mention for providing a supportive environment in which to complete the manuscript's final preparations. I am also indebted to the university librarians for their excellent assistance. Finally, I would like to thank my parents, Kayoko and Kazuo, and my sister, Keiko, for their unfailing support and understanding. Without them, I could not have continued this intellectual exploration.

Note on Asian Languages

Chinese, Taiwanese, and Japanese personal names are given in the text in the customary order, family name first. Works published in English by Chinese, Taiwanese, and Japanese authors are given in Western order, surname last. Chinese is romanized in pinyin unless the English-language work has employed a different system. Very well-known Chinese, Taiwanese, and Japanese cities and districts use the customary English spelling (e.g., Keelung, Taipei, Tokyo), and the rest are romanized using pinyin or as pronounced in Japanese. Japanese names of Taiwanese cities in proper nouns (e.g., Taihoku Imperial University) are romanized by Japanese pronunciation.

Introduction

On December 1, 2011, the Ryukyuan fisherman statue was unveiled in Heping Marine Park in Keelung City in northern Taiwan, where the largest Okinawan fisher community was located during the Japanese colonial era. The statue was a gift from Okinawan residents, former residents living in Taiwan and their descendants, and entrepreneurs who regarded Taiwan as an important export market for Okinawan products and wished to improve business relations with it. More than fifty Okinawans, including the mayor of Miyakojima City, many Taiwanese, Keelung government officials, and the mayor of Keelung City, participated in the unveiling ceremony. At the time the statue was erected, Heping Marine Park was in the midst of redevelopment, and when redevelopment was complete, it was expanded and equipped with modern amusement facilities. The Ryukyuan fisherman statue is situated in an open square inside the park, as though it is the symbol of the redeveloped marine park. Although tourists are not likely to take the statue seriously, the Ryukyuan fisherman monument provides the site with its historical identity.

Interestingly, the engraving beneath the monument makes no reference to the Japanese occupation or Japanese exploitation of Taiwanese land. Instead, it emphasizes the gratitude present-day Okinawans feel toward the Taiwanese for their "generosity" in allowing Okinawan colonial immigrants to settle on their land. In other words, the Ryukyuan fisherman statue best embodies the officially recognized and idealized historical identities of contemporary Okinawa and Heping Island. Both the Keelung Municipal Government and the Keelung Municipal Council recognized the monument as a suitable symbol of the new park. Their acceptance and recognition of the statue may have been due to the fact that it depicts an Okinawan instead of a Japanese. As Okinawans are an ethnic minority in Japan and discriminated against by the Japanese, they are deemed to have undergone discrimination similar to that experienced by the Taiwanese under Japanese rule. For that reason, the Okinawans, who had settled in Keelung during Japanese colonization, are perceived as less dominant and exploitative than the

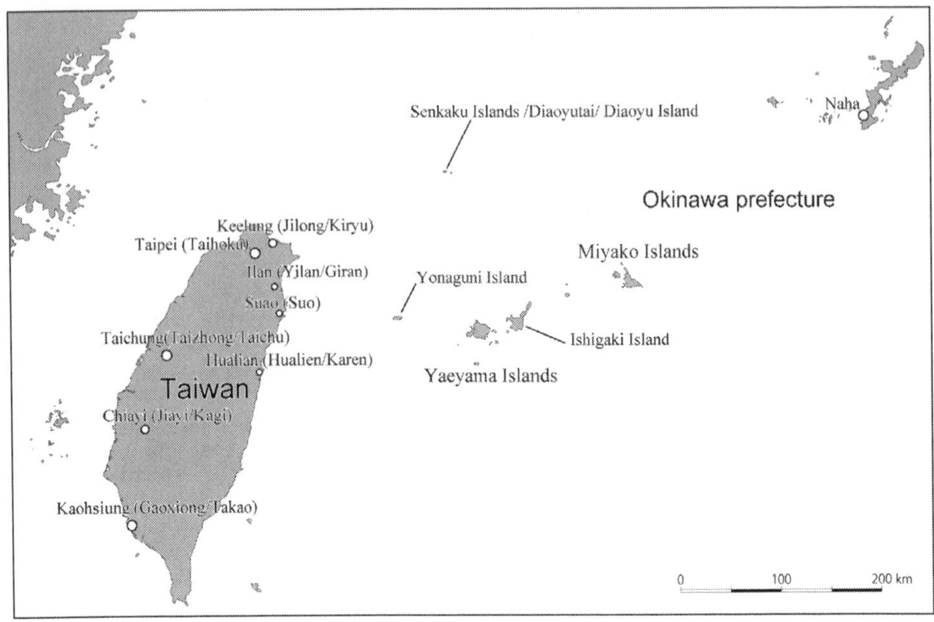

Taiwan and Okinawa Prefecture. Map by Mizuta Kenji.

Ryukyuan fisherman's statue, Heping Marine Park, Keelung. Photo by author.

Japanese. Moreover, Ryukyuan fishermen are regarded as modernizers and educators who selflessly impart their fishing techniques to Taiwanese fishermen. The peaceful coexistence between Taiwanese and Okinawan fishers also fits very well with both the contemporary Taiwanese discourse of multiculturalism and Keelung City's official self-image as a great international port city.

Invaders, colonizers, modernizers, educators, ethnic minority, and friends of the Taiwanese are among the many faces of Okinawans represented by the Ryukyuan fisherman statue; thus, it demonstrates the many different interpretations of the Okinawan immigrants' reasons for residing in Taiwan. Above all, the erection of the statue proves that Okinawan migrants are remembered as uniquely important subjects and should be distinguished from other Japanese migrants who arrived during the colonial period. This book aims to give a historical account of Okinawan migrants in Taiwan under Japanese colonial rule. By showcasing the particular experiences of Okinawans who made their careers in colonial Taiwan, this book provides an alternative to Japanese imperialist nationalism.

The ideology of Japanese nation building in the late nineteenth century is often characterized as "imperialist nationalism." Nationalism contradicts imperialism by definition: the former advocates equality and solidarity among a nation of "community" members, and the latter emphasizes the difference between the ruler and the ruled in order to justify domination and exploitation of one by the other. Nonetheless, survival in the competitive capitalist world of the late nineteenth century necessitated the amalgamation of nationalism and imperialism, so much so that the resulting ideology became the driving force of Japan's imperialistic expansion.[1] Japan's annexation of the Ryukyu Kingdom is the most common example of Japanese imperial and official nationalism. Although the Edo Bakufu, the government of the Tokugawa Shogunate, recognized the Ryukyu Kingdom's subordination to the Shimazu Domain, it did not consider the Ryukyu Islands to be an integral part of its territory. Early modern Japan had an isolationist policy and never felt an urgent need to clarify the borders between Japan and its neighboring countries. However, the international climate compelled the newly established Meiji government to reconsider the status of the Ryukyus. Though the region had been dominated by a Sinocentric world order for centuries, it eventually yielded to pressure from the Western powers to adopt the nation-state system. Accordingly, the Meiji government decided to end the Ryukyu Kingdom's tributary relationship with Qing China and formally annex it to Japan. Even though the Ryukyu Islands were incorporated into the Japanese nation, today these acts are considered the first step in Japanese imperial expansion.

The annexation of Okinawa raises the fundamental question of whether Okinawa—administratively one of the Japanese prefectures—should be regarded as an internal colony rather than an integral part of the Japanese nation.[2] There is no scholarly consensus on Okinawa's status in the late nineteenth and early twentieth centuries. Prasenjit Duara calls Okinawa "neither colony nor quite of the nation."[3] Benedict Anderson interprets Japanese nationalism of the time as an official nationalism that was "a means for combining naturalization with retention of dynastic power, in particular over the huge polyglot domains accumulated since the Middle Ages, or, to put it another way, for stretching the short, tight, skin of the nation over the gigantic body of the empire."[4] While the Ryukyu Islands may be compared to a "seam" of this short, tight skin, the analogy best demonstrates the liminality of the Japanese Empire. This book illustrates the ways in which Japanese imperialist nationalism made the Ryukyu Islands the liminal zone and the extent to which liminality defined Okinawan migration to colonial Taiwan.

The concept of liminality was first theorized by Arnold van Gennep, a French anthropologist known for his unique analysis of ceremonial processes. In his seminal book *The Rites of Passage,* he discusses the schema of the rite of passage as it proceeds from preliminal rites (rites of separation), to liminal rites (rites of transition), to postliminal rites (rites of incorporation).[5] By theorizing rites of passage, he posits that transitional moments can be observed universally. An English social anthropologist, Victor W. Turner, subsequently developed van Gennep's theory conceptually by applying the idea of liminality to a variety of contexts in order to analyze the traditional ceremonies of primitive societies and understand the different human conditions and activities in modern societies. Turner articulates the notion of liminality thus: "The attributes of liminality or of liminal personae ('threshold people') are necessarily ambiguous, since this condition and these persons elude or slip through the network of classifications that normally locate states and positions in cultural space. Liminal entities are neither here nor there; they are betwixt and between the positions assigned and arrayed by law, custom, convention, and ceremonial."[6] Turner encountered van Gennep's study on rites of passage when he was investigating the traditions of the Ndembu of northwestern Zambia in the 1950s. In applying liminality to his analysis of Ndembu rituals, he frequently makes comparisons to cases in Western societies.[7] Consequently, he opened the possibility of applying liminality to the study of larger-scale modern societies.

Anthropologists, sociologists, historians, social scientists, and other scholars in the humanities are still inspired by Turner and have utilized the concept of liminality in their studies. Indeed, liminality may be applied to transitional moments or periods of both single individuals and larger groups such as cohorts and villages or to whole societies. Moments of liminality may be very brief, or they could last a week, a year, or even longer.[8] Some historians of modern empires use liminality to explain certain groups of people and communities that cannot fit into existing historical categories. These studies typically are interested in the in-between colonial subjects such as multiracial people, poor white settlers who did not fit into the idealized image of the rulers, and native people who collaborated with colonial authorities and took part in colonial policies.[9]

Increasing scholarly interest in the liminal subjects of modern empires is not irrelevant to the general trend of colonial studies of the past couple of decades. For the longest time, "metropole" and "colony" were solid historical categories in colonial studies, and the metropole was deemed to be unquestionably superior. Yet contemporary scholars now seek to present a more dynamic picture of modern empires by exploring the metropole and colonies within a single analytic framework. Ann Laura Stoler and other contemporary colonialism scholars have shown that the superiority of the colonizers was neither inherent nor stable.[10] Instead of studying European domination through the traditionally accepted categories of the colonizers and the colonized, they suggest that scholars examine the very process in which these categories were created with the intent of justifying European superiority over colonized Asian and African nations. Contemporary scholars of Japanese colonial history are similarly interested in the liminal subjects of Japanese empire.[11] Placing this book in a cohort of colonial histories that focus on the in-between subjects allows me to offer an alternative approach to Japanese Empire by exploring it through the eyes of people living in the southern border islands of the Japanese nation.[12]

Numerous books and articles on Okinawa have been published to date, but many of these studies identify Okinawa as the "periphery," "internal colony," or "margins" of the Japanese nation—an identification that holds true even in those that consider Okinawa in relation to countries other than Japan.[13] By utilizing the concept of liminality, this volume sheds light on the malleable nature of the relationship between the ruler and the ruled. In so doing, it will not only demonstrate the marginalization of the Ryukyuan people within the Japanese Empire but also illustrate their dynamic use of the border between the Inner Territory and the Outer Territories.

Liminality and National Borders

In short, *Liminality of the Japanese Empire* focuses on the manner in which common people lived in the borderland between the nation and the colony during the late nineteenth and early twentieth centuries. The borderland paradoxically creates distinctions between the nation and the colony while simultaneously generating interactions across them. This book will explore that paradox by uncovering the distinctions and interactions created by the people living in the borderland.

Border studies are currently among the subjects of most interest in the humanities and social sciences. The history of border studies goes back to the 1960s, when scholars from various disciplines started to question the passive nature of territorial and sovereign borders in the age of decolonization and national independence. The end of the Cold War, followed by the rapid increase in human interactions and mobility accompanying globalization, further impelled scholars to reconsider the nature of borders and boundaries.[14] Traditionally, border studies were dominated by legal, geographical, or geopolitical scholarship that usually adopted the views of governments and other political authorities.[15] Yet scholars in other disciplines are increasingly paying attention to those social dynamics and historical development in border regions that are not necessarily related to the intentions of the "center."[16] *Liminality of the Japanese Empire* aligns with such recent developments by exploring the unanticipated social consequences of the Japanese national border as it overlapped the boundary delimiting the nation and the colony.

In studies on Japanese history, Japanese national boundaries have long been considered natural, due to the country's geographical isolation, and thus were not the subject of scholarly investigations. Recent works in both Japanese and English have challenged the static image of Japanese borders by revealing the extent to which these boundaries were historically constructed rather than established by nature.[17] Furthermore, the territorial disputes along Japanese borders in recent years have caused Japanese scholars and journalists to debate the exact borders and boundaries of Japan and Northeast Asia.[18] While the mass media highlight territorial disputes over the Diayutai/Senkaku Islands, some Japanese anthropologists and journalists have discovered that the close, dynamic interactions between the people of Okinawa and neighboring countries have been overshadowed by diplomatic conflicts.[19] Additionally, some recently published books delve into the survival of the common people in the borderlands immediately after the fall of the Japanese Empire.[20] However, these studies focus on the circumstances of the immediate postwar period and do not cover the border shifts that occurred between Japan's annexation of the Ryukyus and the beginning of US military rule in Okinawa.

As Edward Said points out, discourses of modern imperialism divide us from them.[21] Contemporary historians of the empires of Western Europe have examined the borders of these empires by distinguishing them from the national borders of the metropoles.[22] In East Asia, however, the borders between the metropolitan nation and the colony were intertwined with the everyday lives of people who lived in the frontier zone. While social practices were constrained by the border, people also produced and reproduced it. This is, as Hannah Arendt puts it, a product of "continental imperialism" whereby colonizers dominate those who are geographically close and culturally akin.[23] This book sheds light on the Japanese national border zone where the politics of distinction between colonial rulers and colonized subjects were closely intertwined with people's everyday lives.

While many works on Japanese borders and boundaries have been published in the past two decades, Oguma Eiji's *Boundaries of "the Japanese"* (*Nihonjin no kyōkai*) may be the most relevant to this study. In questioning the preexisting divide between "Japan" and "the colonies," Oguma analyzes how policy and political discourses shifted the notions of "Japan/Japanese" and "the colonies." In other words, he examines the discursive construction of the boundaries of Japan/Japanese by opinion leaders, intellectuals, and policy makers in the late nineteenth and early twentieth centuries.[24] Oguma's book is rightly titled *Boundaries of "the Japanese,"* as his emphasis is on the discursive construction of the boundaries of Japan/Japanese rather than an investigation of the people on the national border. Although I agree with him that the notions of Japan/Japanese and the colonies should not be presumed, our research methods vis-à-vis the boundaries are vitally different.

In this book, the term "boundary" indicates discursive limits or lines that are not limited to physcial borders, whereas the word "border" refers to geographical borders. Moreover, *Liminality of the Japanese Empire* takes an ethnographic approach to the border islands rather than exploring policy and political discourses because I share the view that "we can properly understand the often unintended and unanticipated social consequences of national borders only by focusing on border regions."[25] This volume analyzes the intricate relationship between the geographical border and the boundaries of Japan and the Japanese by examining the narratives and practices of people living in the border zone.

The circumstances of Okinawans could be compared to those of the Irish in the British colonial empire. It has been pointed out that the two have some commonalities—both were colonized by people who were racially akin to them and were their geographically proximate neighbors; both sent a number of emigrants overseas against a backdrop of poverty, underdevelopment, and increasing population. Ireland is often deemed the first victim of British colonial expansion, yet recent developments in British imperial history have revealed that the Irish—as merchants, adventurers, soldiers, administrators, missionaries, and other professionals—have played active roles in the expansion of the British Empire.[26] This refreshing viewpoint is certainly helpful in understanding Okinawa's ambivalent position as "not only a half-hearted colony" but "also a half-hearted component of the imperial metropolis."[27] Nevertheless, there is an apparent contrast between the Irish and the Okinawans in terms of their respective colonial empires. As part of the so-called maritime empire, the connections of Ireland's local communities to the British colonies were partial and indirect, if not insignificant. In contrast, Okinawa's local communities maintained close and direct connections with the colony next door. Unlike the majority of colonial and postcolonial studies on liminality that focus on the colonial/colonized individuals, this volume illustrates the experiences of Okinawa's local communities as they straddled the space between the Inner Territory and Outer Territories of the Japanese Empire.

Okinawa and Japanese Settler Colonialism in Taiwan

Mass migration from the countryside to the expanding cities is one of Okinawa's most tangible modern phenomena in the early twentieth century, as it was closely associated with rapid growth in the production of goods for exchange, the rise of the money economy, and the development of specialized division of labor. According to Steve Rabson, large-scale migration from Okinawa to Mainland Japan began around 1900; by 1940, there were 88,319 Okinawans residing in Mainland Japan, accounting for approximately 15 percent of the prefecture's residential population.[28] Due to the increased popularity of mass migration overseas from the 1900s onward, 10 percent of the residential population was living abroad by 1940. Earlier studies have already shown the financial, social, and political importance of mass migration from Okinawa to Mainland Japan in the early twentieth century.[29] However, little attention has been paid to the uniqueness of migration to Taiwan, modern Japan's first settler colony.

After Qing China sued for peace and the Treaty of Shimonoseki (also known as the Maguan Treaty) was concluded in April 1895, Fukuzawa Yukichi—one of the most influential political thinkers of modern Japan—presented his ideas on the principles of Japanese rule over Taiwan:

> Throughout history, foreign states were interested in Taiwan for different reasons. Some established fortresses along the coast and developed military ports to serve their own military vessels. Others reclaimed lands and developed industries for commercial purposes. They intended to appropriate Taiwan for the maintenance of particular purposes. In contrast, Japan

> acquired Taiwan by chance as a result of the Sino-Japanese War. . . . Today, everybody recognizes the need for Japanese emigration overseas. Hence, the ultimate goal of Taiwan's cession is to gain its land and to bring Japanese people onto it. It is clear that our target is the land, and not the people, of Taiwan.[30]

This statement indicates that Taiwan was intended for settler colonialism, which is characterized by "the dispensability of the indigenous person."[31] Although there are variations in settler colonialism, the phenomenon should be distinguished from imperialism and colonialism in the sense that "the presence of a settler population [is] intent on making a territory their permanent home while continuing to enjoy metropolitan living standards and political privileges."[32] While settler colonialism is closely associated with colonialism and migration, it is not the same as either of them. According to Lorenzo Veracini, settlers should be distinguished from immigrants, as they are "founders of political orders and carry their sovereignty with them," whereas migrants are "individually co-opted within settler colonial political regimes" and do not "enjoy inherent rights and are characterized by a defining lack of sovereign entitlement."[33]

For instance, Japanese labor immigrants in the United States should be distinguished from white Western European settlers. The Japanese immigrants made great contributions to settler colonialism in the United States but did not enjoy the same inherent rights as white European settlers, as they were co-opted within settler-colonial political regimes.[34] In contrast, Japanese immigrants in Japan's own colonies maintained a different status. The Japanese were certainly the founders of their colonial order and enjoyed inherent rights in Taiwan, Korea, and Manchuria.[35] However, it is doubtful that all these Okinawans were "colonial settlers" who intended to make Taiwan their permanent home.

When Japan lost World War II in August 1945, there were approximately 320,000 Japanese civilians and 160,000 military personnel in Taiwan, about 25,000 to 30,000 of whom had registered their addresses in Okinawa Prefecture. These people were fairly diverse. Some had emigrated from Okinawa before the war broke out, others were drafted and came to Taiwan as members of the Japanese military, and still others were born in Taiwan as second- or third-generation Okinawan immigrants or settlers. It should be emphasized that these Okinawans were involved in both temporary and long-term Japanese settler colonialism,[36] which was integral to the Japanese rule of Taiwan for fifty years. Nevertheless, it is hardly possible to identify all Okinawans in Taiwan as either "settlers" or "migrants." While Jun Uchida and other scholars of Japanese history question the Europeancentric definition of settler colonialism,[37] this book further reconsiders the nature of settler colonialism by highlighting the Okinawans' subjectivities and forms of agency through the notion of "imperial careering." In this, I emphasize an individual migrant's agency in using the imperial structure for the purpose of establishing himself or herself in life or for making advancements. While Okinawans are noted as settlers and immigrants or migrants in this volume, the distinction between the categories is blurred, and the categories also overlap.

When the Kuomintang (KMT) government took over Taiwan, the country's former Japanese colonizers were told to leave for their "home country." However, the US government did not allow them to land on Okinawa Island. While other Japanese were sent back to Mainland Japan in early 1946, Okinawans were left behind without knowing when and where they were going to resettle. In October 1946, more than a year after the end of World War II, there were still more than 10,000 Okinawans stranded in Taiwan. Some of the elite took on leadership roles by organizing the Association for People from Okinawa, or Okinawan Association, a mutual aid society, and petitioned the US government to improve the situation of Okinawans left behind in Taiwan.

More than 120,000 Okinawans, including over 94,000 civilians, died during the devastatingly fierce battle on Okinawa.[38] As a result, Okinawa lost many men, not only those who held leadership positions during the war but those who would have become society's leaders in the future. Moreover, most of the settlers from Mainland Japan islands, who had occupied executive positions, left Okinawa before the battle. In contrast, most Okinawan immigrants in colonial Taiwan had escaped the battle and could be safely repatriated to their home islands after the war. In October 1946, before official repatriations from Taiwan to Okinawa began, the American consulate in Taipei foresaw the potential for future leadership roles for the Taiwan repatriates: "The receptive and articulate leaders among 10,000 Okinawans on Taiwan may well become leaders of influence after repatriation. They are demonstrating a capacity for organization and leadership. The management for Okinawan affairs (Okinawan Association), voluntarily set up, has minimized difficult problems of administration and public order and welfare."[39]

As the American officer had predicted, some of the repatriates took up leadership positions. For instance, Yara Chōbyō (1902–1997), the first democratically elected governor of the Ryukyu Islands under US occupation, who later became the first governor of Okinawa Prefecture after returning to Japan in 1972, was an Okinawan repatriate from Taiwan. He is one of the most well-known Okinawans and frequently noted in Okinawan modern history books. Yet very few historians have paid serious attention to the fact that he had moved to colonial Taiwan in 1938 and worked as a high school teacher until the end of the war. Therefore, *Liminality of the Japanese Empire* aims to articulate the tangled threads of Okinawan local history and Japanese imperial history, which are conventionally studied as two separate fields. By focusing on Okinawan migration during and after the Japanese imperial period, this book demonstrates how Okinawa's modernity has been entangled with Japanese colonialism in Taiwan.

Indeed, the history of immigration to colonial Taiwan was little known in Japan until Matayoshi Seikiyo, an Okinawa-based local historian, published his seminal work *Taiwan and Okinawa under Japanese Colonial Rule* (*Nihon shokuminchika no Taiwan to Okinawa*) in 1990.[40] Since then, some geographers, sociologists, literalists, and historians have studied Okinawan migration to colonial Taiwan, in particular, groups of Okinawan immigrants during a certain period of time.[41] It can be said that Matayoshi's work is the most comprehensive work on Okinawan migration to colonial Taiwan to date. While I have learned much from the excellent archival and fieldwork research in Matayoshi's work, *Liminality of the Japanese Empire* provides an alternative understanding of the relationship between Japan, the Ryukyus or Okinawa, and Taiwan. In Matayoshi's book, the ethnic boundaries of the Japanese, Okinawans, and Taiwanese are predetermined, and the relationships between the three are mostly fixed. He presents the hierarchical relationships with the proper Japanese positioned as the superior, the Taiwanese as the inferior, and Okinawans between the two. However, Okinawa's unique position in Japan's colonial empire cannot be adequately understood through this inflexible hierarchical structure. To better understand Okinawans' place in the Japanese Empire, this volume emphasizes the liminal character of Okinawa and Okinawans instead of labeling them as second-class imperialists or colonialists inferior to the Japanese.

Memories of Liminal Subjects

As it has been frequently noted, lack of historical sources is the biggest obstacle to studying non-elite people. *Liminality of the Japanese Empire* uncovers the experiences of people from this border community by relying heavily on subjective documents that showcase individuals' views of their experiences. According to Virginia Yans-McLaughlin, subjective documents include autobiographies, life histories, letters, oral narratives, interviews, and court records.[42] By analyzing migration and ethnicity through oral history, Yans-McLaughlin stresses that subjective documents—whether written or orally produced—are collaborative constructs of informants and investigators, as well as the products of power relations. Employing Alfred Schutz's social hermeneutics theory, she came to two conclusions on social and historical inquiry. First, an interview should be considered not purely an act of discovering an informant's memory but also a social act in which the interviewer produces a text with the informant. Second, subjective documents should be interpreted within a larger context that comprises the social and cultural contexts, family lives, life experiences, educational experiences, and narrative traditions in which interviews between investigators and informants take place. When these aspects of an informant's narrative are taken into account, the subject matter of the oral interview is no longer merely a reflection of past reality; instead, it emerges from social interactions between the informant and the investigator as constructs of the former's self-representation.[43]

As there are limited written materials demonstrating the social and cultural conditions of Okinawa during the late nineteenth and early twentieth centuries, subjective documents are important to the reconstruction of the history of the boundary between Okinawa and Taiwan. In addition to examining local newspaper articles, government documents, and reports written by researchers of the time, I relied on autobiographies by former colonial settlers and oral historical materials to show how Okinawans left their home islands, spent their time in Taiwan, and were repatriated after World War II. I also conducted independent interviews with forty-four women and men on several of the Ryukyu Islands and Mainland Japan between 2003 and 2006 and 2008 and 2012 (see appendix). Each of these informants spent more than a year in Taiwan and repatriated to either Mainland Japan or the Ryukyu Islands under US military administration. These recorded interview materials were augmented by informal conversations with former immigrants to Taiwan.

From the time oral history became popular in the 1970s, compilation of the neglected experiences of non-elite classes has been the foremost justification for recording oral history. However, the credibility of oral histories has been seriously challenged by traditional historians who rely exclusively on document as sources.[44] In responding to skeptics, Alessandro Portelli argues, "Oral sources are credible, but with a different credibility."[45] He defends oral sources because they tell historians less about the actual chronology of a certain event and more about the meanings, imaginings, symbolisms, and desires of the individuals involved. Oral histories may not prove what people did, but they certainly reveal what people wanted to do and how they interpreted the events of the past.[46] The Popular Memory Group at the Birmingham Centre for Contemporary Cultural Studies, United

Kingdom, further discusses the complexity of oral historical sources by treating them as more than mere alternatives to documented materials. The Popular Memory Group acknowledges both the significance of oral sources and the inevitably relational nature that characterizes the study of popular memory or oral sources. Rather than understanding oral sources as a mere tool for reaching past events, they pay attention to the process by which popular memories are produced through everyday interactions as well as the effect of dominant historical discourses.[47] Having gone through this intellectual evolution, many present-day oral historians integrate memory studies into their historical investigations. In so doing, they provide a reflective account of memory production in their studies.

The oral historical materials directly quoted in this book are the narratives of those who were born in either Okinawa Prefecture or Taiwan and raised by parents with Okinawan backgrounds. Introductions from local residents provided my initial contacts with potential interviewees. I also approached individuals who had published accounts of their experiences in colonial Taiwan. Others were contacted by snowball sampling. I also met informants at the annual meetings of the Taiwan Association in Okinawa (Okinawa Taiwan-kai), which consists largely of Okinawan repatriates from Taiwan. Interviews were usually conducted individually and sometimes in groups of two to six people. Each interview ranged from an average of two hours to more than four hours. Some of the interviews were audio recorded, while others were recorded through note-taking. I am aware that interview materials are socially constructed through interactions between narrators and an investigator and that they are represented by an author with a particular interest. Nonetheless, rather than showing total unrepresentability here, I attempt to recover a past that has been ignored in previous historical studies.

As with people in many other regions and countries, memory has occupied a central position in Japan for the past two decades, not only among humanities and social science scholars but also in national and international political arenas. The multifarious debates over the Japanese politics of memory often involve court cases because they are invariably related to the claims of other Asian countries in relation to Japan's war responsibility. These heated debates have given rise to numerous books and articles on Japanese colonial and war memories,[48] yet historians rarely rely on oral historical material in reconstructing Japanese imperial history despite their recognition of the crucial roles played by ordinary Japanese during colonial rule. *Liminality of the Japanese Empire* is the first English-language book to explore Japanese colonial rule in Taiwan by relying heavily on the oral historical materials of former colonial migrants and settlers. It not only sheds light on Japanese colonial rule from their perspective but also reveals how the postcolonial discourses of former Okinawan migrants and settlers were constructed under the political and economic constraints of the imperial era and beyond.

Furthermore, contemporary Okinawan collective identity is shaped and maintained by memories of World War II, among both residents of Okinawa Prefecture and Okinawan diasporic communities.[49] These war memories are important to the maintenance of Okinawan identity because they highlight the differences between "Okinawans" and the "Japanese."[50] Most scholarly disputes arise from the fact that Okinawans' private and personal memories of the war are often at variance with Japanese public discourse and the "official" history of Japan. Through the memories of Okinawan colonial settlers, most of whom did not experience the tragic battle for the island, this study reveals not only the alternative war experience of the Okinawan people but also the way that these colonial memories are narrated in the politics of war memory in the public space of contemporary Okinawa.

Making Taiwan into a Japanese Settler Colony

Before proceeding, I should clarify the usages of the key terms in this volume, including "Ryukyu," "Okinawa," "Mainland Japan," "Inner Territory," and "Outer Territories." The geographical name "Ryukyu" appears in Chinese historical documents such as the *Book of Sui*, which was written in the seventh century. In the fifteenth century, "Ryukyu" became the official name of the kingdom unifying the archipelagos of Amami, Okinawa, Miyako, and Yaeyama, known today as the Ryukyu Islands or Southwest Islands. Under the Ryukyu Kingdom's rule, the name "Okinawa" indicated the main island of Okinawa and surrounding small islands. In 1872, Japan's Meiji government changed the kingdom's status to that of a domain (*han*) by fiat; the government then declared the abolishment of the kingdom and the establishment of Okinawa Prefecture in 1879. However, as Wendy Matsumura explains, the word "Okinawa" is not a neutral geographical title referring to a Japanese prefecture but a term that implies a cultural community distinct from the Japanese nation-state.[51] This volume loosely defines "Okinawans" as people whose families and relatives originated in Okinawa Prefecture or the Ryukyu Islands. The term "Okinawans" therefore encompasses people of diverse backgrounds, including those born in Okinawa Prefecture and those born and raised in Taiwan whose parents were born in Okinawa Prefecture. In fact, people from the Yaeyama and Miyako Islands often distinguish themselves from "Okinawans" even though they are part of Okinawa Prefecture, identifying themselves as people of Yaeyama and Miyako rather than as Okinawans. Nonetheless, in this volume, the term "Okinawans" includes people with Yaeyama and Miyako backgrounds unless otherwise indicated.

Likewise, in this volume, the term "Mainland Japan" loosely indicates the islands of Honshu, Shikoku, and Kyushu. As the following chapters reveal, the word "Japanese" occasionally includes and excludes "Okinawan." In other words, the social and cultural categories of "Japanese/the others" and "Okinawan/the others" have been persistent, although the categories are malleable and changeable. Mainland Japan is geographically ambiguous, but the notion of such a place suggests that Okinawans are "the others," as Mainland Japan was considered dominant over the local islanders. In Okinawa Prefecture, Mainland Japan has customarily been called the "Inner Territory" (Naichi). However, to avoid confusion, this volume defines the Inner Territory as the territory under the rule of the Meiji Constitution (Constitution of the Great Japanese Empire). The notion complements the idea of the "Outer Territories" (Gaichi), which refers to the territories excluded from the Meiji Constitution.

When the First Sino-Japanese War (1894–1895) ended, there were approximately 2,119,000 people living in Taiwan, excluding Taiwanese aborigines.[52] Although Taiwan had fallen under Qing Chinese rule in 1683, residents rarely developed a strong sense of Chinese identity, and there were frequent riots against the Qing government.[53] At the same time, they did not develop a group identity as Taiwanese because the island was dominated by several different regional authorities.[54] Much as the common Okinawans did not know about diplomatic negotiations over the Ryukyu Islands, the common Taiwanese were unaware of the outcome of the First Sino-Japanese War. The Taiwanese gentry and Qing officials dominating the island were indignant about the Qing government's decision to cede Taiwan to Japan even though Taiwan had scarcely been affected by the war. They appealed to the Qing government to reverse its decision but were ignored. Hoping to gain support from European countries, they resisted Japanese rule and declared independence as the Republic of Formosa on May 23, 1895. Two days later, on May 25, Tang Jing Song (Tang Ching-sung), the former governor of the Chinese province of Taiwan, was appointed president of the Republic of Formosa.[55]

Despite its determination, the Republic of Formosa did not have the military capacity to compete with Japan. Moreover, it comprised several different regional groups and was unable to present a united front in opposing Japanese rule. On May 29, the Japanese landed on Taiwan and were met by Taiwanese private armies, which proved ineffective against the Japanese military. On June 7, without engaging in armed conflict, the Japanese military entered Taipei Castle, formerly occupied by the government of the Chinese province of Taiwan. Tang Jing Song fled to Amoy (present-day Xiamen), and the Republic of Formosa fell. In its place, the Japanese established the Colonial Government of Taiwan (Taiwan Sōtokufu) inside Taipei Castle and held the ceremony inaugurating Japanese rule on June 17.[56]

Despite the official inauguration, the Taiwanese never ceased fighting against Japanese rule. The first governor-general, Kabayama Sukenori, spent another five months suppressing a number of small- and large-scale revolts across the island before declaring victory over Taiwan.[57] By the end of March 1896, Japan had marshaled approximately fifty thousand soldiers and twenty-six thousand military laborers. An estimated thirty-three thousand Taiwanese had joined the resistance by mid-May 1895, but it is unclear how many had lost their lives by then.[58] In addition to the Sino-Japanese War, the Japanese fought another war with Taiwanese residents and managed to conquer the island by killing thousands. The rebels were composed not only of local bandits and former Qing Chinese soldiers who remained in Taiwan after the end of the Sino-Japanese War but also of ordinary Taiwanese who had hitherto avoided politics and armed conflicts.[59] In the early stage of Japanese rule, Japanese administrators found it particularly difficult to communicate with local residents, as few Japanese comprehended the local languages and few Taiwanese understood Japanese at that time. The resultant miscommunications and misunderstandings created tension and frustration. Moreover, the tyranny of the Japanese and their sense of superiority exacerbated local Taiwanese anger, which led them to participate in violent resistance activities.[60]

Having observed the colonial government struggling to control local resistance without making any headway, concern grew as to whether it was worth Japan's while to hold on to a colony that created trouble rather than benefit. Japan had not fought the Sino-Japanese War in order to win Taiwan, but the cession of the island was an unsought gain from its victory. Japanese public opinion on the first colony turned favorable only after Kodama Gentarō and Gotō Shimpei took their positions in the colonial government.[61]

Still, for the first ten years of Japanese rule, there were various legal and political concerns about Taiwan's status. The Constitution of the Great Japanese Empire, or Meiji Constitution, promulgated on February 11, 1889, did not include any articles on changes of sovereign territories. While the colonial government struggled to suppress the Taiwanese rebels, the Tokyo government continued to search for the best political direction in governing Taiwan. At that time, two very different options were proposed: first, Taiwan should be ruled as a "colony"; second, Taiwan should not be ruled as colony but should have institutions that were slightly different from those of the Inner Territory. It was suggested that many European powers took the first option in governing their colonies, and should Japan adopt it vis-à-vis Taiwan, it would allow the colonial government to hold legislative power while Taiwan maintained relative autonomy. The second option was understood to be similar to German rule of Alsace-Lorraine and French rule of Algeria. This policy was grounded on the idea that there should not be a big gap between Taiwan and the Inner Territory.[62] In the end, on March 30, 1896, the Act on the Enforcement of Laws and Orders in Taiwan, commonly known as Law Title 63 or Law No. 63, was issued. Law Title 63 stipulates that Taiwan is excluded from the Meiji Constitution, but delegates legislative power over the island to the colonial government of Taiwan.[63]

After suppressing several Taiwanese rebellions against Japanese colonial rule, the fourth governor-general, Kodama Gentarō, along with Councilor of Civil Affairs Gotō Shimpei, inaugurated various projects designed to improve infrastructure and establish the foundation of colonial industries to come. As the Japanese population grew, the number of shops and restaurants increased, and entertainment industries flourished. For the first ten years, colonial Taiwan was considered not a territory where families settled down but a place where Japanese men went on their own to seek their fortunes for a short period of time. Work opportunities for women were fairly limited, so most Japanese women in Taiwan worked in the entertainment industry.

In an attempt to restore order in Taiwan, Governor-General Kodama reformed the police system and implemented the *hokō* system, based on the Chinese *baojia* system, which introduced community-based law enforcement and civil control integrated with public police authority. Due to Kodama's successful security policies, local rebels and resistance activities initiated by Han Chinese were largely suppressed by 1902.[64] According to Japanese records, 8,300 rebels were arrested between 1897 and 1901, and 3,473 were executed.[65] While the governors-general of Taiwan were fighting the Han Chinese insurgents, it took a nonviolent and placatory approach with the aborigines in mountainous areas. After Japanese troops quelled the uprisings, Sakuma Samata, who was appointed fifth governor-general in 1906, shifted the government's focus to conquering the aborigines. The colonial government spent 16 million yen and carried out a five-year plan for conquering the most insubordinate aborigine communities between 1910 and 1914. After marshaling about ten thousand soldiers and policemen, the colonial government managed to take control of aborigine communities across the island.[66]

Chapter Outlines

The following chapters focus on Okinawa and Taiwan after the suppression of both Han Taiwanese and Taiwanese aboriginal resistance. Okinawa is known as the prefecture of emigration (*iminken*), so it is possible to claim that crossing the border to colonial Taiwan was one form of Okinawan population movement overseas in the early twentieth century. By comparing migrations to other popular destinations, including the Philippines and the South Sea Islands, chapter 1 elucidates the characteristics of Okinawan immigration to colonial Taiwan. It begins by illustrating how Tōyama Kyūzō, a pro-democracy campaigner, initiated the enterprise of sending Okinawan indentured laborers to sugar plantations in Hawaiʻi. Because of their economic success, overseas immigration became popular among ordinary islanders across Okinawa Prefecture. After the United States closed its doors to Asian immigrant labor, Brazil, the Philippines, and the South Sea Islands became the most popular destinations for Okinawans, partly because immigration agencies recruited Okinawans to work for certain industries in these destinations. In contrast, neither the government nor private agencies recruited Okinawans to work for industries in Taiwan. Consequently, Okinawans in colonial Taiwan came from diverse social and regional backgrounds, and they were associated with various industries. By comparing the similarities and differences of immigrants in the other major destinations, chapter 1 illustrates the overall picture of Okinawan immigrants in colonial Taiwan.

Chapter 2 focuses on emigration from the Yaeyama region, which is known for sending a number of immigrants to colonial Taiwan between the 1920s and early 1940s. Before the First Sino-Japanese War, Yaeyama—located at the southwestern end of the Ryukyu Islands—was the only tropical region in Japanese territory. Its uncultivated lands attracted people from Mainland Japan and the main island of Okinawa. After Taiwan was ceded to Japan, the Yaeyama Islands became the borderland between the Inner Territory and the Outer Territories, the lands belonging to the Japanese Empire. The chapter explores the local history of Yaeyama following the annexation of the Ryukyu Islands to Japan and elucidates Yaeyama's liminal place between the Japanese nation and its colonial empire by examining the ways in which local farmers—marginalized in the new capitalist economy of the islands—migrated to the colony next door.

Ann Laura Stoler pays particular attention to poor white settlers and *métissage* (miscegenation) in her study, as these were considered threats to the fixed boundary between the colonizer and the colonized.[67] Although Japanese colonialism also shared a concern with similar issues, "Okinawan" is another social category that cannot be understood as the simple dichotomy of the colonizer and the colonized. Indeed, a number of scholars have discussed the malleability of the ruler-ruled divide and shed light on liminal subjects in colonial empires.[68] While many works have investigated colonial policies and representations of liminal subjects, there are few ethnographic works illustrating liminal subjects' construction, maintenance, and negotiation of the boundary between the ruler and the ruled. With a particular focus on Okinawan youth migrants, both male and female, chapter 3 explores Okinawans' attempts to advance socially within the colonial context. Such advancement suggests not only a rise in economic status but also the acquisition of standard Japanese, which was based on Japanese spoken by the middle class in Tokyo, or other forms of culture and traditions maintained by upper- and middle-class immigrants from Mainland Japan. It also illustrates the ways in which the politics of distinctions played out in the contact zone of Taiwan. Struggles over classification were more intense at the social margins and manifested themselves in the everyday lives of unskilled laborers and people from rural areas or among ethnic minorities like the Okinawans.

Taiwan was the destination not only for desperate Okinawan youths eager to make their fortunes but also for young Okinawans seeking tertiary education. In particular, the medical school in Taipei was one of the most popular schools for youths who had completed their secondary educations in Okinawa Prefecture and were eager to establish themselves in the medical profession. Chapter 4 demonstrates how Okinawan youths overcame great disadvantages by exploiting the imperial structure to advance their school careers in the colony, a phenomenon I call "imperial schooling." The chapter elaborates how Okinawan youths' imperial schooling in Taiwan reflects Okinawa's liminal position in the Japanese colonial empire. Indeed, on the one hand, modern medicine in Okinawa was marginalized within the scientific network of the Japanese Empire, but, on the other, Okinawans gained the greatest benefit from the imperial school network due to their liminal position.

The assimilation of Okinawan immigrants into Japanese culture is one of the most thoroughly discussed issues in Okinawan history studies,[69] partly because this assimilation is considered the root cause of the "mass suicides" that took place during the Okinawan ground battle of World War II.[70] Earlier studies have described the discrimination faced by Okinawan immigrants in Taiwan and their efforts become more Japanese so as to avoid unfair treatment.[71] However, these studies tend to focus on the experiences of first-generation immigrants. In so doing, they dismiss the fact that second- and third-generation Okinawan immigrants maintained different attitudes toward Japanese culture. Indeed, a significant number of Okinawans with dependent families also headed to Taiwan in hopes of making better lives for themselves. In demonstrating the heterogeneity of Okinawan immigrants, who often suffered the negative label "Okinawans" and "Ryukyuans," chapter 5 examines how second- and third-generation Okinawans shaped their identities quite differently from their parents, who were born and raised on Okinawa. This chapter also shows the ways in which some Okinawan immigrants asserted their pride in Okinawan culture with the support of Japanese mainlanders, thereby challenging the conclusion in previous studies that assimilation into the Japanese settler community in Taiwan was the only way for Okinawan immigrants to overcome their inferior status. Unfortunately, their pride in their Okinawan cultural heritage and ethnicity did not take hold among fellow Okinawans.

Chapter 6 examines the survival of Okinawan immigrants at the critical juncture following the collapse of the Japanese Empire and the reterritorialization of East Asian countries under the newly emerging Cold War regime. When the KMT government took over Taiwan, the country's former Japanese colonizers were told to leave for their "home country." While other Japanese migrants in Taiwan were sent back to Mainland Japan in early 1946, Okinawans were left behind without knowing when and where they would be resettled. In October 1946, more than a year after the war ended, over ten thousand Okinawans were still stranded in Taiwan. The identities of these Okinawans were critically reshaped by their experiences in Taiwan in the immediate aftermath of the war. In considering individual reactions to these new circumstances, this chapter examines the views on repatriation held by different Okinawan settlers in Taiwan. It also analyzes the ways in which Okinawans' colonial experiences have been marginalized vis-à-vis the memories of those who survived the Battle of Okinawa, as well as the vital role those experiences and memories have played in reshaping postwar Okinawan identity.

CHAPTER 1

Migration in the Age of Modern Colonialism

> The Discovery of the Okinawan diaspora was a surprise for this sansei Okinawa born and raised in Hawai'i. I knew that there were Okinawan communities in Hawai'i, the mainland United States, and Brazil. But I was surprised to learn that the Okinawan presence extended to the Philippines, Micronesia, and Fukien, China, and Manchuria. I was fascinated to learn of Okinawans living as far away as Singapore, Java, Cuba, and New Guinea.
>
> —Robert K. Arakaki, "Theorizing on the Okinawan Diaspora"

In 2016, there were more than 411,000 people of Okinawan descent outside Okinawa Prefecture.[1] Through the proud claim that it is the "prefecture of emigration" (*iminken*), the Okinawa prefectural government has been holding the Worldwide Uchinanchu Festival every five years since 1990. The life histories of Okinawan emigrants and their descendants are narrated and transmitted across Okinawa during the Uchinanchu Festival. The festival is a time for Okinawans to recall the struggles of previous generations of Okinawans who left their home islands, struggled to survive in a foreign country, sent their hard-earned money back to Okinawa, and maintained their Uchinanchu identity throughout the adversities they encountered. Memories of Okinawan emigrations are well narrated and remembered by Okinawan descendants in Hawai'i and South and North America.

The many scholarly efforts aimed at uncovering the unique experiences of Okinawan immigrants correspond to the rise of ethnic Okinawan consciousness across the globe.[2] By locating itself in the field of contemporary "diaspora studies," *Okinawan Diaspora,* edited by Ronald Y. Nakasone, articulates the ways in which Okinawan diasporas living in diverse regional contexts share the experience of being a "double minority";[3] that is, they have commonly been seen as "second-class Japanese" or "the other Japanese" by both immigrants from mainland Japan and residents of their host societies, so much so that their wages were sometimes lower than those of Japanese immigrants.[4]

While stressing their common experiences as a "double minority,"

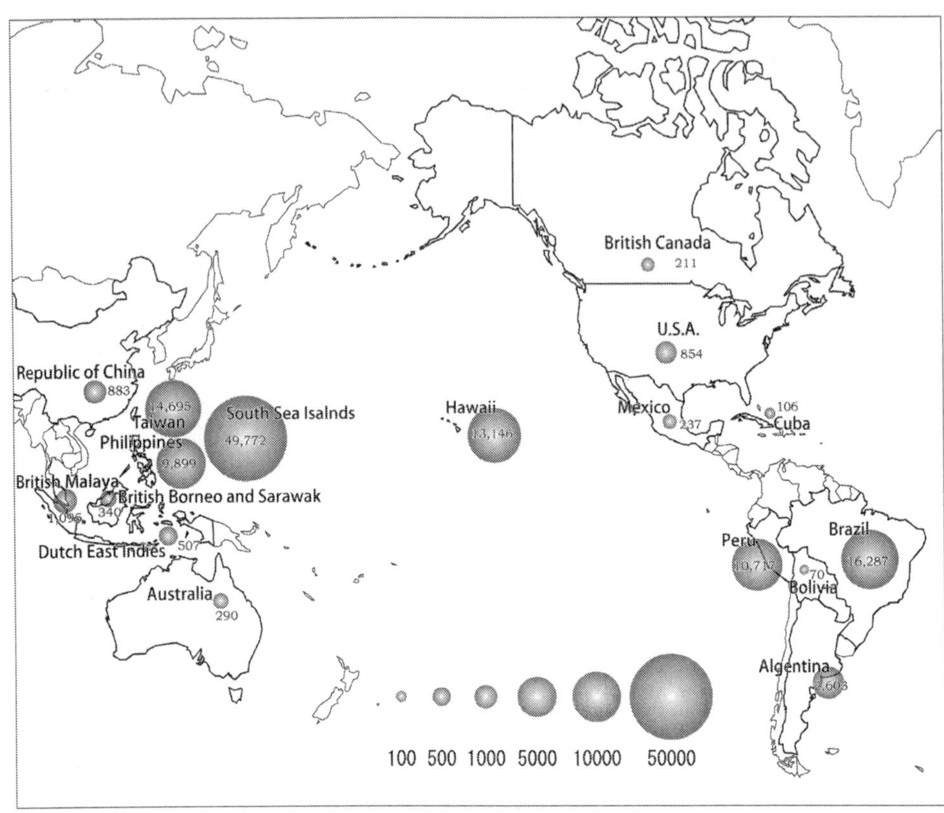

Worldwide distribution of Okinawan immigrants, 1940. Sources: *OKK*, 351, 406; Okinawa-ken Kyōiku Īnkai, *Okinawa-kenshi*, vol. 7, 14. Map by Mizuta Kenji.

Arakaki distinguishes the four contexts that shaped Okinawan identity in the past: in Okinawa under Japanese colonial rule, in Mainland Japan under the Japanese majority population, in the wider diaspora alongside the Japanese diaspora and the native population under Japanese colonial rule, and in the Okinawan diaspora within both the Japanese diaspora and the native population outside the Japanese polity.[5] Although the contexts are helpful in mapping the fairly diverse experiences of the Okinawan diaspora across the globe, the dissimilar experiences of the Okinawan diaspora under these different political contexts remain unclear. It is therefore important not to simply compare the migrants' experiences in different regional contexts but also to pay attention to the interconnectivity of the diasporic flows, even though the migrants themselves were rarely aware of the structural connections.

This chapter first describes the beginning of Okinawan migration overseas and explicates the reasons for the organized migration to Hawai'i and its popularization in Okinawa. It then elucidates the ways through which Okinawans migrated to many different destinations after the enactment of the Gentlemen's Agreement between Japan and the United States and explores their common experiences as a "double minority." Finally, it demonstrates how the experiences of Okinawan immigrants in Taiwan were shaped by that country's particular political and geographical settings. Okinawan immigration to colonial Taiwan is characterized by its spontaneity and diversity in socioeconomic background. Unlike first-generation Okinawan immigrants in other major destinations, those in Taiwan found employment in various industries, including government offices, commercial businesses, and fisheries. Additionally, immigrants from diverse backgrounds formed the minority of the Japanese settler population, which made it difficult for them to create a powerful ethnicity-based community in Taiwan.

Emigration as the Breakthrough for the Okinawan Economy

Japanese government policies toward Okinawa Prefecture during the first two decades of its annexation were never straightforward, as Qing China disapproved of the Japanese takeover of the Ryukyu Islands. Additionally, the majority of the *shizoku* (the Ryukyu Kingdom's former ruling class) strongly opposed the new Japanese administration. Hoping that China would aid them in recovering their kingdom and reinstating the previous regime, some members of the *shizoku* formed an opposition movement against the Japanese government, while others traveled secretly to China to request assistance.

In order to establish its rule in Okinawa, the Japanese government swiftly founded a conversational-Japanese school and normal school (*shihan gakkō*). It also allowed local authorities to maintain the former regime's customs and institutions because disaffected local authorities were strongly opposed to the new government, and it did not want to further fuel their resentment. Tokyo officials justified the delay in normalizing Okinawa, compared to the other prefectures, by citing Okinawa's "low level of civilization."[6] The tax system, which had a heavy impact on farmers, was not modernized in Okinawa until the land reform of 1902, whereas reforms were fully implemented in the other prefectures in 1873. Due to its tax system and different administration, Okinawa Prefecture was excluded from the national election until 1912.[7]

The delay of structural reforms widened the already deep economic divide between Okinawa and the Japanese mainland. Hoping to alleviate Okinawa's devastating economic situation, first-generation youth leaders who received a modern education in Mainland Japan proposed sending emigrants overseas. Tōyama Kyūzō (1868–1910), now known as the Father of Okinawa's International Migration, began by teaching in an elementary school in his home village. He later went to Tokyo with the intention of receiving tertiary education. In Tokyo, he met Jahana Noboru (1865–1908), a fellow Okinawan who was studying agriculture at the Imperial University in Tokyo. At the time, the people's rights movement was developing across Japan. Under its influence, Tōyama and Jahana were indignant at the dominance of immigrants from the other prefectures and were convinced that Okinawans should promote their own people's rights movement, to achieve democracy on their home island. On their return to Okinawa, they organized the Okinawa Club (Okinawa Kurabu), a political organization, and initiated a suffrage movement in 1899. While devoting himself to the liberation movement with Jahana and other fellow political activists, Tōyama organized another project that sent migrants to Hawai'i. He learned about the history of European colonization when he was in Tokyo and was greatly attracted to the prospect of colonizing uncultivated lands.[8]

Although there had been sporadic migration to the US mainland since the mid-nineteenth century, the demand for Japanese laborers sharply increased after Chinese immigration was banned in 1882. Japanese migrant workers came to the fore against this backdrop and consequently were regarded as alternatives to Chinese coolies. In 1886, the Japanese government concluded the Immigration Convention with the Hawaiian Kingdom and sent the first Japanese immigrants to Hawai'i, which was suffering a serious labor shortage. Furthermore, Japanese laborers were needed to replace the Chinese migrant workers toiling in railway construction and on large-scale plantations along the US west coast. Thus, there were approximately 1,700 Japanese immigrants in the United States in 1889.[9]

Conscious of the difficulty of improving the living standards of Okinawans in a short period of time, Tōyama was convinced that participation in colonization projects through international migration would lead to the salvation of the impoverished Okinawan people. Although the governor of Okinawa Prefecture, Narahara Shigeru, initially opposed this plan, Tōyama managed to convince him otherwise.[10] In other words, it was not the local or national government but the people's initiative that inaugurated international migration.

In 1899, Tōyama called on Okinawan volunteers to migrate to Hawai'i as indentured laborers, and nearly two hundred people came forward.[11] He eventually selected thirty male Okinawans from different regions and dispatched them to Hawai'i. In fact, they were not the first Okinawans to travel overseas. Following Okinawa's annexation to Japan, several Okinawans traveled independently to foreign countries, including the United States and Canada. Tōyama's group of Okinawan laborers, however, was the inaugural group of indentured laborers departing for foreign countries. The first group of Okinawan migrant workers left Okinawa on December 5, 1899, and headed to Yokohama, where they were to board the ship for Hawai'i. Four men failed the health examination and were removed from the group, and the remaining twenty-six arrived in Honolulu on January 16, 1900.[12]

These twenty-six pioneer Okinawan migrant workers—all males between the ages of twenty-one and thirty-five—were sent to the Ewa Sugar Plantation on the island of Oahu. The immigrants who had no farming experience found the labor particularly hard; those from farming families also found life in Hawai'i difficult and humiliating. Accordingly, some of the pioneer immigrants prepared a formal request for the governor of Okinawa and the immigration agency that their contracts be cancelled so that they could return to Okinawa immediately. However, before they could present their request, they were told that their contracts would soon be cancelled because the United States had extended its prohibition of indentured migration to Hawai'i, which became a US territory in 1900. Thus, the twenty-six pioneer immigrants were released from their contracts three months after their arrival. Once freed from the Ewa Plantation, they sought better employment elsewhere in Hawai'i, and some eventually moved to the US mainland.[13]

Meanwhile, Okinawans at home were deeply concerned about the fate of the twenty-six pioneer immigrants because nobody had heard any news of them. Once reports from Hawai'i reached Okinawa, their anxieties were allayed, and Okinawans again saw international migration as an opportunity for achieving a better future. This positive outlook was bolstered when some of the pioneer immigrants returned to Okinawa and told their neighbors about their lives in Hawai'i. Their neighbors observed that some returnees bought rice fields and farms, while others built luxurious residences. Their stories and actions provided the most effective promotion of migration overseas. Moreover, the Sino-Japanese War and the cession of Taiwan to Japan drew the common people's attention to international affairs, which in turn ignited migration fever in Okinawa. Consequently, a great number of people applied to participate in Tōyama's second migration project to Hawai'i.[14] After the great success of the second immigrant group at the Ewa Plantation, migration to Hawai'i became increasingly popular in Okinawa. In 1904, the number of Okinawan immigrants to Hawai'i was 262; it increased to 1,233 in 1905 and 4,467 in 1906. However, the Gentlemen's Agreement of 1908 between the United States and Japan severely restricted the number of immigrants to the United States, and the number of Okinawan immigrants dropped to 2,525 in 1907 and 678 in 1908.[15]

Okinawan Migration in the Time of Colonialism and Racism

Before migration to the US mainland became popular in Okinawa, anti-Japanese sentiment spread across the West Coast, where the Japanese population had increased rapidly at the turn of the twentieth century. After the enactment of the Gentlemen's Agreement in 1908, Okinawans were unable to enter the United States as migrant laborers. Thus, very few Okinawans followed the thousands of Japanese who had migrated to the US mainland. The few who did so during this period were youths pursuing higher education. Some went to the US mainland via Hawaiʻi, Canada, and Mexico; a few traveled directly from Okinawa. As the Gentlemen's Agreement allowed only families of migrants to enter for the purpose of reuniting with husbands and fathers, some female Okinawans arranged to immigrate and join their grooms in the United States as picture brides.[16]

Elderly Okinawans have a saying that best sums up these migration trends: "The richest people were able to immigrate to South America; people with some money migrated to the Philippines; and the poorest worked on mainland Japan."[17] Indeed, when it proved too difficult to enter the United States as migrant workers, the Japanese turned to South America—especially Brazil—and the Philippines as alternative destinations. Later, the South Sea Islands became popular as the South Seas Development Company (Nan'yō Kōhatsu) targeted and recruited Okinawan laborers for its sugar industry. While Brazil, the Philippines, and the South Sea Islands were under different governments and Okinawan immigrants there worked in different industries, there are some commonalities among them. First, the initial immigrants in these countries worked in manufacturing and commercial crop industries such as coffee (Brazil), abaca (the Philippines), and sugarcane (the South Sea Islands). Second, Okinawan immigrants accounted for the majority of Japanese immigrant communities in these countries despite their treatment as "second-class Japanese" and "the other Japanese."

South America

Japan sent the first indentured migrant farmworkers to Brazil in 1908. Okinawans accounted for more than 40 percent, 325 of the 781 immigrants, of that inaugural group of economic immigrants to Brazil.[18] In fact, many of the first Okinawan immigrants left the plantations to which they were allocated shortly after their arrival. This gave a negative impression to both the Japanese and Brazilian governments. In 1913, the Japanese government refused to

Table 1.1. Occupations of Japanese Immigrants in Hawai'i, Brazil, Philippines, and South Sea Islands, 1928

Occupation	Hawai'i	Brazil	Philippines	South Sea Islands
Agriculture (farming, horticulture, cattle breeding)	19,845	14,666	5,655	2,438
Forestry	0	2	251	115
Fishery	773	78	715	166
Manufacturing	1,168	220	364	346
Factory laborers	2,857	56	98	89
Business (including geishas and waitresses)	5,347	527	1,223	714
Transportation	2,408	312	109	180
Government officials	26	35	7	449
Professional and freelance workers	720	147	140	181
Students	0	7	8	0
Others	8,684	843	1,199	1,406
Total	41,828	16,893	9,769	6,084

Source: Gaimushō Tsūshōkyoku, *Kaigai kakuchi zairyū honpōjin shokugyōbetsu jinkōhyō*, table, 17, 24, 28, 36.

accept Okinawans wishing to travel to Brazil as indentured laborers, citing their propensity to leave the plantations and their cultural difference from Japanese workers from the other prefectures, but when migration agencies were unable to recruit enough laborers from the other prefectures, Okinawans were once again permitted to go to Brazil as indentured migrant workers. However, as was the case in the United States, Okinawan migration to Brazil was prohibited in 1919, and only immigrants who were currently in Brazil were allowed to send for their families.[19] According to the record of 1940, 16,287 Okinawan females and males resided in Brazil, composing nearly 10 percent of the total number of Japanese immigrants to Brazil. Most of the Okinawan immigrants were first employed on large-scale plantations, and some later became successful independent farmers.[20]

In addition to Brazil, Okinawa sent a significant number of immigrants to other Latin American countries. For instance, Peru quickly became

Table 1.2. Occupations of Okinawan Households in Brazil, June 30, 1936

Occupation	Number of Okinawan households
Agricultural workers (farming, horticulture, forestry, cattle breeding)	2,455
Peddlers	432
Dockside laborers	70
Shop owners	58
Transportation workers	55
Brokers (agricultural products and others)	51
Barbers	30
Laundry operators	28
Other	154
Total	3,333

Source: Yabiku, *Burajiru Okinawa iminshi,* 110–112.

one of the most popular destinations for Okinawan migrant workers after the first group of Okinawan immigrants arrived there in 1899. Between 1899 and 1941, Okinawa sent 11,461 immigrants to Peru, accounting for nearly 30 percent of the total number of Japanese immigrants. Although the immigrants were initially employed on plantation farms, many later moved to urban areas, where they became grocery store or restaurant owners.[21]

Similarly, most Japanese immigrants to Argentina were Okinawans. This is despite the fact that Japanese immigrants had been arriving in Argentina since 1910. There were 1,831 Okinawans in Argentina in 1940, accounting for approximately 45 percent of the Japanese population in the country. Not all Okinawans in Argentina had migrated directly from Okinawa; in actuality, many ended up in Argentina after traveling to Brazil and Peru. In Argentina, many Okinawans initially found work as factory laborers or porters A sizeable number eventually set up small businesses such as coffee shops and laundries.[22]

The Philippines

As the doors to North America and Hawai'i were closed, Okinawans sought other destinations on and near the South American continent. After visiting and observing the hardships experienced by Okinawan settlers in Hawai'i, Tōyama Kyūzō realized that although there was great potential for success for Okinawan migrants in Hawai'i, the islands were apparently too small to accommodate a large number of immigrant laborers. He also had the foresight to recognize that harsh anti-Japanese sentiment in the United States and Hawai'i could very possibly result in the eventual restriction of Okinawan migration. In seeking other destinations, Tōyama found the Philippines a suitable alternative and subsequently entrusted Ōshiro Kōzō, his former student at Kin Elementary School, with the task of organizing a group of migrant workers who would leave for the Philippines in 1904.[23]

After more than four centuries of Spanish colonial rule, the Philippines came under the control of the United States in 1898. Eager to improve the economic infrastructure of the islands, the United States launched numerous public works. The most famous is the construction of Benguet Road, leading to Baguio City. As a labor shortage was the biggest obstacle to the project's completion, the US governor-general schemed to augment Filipino and American workers with foreign laborers.[24] In June 1903, the governor-general requested the consulate of Japan to recruit a thousand Japanese migrant laborers to join the workers at the Benguet Road construction site. It is notable that the US governor-general made this request in spite of the Alien Contract Labor Law (1885) and Immigration Act (1891) strictly regulating the entrance of Japanese migrant workers to the United States. The governor-general granted special dispensation for the Benguet Road construction project, as additional workers were the only means of resolving the serious labor shortage. While the exact number of Japanese laborers who worked on Benguet Road is unknown, it is estimated that more than half the nearly five thousand Japanese visitors to Manila between 1903 and 1904 worked on the road or related works.[25] In addition to the hundreds of Japanese immigrants already employed at the construction site, Ōshiro brought about 360 males from Okinawa to work on the road.[26]

Meanwhile, American and European planters were trying to develop the abaca industry in Davao, on Mindanao island, as abaca had become the major cordage fiber in the world market in the mid-nineteenth century. Despite strong resistance from native tribes in Davao, Americans and Europeans cultivated the land for this profitable cash crop.[27] While the plantations in Davao suffered from a grave labor shortage, Japanese and Okinawan workers at Benguet Road fretted over their future employment opportunities after the road-building project was completed. On learning of the labor shortage in Davao, Ōta Kyōsaburō, who was in charge of Japanese workers at Benguet Road, transported 180 Japanese laborers to Davao in September 1904.[28] Later, in May 1907, Ōta established the Ōta Development Company; Ōshiro Kōzō, who coordinated the migration of a group of Okinawans to the Philippines, became the vice president.[29] As a result of Ōshiro

Kōzō's recruitment efforts, the number of Okinawan immigrants rapidly increased during the 1920s, from 1,260, approximately 22 percent of the total Japanese population, in 1920, to 4,447, more than a half of Davao's total Japanese population, in 1928.[30]

The South Sea Islands

The South Sea Islands received the greatest number of Okinawan immigrants in the early twentieth century. Several Japanese trading companies were founded in the islands in the late nineteenth century, and a small number of Japanese were living there at the outbreak of World War I (1914–1918). In 1914, Japan declared war on Germany and occupied German possessions in Micronesia. Between Japan's occupation of the islands and its eventual acquisition of sovereignty over them, the Japanese population there rapidly increased, with some settlers establishing sugar production companies. In 1916 and 1917, two Japanese entrepreneurs founded the Nishimura Development Company (Nishimura Takushoku) and the South Seas Production Company in Saipan and brought in hundreds of Japanese and Korean laborers to develop sugarcane plantations. However, with little knowledge of sugar production in a tropical climate, both companies failed. At the end of the war, Japan was given a League of Nations Class C mandate and formal recognition of its occupation of these South Sea Islands.[31]

The first recorded Okinawan immigrants to the South Sea Islands were Itoman fishers. A party of seventeen fishers sailed to Saipan in November 1915 and eventually came to dominate fishing in the region. Okinawan fishers played a vital role in the development of fishery in the region.[32] Nevertheless, the rapid increase in Okinawan immigrants cannot be explained without the development of the sugar industry in the South Sea Islands. In 1921, Matsue Haruji (1876–1954), an immigrant from Fukushima Prefecture, established the South Seas Development Company (Nan'yō Kōhatsu), utilizing the assets of the Nishimura Development Company and the South Seas Production Company. Unlike the founders of the Nishimura Development Company and South Seas Production Company, Matsue had practical experience in the sugar industry in the United States and Taiwan. Moreover, he obtained financial support from Ishizuka Eizō, president of the Oriental Development Company in Korea. In March 1922, the South Sea Government (Nan'yō-chō) was established to govern the islands. The government provided the South Seas Development Company with much support and benefits, including nearly rent-free use of land in its early years and a favorable tax policy. As a result, the company grew rapidly and became the major South Sea company in the monoculture sugarcane production economy. In return for this favorable treatment, the company did its utmost to support the government's development policies on the islands.[33]

The South Seas Development Company brought nearly two thousand migrants from Okinawa in 1922. They joined the Okinawan immigrants who had been employed by the Nishimura Development Company and South Seas Production Company before those two companies failed and worked in reclamation and construction of infrastructure for a large-scale sugar production enterprise. There were several reasons for Matsue's decision to recruit immigrant laborers from Okinawa. First, there was already a significant number of Okinawan immigrants in Saipan who had been employed by the two companies that failed. Second, Okinawans had experience on sugarcane plantations and in sugar-related industries at home. Third, Okinawa Prefecture was overpopulated, and the common people suffered from severe economic depression. Matsue believed that the economic migration of laborers from Okinawa Prefecture would alleviate these serious social problems.[34]

During the 1920s and 1930s, the Japanese population grew rapidly, as there was a common belief that natives would not be suitable workers, and thus it was necessary to bring immigrant laborers to the islands. By the 1930s, a growing number of Okinawans had migrated without contracting with any company, relying instead on networks of friends and family. As the

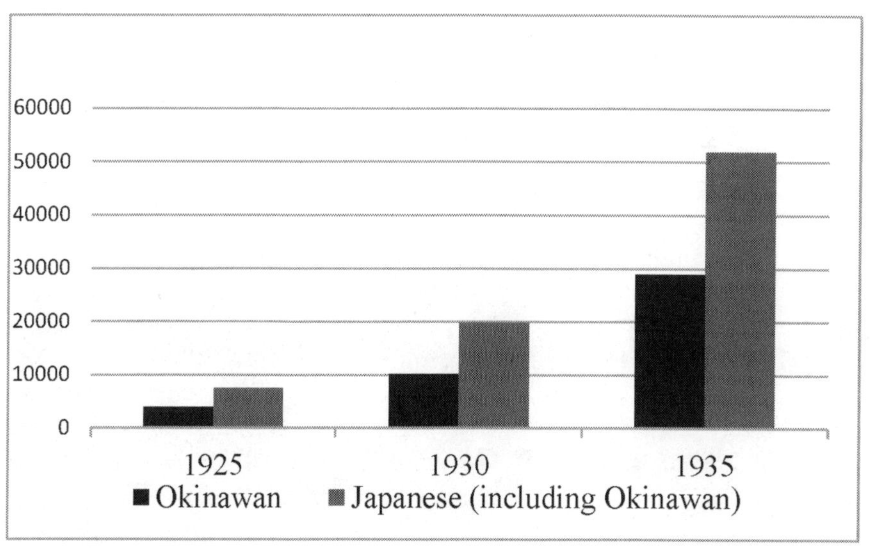

Okinawan and Japanese populations in the South Sea Islands. Sources: Nan'yōchō, *Nan'yō guntō tōsei chōsa hōkoku,* 160–161; Nan'yōchō, *Nan'yō guntō tōsei chōsasho,* 452–453; Nan'yōchō Chōkan Kanbō Bunshoka, *Nan'yō guntō tōsei chōsasho,* 140–141.

Okinawan population increased, shops and restaurants catering to Okinawan immigrants appeared. Some South Seas Development Company employees became independent and opened their own businesses, while some women arrived as spouses or picture brides of Okinawan male immigrants who had chosen to settle in the South Sea Islands.[35]

OKINAWANS AS "SECOND-CLASS JAPANESE"

As earlier studies have pointed out, Okinawan immigrants suffered so much prejudice and discrimination in their host countries that their memories of marginalization and suffering formed the basis of present-day Okinawan diasporic identity. In Brazil, Okinawans were frequently prohibited from immigrating because the Japanese government continued to hold negative views of them. The government was wary of Okinawan immigrants to Brazil because Okinawan migrant workers created fake families during the initial stage of immigration for the sole purpose of entering Brazil, only to break their contracts and leave their allocated plantations in search of better-paying jobs. Furthermore, the government had grave concerns about their low level of literacy and Japanese-language ability. Okinawa's unique customs and traditions were also frequent targets of criticism. Because of the repeated suspensions, the number of Okinawan immigrants to Brazil constantly changed over the years.[36]

Okinawans were treated as second-class Japanese in the Philippines, where the majority of Okinawan immigrants worked for the abaca industry in Davao. The Filipinos noticed the marked difference between Okinawans and Japanese immigrants from the other prefectures and consequently came to refer to Okinawans as "the other Japanese."[37] Naturally, Okinawans in the Philippines chafed at the negative perceptions maintained by Japanese from the other prefectures and tried to emphasize Okinawan integration with mainstream Japanese society. For instance, in 1916, three female Okinawan migrants were sent home by the Okinawan Migrants' Association because they had tattoos on their hands. The association's representatives contended that previous Okinawan migrants were no different from the Japanese of the other prefectures because "none of the other Okinawan wives had tattoos, and their lifestyles were identical to that of the Japanese from the other prefectures."[38] The association expelled these new female Okinawan migrants because they were objects of derision among Japanese migrants from the other prefectures and had a negative impact on their relationship with other Japanese immigrants. The *Ryukyu News* (Ryūkyū shinpō) commented: "Sharing the same culture and language creates a deep emotional tie among people. Similar cultural and linguistic identification are the cornerstones of solid national unification. . . . It is understandable that Okinawans frequently accuse Japanese immigrants from the other prefectures of prejudice and unfair discrimination. Nevertheless, an objective analysis of this treatment reveals that Okinawans are greatly responsible for its perpetration. Although Okinawan customs and languages have been gradually reformed over the years, there is still a great gulf between Okinawans and Japanese from the other prefectures."[39] After pronouncing the three women's expulsion a "tragedy," the author called for urgent cultural and language reform among Okinawans. The *Ryukyu News* proposed implementing an educational program especially for Okinawan migrants so that their behavior would not "bring shame on the prefecture and affect the dignity of Okinawans as the national subjects of Imperial Japan."[40]

Furthermore, in 1927, the Japanese consulate in the Philippines submitted a report to the Minister of Foreign Affairs, revealing the common view of Okinawans among elite Japanese from the other prefectures. On the one hand, the report celebrates the Okinawans' humble and simple lifestyle by noting, "Unlike Japanese immigrants who immediately returned home after saving a small amount of money, Okinawans are determined to settle down in the Philippines, probably because their lives here would be easier and more comfortable than in Okinawa."[41] The consulate official also adds, "Okinawans are the best farmers in a tropical climate. They are good savers, unsophisticated, religious, and respectful towards their elders." On the other hand, the report points out, "Their simple lifestyle is the Okinawans' biggest weakness as well as their strength." The consular official claims that even local Filipinos despise Okinawans because "their culture is less sophisticated," "they maintain their own distinctive local culture," and "they maintain strong emotional ties with those from the same prefecture and rarely cooperate with those from the other prefectures."[42] The Okinawan Association in Davao reacted strongly to the Japanese consulate's report. On January 3, 1928, it introduced the consular official's report at its annual meeting, which was attended by nearly 1,500 Okinawan immigrants.[43] The association's members then formed a special committee to make their objection to this report known to the Ministry of Foreign Affairs because "this was not only a serious matter to all Okinawans resident in the Philippines but would also affect the 600,000 people in Okinawa."[44] The committee presented a petition to the Okinawa prefectural government and the Ministry of Foreign Affairs, insisting that the report was based on the prejudicial and discriminatory attitudes of immigrants from the other prefectures.[45]

Okinawans in the South Seas were treated no differently than those in the Philippines and other host countries. Japanese rule in the South Seas would not have been possible without the large Okinawan labor force. Nevertheless, they were continually regarded as second-class imperial migrants and were subjected to prejudice and discrimination. In order to better endure such indignities outside their home country, Okinawans founded prefectural associations (*kenjinkai*) on each island, which fostered and maintained solidarity among immigrants from the same region. While most prefectures established their own associations, the Okinawan associations were particularly large and very well organized. Whereas many Okinawan prefectural associations overseas simply offered cultural activities and communal welfare, the association in Saipan occasionally played a political role. During the late 1920s and early 1930s, the Okinawan prefectural association in Saipan organized three large-scale strikes against the South Seas Development Company, protesting the company's management and criticizing racial discrimination against Okinawans in the workplace. Because the company relied heavily on the Okinawan labor force, these association-led strikes were successful in compelling the company to compromise. The prefectural associations also played an important part in encouraging Okinawan immigrants to assimilate into the culture of Japan's main islands. The younger members of Saipan's prefectural association established a youth group and volunteered to teach "standard spoken Japanese" to others in order to combat unfair discrimination and prejudice.[46]

Immigrants and Settlers in the Kingdom of the Governor-General

In contrast to major migration destinations such as Hawai'i, Brazil, the Philippines, and the South Sea Islands, Okinawans had been traveling to Taiwan since the late 1890s. In March 1896, a year after the end of the First Sino-Japanese War, four or five Okinawan women appeared at the Port of Keelung, located at the northernmost tip of the island of Taiwan. This marked the first recorded arrival of Japanese females in Taiwan. They excited much interest, as, it was noted, "their style differed from local women's. They tightened an obi at their waists and wore sandals. The local residents were astonished by the sudden appearance of women in exotic clothes."[47] Whereas immigration to other host countries was planned and coordinated by community leaders or the companies in need of Okinawan labor, early migrations to colonial Taiwan were characterized by their spontaneity.

After declaring Japan's complete conquest of Taiwan on March 23, 1896, the colonial government relaxed the travel restrictions on Japanese civilians arriving in Taiwan.[48] Early Japanese migrants came from all walks of life. Some were in Taiwan for specific purposes, such as working for the

Table 1.3. Occupations of Okinawan and Japanese Visitors to Taiwan, 1897

Occupation	Okinawan	Japanese (including Okinawan)
Government officials	38	3,821
Agriculture	7	2,066
Commerce	535	13,385
Manufacturing	66	4,113
Miscellaneous	103	6,465
Unemployed	59	2,376
Total	808	32,226

Source: Taiwan Sōtokufu Minseibu Bunshoka, *Taiwan sōtokufu daiichi tōkeisho,* 52–55.

the colonial government or starting new businesses, but many arrived without jobs waiting for them. It is recorded that 499 males and 309 females from Okinawa landed on Taiwan in 1897, more than half of whom were merchants.[49] On November 22, 1899, a brothel called "Okinawa House" (Okinawa-rō) was mentioned in an article in the *Taiwan Daily News* (*Taiwan nichinichi shinpō*).[50] These numbers indicate that the majority of Okinawan visitors visited Taiwan for commercial purposes during this time.

In August 1910, the *Okinawa Daily News* (*Okinawa mainichi shinbun*) serialized an essay by an Okinawan settler in Taiwan. According to his memoirs, he arrived in Taiwan in August 1899, caught up in "Taiwan fever." He was born in Okinawa and was a feckless youth who had never had a single proper job until he moved to Taiwan at the age of thirty.[51] He candidly observed, "Most of the Okinawan migrants had been jobless and despised at home for leading idle lives. Some came to seek their fortunes, while others were hopeless losers. Real ambitious men with concrete plans were few and far between."[52] His essay reveals that early Okinawan migrants, like the pioneer Japanese immigrants, came from diverse backgrounds and included many struggling civilians as well as people from the lowest rung of society seeking new opportunities.

While the total Japanese population in Taiwan steadily rose during colonial rule, the Okinawan population grew at a brisker pace between the mid-1920s and the mid-1940s. In contrast to Okinawans initially recruited to the other host countries as laborers or farmers, the social and economic backgrounds of Okinawan immigrants in Taiwan were more diverse. Some were employed in public offices, others worked for commercial businesses in the Japanese settler communities, and a few were fishers. Like the rest of

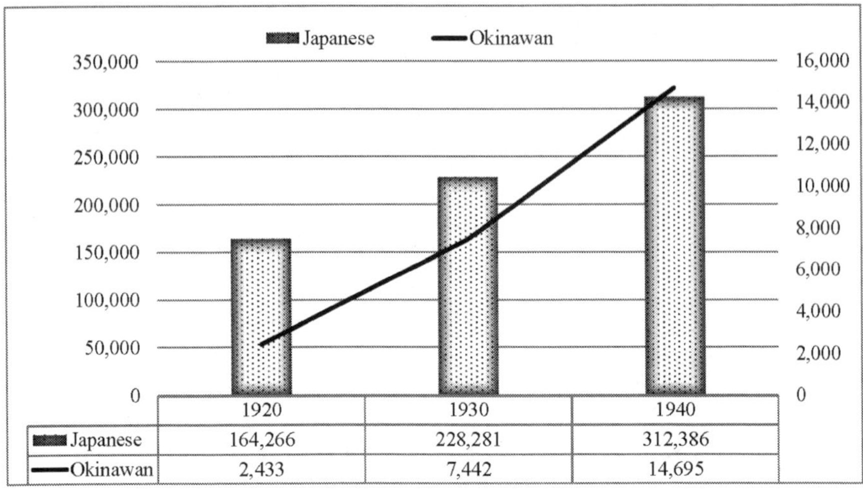

	1920	1930	1940
Japanese	164,266	228,281	312,386
Okinawan	2,433	7,442	14,695

Okinawan and Japanese populations in Taiwan, 1920–1940. Sources: Taiwan Sōtokufu Kanbō Rinji Kokusei Chōsabu, *Taiwan kokusei chōsa shūkei genpyō,* 826–827; Taiwan Sōtoku Kanbō Rinji Kokusei Chōsabu, *Kokusei chōsa kekkahyō, Showa 5-nen, Zentō-hen,* 438–439; Taiwan Sōtokufu, *Taiwan tōsei yōran,* 32–33.

the Japanese immigrant population, most Okinawans settled in Taipei or Keelung.

Although Okinawans were employed by various industries in colonial Taiwan, the relatively high proportion of Okinawan white-collar workers is particularly noteworthy because first-generation Okinawan immigrants in Hawai'i, Brazil, the Philippines, and the South Sea Islands rarely held white-collar jobs. The reason lay partly with the massive Japanese colonial administration in Taiwan, which hired numerous Okinawan settlers and settlers from Mainland Japan. Unlike the political structure of Japan proper, which was governed by the Meiji Constitution, the colonial government of Taiwan controlled all the judicial, legislative, and executive power. Without an independent congress, there was no official institution restricting the governor-general's authority. Colonial Taiwan was indeed like the "kingdom of the governor-general."[53] As the colonial government's institutions grew, the number of public officials increased. In 1896, there were fewer than 5,000 public officials. This number exceeded 30,000 in 1920 and finally reached 86,212 in 1941.[54]

In fact, the colonial government also employed Taiwanese who were lower in rank or contract workers. By the end of 1940, there were 44,284 Japanese and 41,928 Taiwanese officials working for the colonial government. The near-equal number of Japanese and Taiwanese officials did not

Table 1.4. Occupations of Japanese and Okinawan Residents of Taiwan, 1930

Occupation	Japanese	Okinawan
Agriculture	4,429	124
Fishery	1,620	383
Mining	418	8
Manufacturing	14,684	426
Commerce	18,135	567
Transportation	9,063	592
Government officials and freelance workers	37,619	750
Domestic service	1,546	415
Others	2,920	174
Total	90,434	3,439

Source: Taiwan Sōtokufu Kanbō Rinji Kokusei Chōsabu, *Kokusei chōsa kekkahyō, Showa 5-nen, Shūchō-hen,* 456–457.

mean they held the same posts. Whereas more than half the Japanese employees were formally hired government bureaucrats, fewer than five thousand Taiwanese officials were appointed to these formal positions, while the rest were employed on a temporary or part-time basis.[55] On the one hand, there were policies in place to assimilate the Taiwanese into the ranks of Japanese imperial subjects in anticipation of the integration of Taiwan into Japan proper. On the other hand, a small number of Japanese controlled the government of Taiwan, and the Taiwanese were given few opportunities to participate in politics. Throughout the fifty years of Japanese rule, it was expected that Taiwan would one day be fully integrated into Japan proper. However, persistent discrimination against the Taiwanese rendered such integration a pipe dream.

It should also be noted that few Okinawan public officials occupied high-ranking positions. This may be due partly to high-ranking Okinawan government officials changing their original registered prefectural addresses for fear of discrimination (discussed in chap. 5). It is therefore possible that there were more high-ranking Okinawan government officials, even though their true origins are not in the public record. Nevertheless, it was likely that most Okinawans held less notable posts, even though they were government employees.

The majority of Okinawan immigrants were concentrated in the city areas, but many assimilated into the Japanese settler community. Partly because of the social and economic diversity, Okinawan immigrants did not form a tight-knit ethnic community, unlike the immigrants in the Philippines and the South Sea Islands, where the majority of Okinawans were associated with the same industry. There was, however, an exception. Although the majority of Okinawan immigrants resided in the Japanese settler community in city areas, Okinawan fishers created several tight-knit ethnic enclaves along the coast. Immediately after the occupation of Taiwan, the Japanese colonial government conducted an investigation into Taiwan's marine resources and tried to develop fisheries by introducing Japanese technologies. Japanese fisher settlements were also encouraged.

The colonial government implemented various policies for developing fisheries in Taiwan and initiated several migration projects targeting Japanese fishers, but Okinawans largely went to Taiwan independent of government policies. At first, Okinawan fishers did not live in Taiwan; instead, they came seasonally to the coastal area of Keelung to gather agar weed (Japanese, *sekkasai* or *kantengusa*).[56] The period between April and September was agar weed in Keelung.[57] On June 13, 1902, the *Taiwan Daily News* reported that Okinawans as well as local Taiwanese gathered agar weed every day for export to Osaka and other cities in Japan through brokers.[58] In the early 1900s, more than three hundred Okinawan seasonal workers were observed, although the number of workers fluctuated with the agar weed's yield and price.[59] Though local Taiwanese and a small number of Japanese also gathered agar weed in Keelung, the more experienced Okinawans were most skilled in the gathering technique and dominated the harvest.[60] Okinawan seasonal agar-weed collectors found that Sharyō Island (Japanese, Sharyōtō), now Heping Island (Mandarin, Hepingdao), was the best place for gathering agar weed and gradually settled there. Okinawan fishers also settled on the island and fished in Taiwanese waters. By 1905, there was an Okinawan community on Sharyō Island.[61]

While Okinawan fishers and seasonal agar-weed gathers frequently came to Taiwan, some eventually settled there, and the Okinawan population slowly increased. In 1930, there were 383 Okinawan fishers, accounting for nearly 10 percent of the total employed Okinawan population in Taiwan.[62] They formed their own fishing communities in different coastal areas, and the Sharyō Island community was the largest in both size and number. Okinawan fishing communities collectively maintained their traditional customs, whereas Okinawans living amid the Japanese settler community largely assimilated into mainstream Japanese culture. Because the largest Okinawan community, on Sharyō Island, was well known across Taiwan, Okinawan settlers in other cities would flock there during traditional annual events—such as the Dragon Boat Festival—to enjoy the festivities together.[63] Therefore, even though the great majority of Okinawan immigrants were not fishers, these fishers were believed to represent the ethnic icon of "Okinawa" in colonial Taiwan.

The fisher communities not only maintained Okinawan traditions and ceremonies but occasionally served as a labor union. In 1935, nearly 600 Okinawan fishers established an ethnicity-based association to protect their common interests. In Kaohsiung (Japanese, Takao) City, the second-largest city in Taiwan, Okinawans formed the bulk of fishers, and most shipowners were Japanese mainlanders. In order to protect their rights and interests, Okinawan fishers established the Mutual Help Fishers' Association of Takao Southward Advancement Fishing (Takao Nanpō Shutsuryō Okinawa Gyomin Gojokai) with the support of Asato Tsumichiyo, a lawyer working in Tainan City, originally from Okinawa Prefecture. In 1935, they went on strike for fifty days, the first strike in colonial Taiwan, to protect their interests against those of the shipowners.[64]

Okinawa is known as the prefecture of emigration, not only because emigration was an integral part of its economic and social policies, but also because Okinawans were a significant part of Japanese immigrant groups in host societies. Unlike Japan proper, where the government initiated labor migration to Hawai'i, Okinawa was excluded from the government's migration project in the 1880s, and Okinawans began migrating to Hawai'i due to the common people's initiative. In 1899, Tōyama Kyūzō, who had also joined the Okinawan suffrage movement with Jahana Noboru, promoted a plan for sending Okinawan immigrants to Hawai'i for the purpose of improving Okinawa's dire economic situation. Labor migration overseas soon became popular in Okinawa. However, along with Japanese mainlanders, Okinawans were also expelled from North America and Hawai'i due to anti-Japanese migration policies.

Suffering from intense racism in North America and Hawai'i, Japanese considered South America and neighboring Asian countries to be the best alternatives for migration. Even though they were free from Western racism against Asians, Okinawans continued to be viewed as "second-class Japanese" in most of their host countries. Despite this prejudice, Okinawans organized ethnic associations to combat such discrimination in countries like the Philippines and the South Sea Islands, where Okinawans composed the majority of Japanese settler communities. Because Okinawan immigrants in these countries were concentrated in a few industries such as abaca farming and sugar production, it was much easier for them to form ethnic organizations to fight discrimination.

While government and private agencies were largely responsible for recruiting and sending Okinawan immigrants to Hawai'i and the Philippines, there was no government or private company initiative sending Okinawans to colonial Taiwan. "Taiwan fever" was spontaneous in Okinawa, and people usually relied on their network of family and friends when immigrating to Taiwan. Consequently, their occupations were fairly diverse in comparison to the jobs of immigrants in the other destinations. Although they faced discrimination in their everyday lives, Okinawans in Taiwan did not form a powerful ethnic community or unions and were rarely able to fight the unfair treatment they experienced at work. Fishers were the only exception, as they formed several Okinawan fisher communities to maintain traditional Okinawan customs. By living and working together, Okinawan fishers could fight collectively for their common interests.

Chapter 2

Crossing the National/Imperial Border

Okinawans were likely to immigrate to countries where their families and friends had already settled. Thus, immigrants from the same country or province of origin tended to concentrate in particular destinations. Many migrants arriving in colonial Taiwan in the 1920s–1940s came from the Yaeyama Islands in the southwestern end of the Ryukyu Islands. According to a survey conducted in 1959, nearly 12 percent of the total residential population of Ishigaki Island, the largest island of the group, repatriated from Taiwan after World War II. The survey also suggests that nearly 95 percent of Ishigaki repatriates had returned from Taiwan, while the rest repatriated from the South Sea Islands, the Philippines, and other former Japanese colonies and occupied territories.[1] Yaeyama also best demonstrates Okinawa's liminal character in relation to the Japanese colonial empire. This chapter elucidates how numerous Yaeyama Islanders migrated to Taiwan during the region's transition from the "southern gate" of the Japanese nation to the border zone of the colonial empire.

Yaeyama consists of thirty-two islands.[2] Totaling 591.97 square kilometers, it accounts for approximately 26 percent of the total area of Okinawa Prefecture (2,275.71 square kilometers).[3] In early modern times, Yaeyama was regarded as a peripheral region and suffered from the Ryukyu Kingdom's discriminatory governing policies In the early seventeenth century, the Tokugawa Shogunate prohibited private trade and exchanges with foreign countries, and the Ryukyu Kingdom followed suit as a vassal of the Satsuma Domain. Yaeyama was considered an important security checkpoint for examining foreign arrivals because of the unstable Chinese political situation and the European colonization of East Asia in the seventeenth century.[4] Evidence of contact between the Yaeyama Islanders and the Taiwanese is difficult to find, and it is unknown if they had regular contact during the Ryukyu Kingdom period.[5]

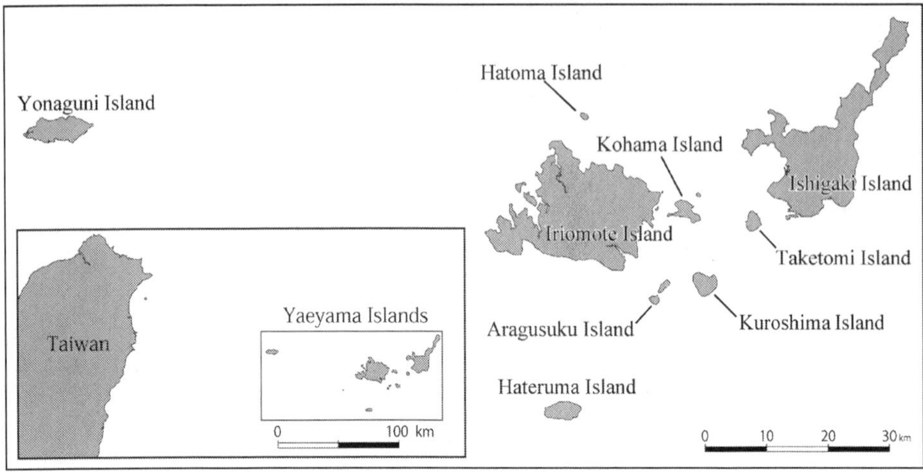

Yaeyama Islands. Map by Mizuta Kenji

After the Ryukyu Kingdom was formally annexed by Japan in 1879 and came under the control of the Meiji government as Okinawa Prefecture, Yaeyama became the "southern gate" of the Japanese nation. Yet Japanese government officials exercised caution in developing Yaeyama, lest they further antagonize the Qing government, which opposed Japan's forcible annexation and establishment of Okinawa Prefecture. Yaeyama's uncultivated lands, however, attracted people from Mainland Japan and the prefecture's main island of Okinawa.

When Taiwan was ceded to Japan, Yaeyama was no longer the southern gate of the Japanese nation; instead, the islands became the border demarcating the Inner Territory of Japan proper and the Outer Territories of the Japanese Empire. By exploring the local history of Yaeyama from the time the Ryukyu Kingdom was annexed by Japan, this chapter examines the changes the region underwent during the late nineteenth and the early twentieth century, which in turn created the preconditions for the large number of Yaeyama Islanders who immigrated to Taiwan in the early twentieth century.

From the Periphery of the Ryukyu Kingdom to the Empire's Border Zone

Under the hegemony of Sinocentrism, early modern Japan recognized "foreign zones" (*iiki*) as well as "foreign countries" (*ikoku*).[6] Yezochi, which was inhabited by the Ainu people, the islands of Hokkaido and Sakhalin, and the Kuril Archipelago as well as the Ryukyu Islands were recognized foreign zones or foreign countries from time to time. While Yezochi was manipulated by the Matsumae Domain and the Ryukyus were controlled by the Shimazu Domain,[7] they were recognized as autonomous regions with separate political, economic, and cultural systems.[8] Unlike the obvious borders demarcating independent states in the modern nation-state system, the Sinocentric world did not necessarily maintain clear boundaries between countries and regions.[9] However, these ambiguous zones became problematic when Japan was pressured to join the modern nation-state system.[10] While the Meiji government tried to erase regional boundaries in establishing the centralized nation-state, it attempted to clarify the national borders in the north and south.

First, Russia and Japan tussled over the northern border.[11] As Russia had been actively exploring Yezochi in the mid-nineteenth century with an eye to one day ruling it, the Tokugawa Shogunate needed to clarify the border between their two countries. In contrast, the southern foreign zone became problematic a little later than the northern border. To show that the Ryukyu Islands had become a formal territory of Japan, the Japanese government designated the archipelago the Ryukyu Domain in 1872, denoting the Tokugawa Shogunate's perception of the Ryukyu Kingdom as one of the Japanese domains.[12] Despite this designation, the shogunate initially did not oppose the Ryukyu Kingdom's tributary relationship with China. Rather, the Japanese government claimed that the Ryukyu Kingdom was not an independent country because it belonged to two countries—Japan and China.[13]

After Japan adopted the modern nation-state system, the government began negotiating the southern border following the dispatch of troops to Taiwan in retaliation for the murder of some fishermen from Miyako, one of the southern Ryukyu Islands, who had accidentally drifted there. In November 1871, the Ryukyu Kingdom's tributary vessels were shipwrecked on their return to Miyako. On December 7, 1871, one of these vessels drifted to the coast of southern Taiwan. Three crew members drowned before landing, but the other sixty-six landed on the island and arrived at one of the Taiwanese aboriginal communities. Because of miscommunication and misunderstanding between the two groups, the Taiwanese aborigines murdered fifty-four crew members. The Japanese government got wind of this tragedy from the twelve survivors, who returned to Miyako by way of China. Despite international opposition, Japanese troops were dispatched to Taiwan in May 1874 to avenge the murder of Japanese subjects. The Qing government strongly remonstrated with the Japanese government over this invasion of its territory. Although the dispute created a diplomatic furor, it was resolved on October 31, 1874, through British arbitration and the signing of the Beijing Agreement. Under the terms of this agreement, China agreed to compensate the survivors of the tragedy monetarily as long as Japanese troops were removed from Taiwan.[14] The peaceful settlement of this dispute was of great significance to the Meiji government, for it implied that the Ryukyus were a Japanese territory. When the Meiji government concluded the Beijing Agreement with China, the Qing government formally acknowledged that the crew members from Miyako were Japanese subjects. Even though the Chinese government never admitted that the Ryukyu Islands were integral parts of early modern Japan, the Qing government's formal acceptance of the terms of the Beijing Agreement implied its tacit acknowledgment of the Ryukyus as a Japanese territory.[15]

The Taiwan expedition and subsequent diplomatic agreement did not necessarily justify Japanese annexation of the Ryukyus; however, it provided the Meiji government with the confidence it needed to carry out its imperialistic plan. China protested Japan's annexation of the Ryukyus, but Japan justified its actions by insisting that the Ryukyus had been under the control of the Shimazu clan since the early seventeenth century.[16] In order to prevent this territorial issue from devolving into armed conflict, both governments sought the arbitration of former American president Ulysses S. Grant. On October 21, 1880, they signed a treaty by which they agreed to divide the Ryukyu Islands: Japan would take the northern islands, including the main island of Okinawa and the surrounding islands, and the southern part of Miyako and Yaeyama Islands would belong to China. Owing to lobbying against the division of the archipelago by Ryukyuan activists and some Chinese officials, the Qing government did not reach a consensus as to formal ratification of the treaty. This proposed division of the archipelago was never realized, and the issue of the Ryukyus' sovereignty was set aside until the end of the First Sino-Japanese War in 1895. This indicates that in spite of the abolishment of the Ryukyu Kingdom and the establishment of Okinawa Prefecture in 1879, the sovereignty of the Ryukyus remained uncertain until the end of the Sino-Japanese War. The Meiji government, however, succeeded in justifying the establishment of Okinawa Prefecture based on the outcome of the Taiwan expedition; this justification was further bolstered by Japan's victory in the First Sino-Japanese War and the cession of Taiwan.[17]

Integration into the Japanese National Economy

While the lives of Yaeyama locals were greatly transformed after Japan annexed the Ryukyu Kingdom, a significant number of settlers had been arriving in the islands since the 1880s. Many of these new immigrants began their own businesses, but some Japanese entrepreneurs rose to the challenge of undertaking land reclamation in Yaeyama. Among these endeavors, Nakagawa Toranosuke's project was the first and foremost development project conducted in Yaeyama. Nakagawa Toranosuke's hometown, Tokushima Prefecture, had been famous for its white sugar industry during the Edo period. He was born into a well-established sugar manufacturing family celebrated for its traditional methods of producing quality white sugar. Domestic sugar manufacturers fell into decline when good, lower-priced sugar was imported in large quantities in the 1860s. In March 1881, Nakagawa attended the Second Industrial Promotion Exhibition in Tokyo and noticed the excellent quality of Okinawan sugarcane. Intrigued, he visited the main island of Okinawa and Ishigaki Island with the intention of developing a sugar industry in Yaeyama. He planned to overcome the slump in the domestic sugar industry by using modern methods of agriculture and industry in Japan's newly acquired territory.[18]

The Okinawa prefectural government rejected Nakagawa's initial request to reclaim land on Ishigaki Island on the grounds that it was too early for Japanese mainlanders to reclaim land in Yaeyama. The government's hesitation on socially integrating Yaeyama into Japan arose from its concerns vis-à-vis the reactions of local authorities and Chinese to its active involvement in reclamation. The Yaeyama local government immediately accepted Nakagawa's subsequent application to reclaim land on Ishigaki Island with nine colleagues in 1891.[19] In the same year, the Okinawa prefectural government implemented its Regulations for Reclamation in Yaeyama (Yaeyama Kaikon Kisoku), and eighteen projects comprising eighty-one Okinawan and Japanese settlers were allowed to reclaim approximately 385 hectares of land in 1891–1893. However, some of them did not start the work of reclamation, and others gave up early in their attempts. In 1894, only eight projects were engaged in actively developing their leased lands. Nakagawa's reclamation project originally spanned 91 hectares of land in the Nagura area of Ishigaki Island. He further leased nearly 2,500 hectares of land in 1893 and founded the Corporation for Yaeyama Reclamation (Yaeyama Kaikon Kumiai), which employed twenty-seven immigrant laborers and five hundred islanders. He paid wages in cash, which spread currency use among Yaeyama locals for the first time.[20]

With an eye to further expanding his project, Nakagawa and eight other founders established the Yaeyama Sugar Industry Corporation in 1895. Nakagawa was chosen to be the executive director, and the renowned Meiji entrepreneur, Shibusawa Eiichi, was appointed auditor. In March 1896, Nakagawa brought fifty-four people from Mainland Japan—including a medical doctor, office workers, farmers, and technicians—and started a business in Nagura, the western part of Ishigaki Island. He employed local islanders

Nakagawa Toranosuke, Ishigaki Island, 1894. Source: Tokushima Kenritsu Hakubutsukan, *Tokushima Kenritsu Hakubutsukan nyūsu.* Used with permission.

as unskilled laborers and brought in skilled workers from outside.[21] According to the corporation's first annual report in 1896, Nakagawa relied on immigrant workers because "it would be more efficient to bring in laborers from Mainland Japan and hire workers from Naha or Ōshima for convenience than employ the natives, who are unskilled and unable to fully communicate with us."[22]

However, many of the immigrant workers and their families were unaccustomed to the environment of Ishigaki Island and could not cope with the working conditions. Many contracted malaria. Some succumbed to the disease, and others returned home. Thus, although a number of people from Mainland Japan came to work for Nakagawa's office, only some of them settled in Ishigaki.[23] In November 1897, the Nagura office was seriously damaged by a typhoon. Four factory buildings and thirty-nine houses were destroyed. As soon as the company recovered from the destruction, the office was hit by another typhoon in June 1898. Due to these two successive natural disasters, the stockholders decided to close Yaeyama Sugar Industry Corporation at their annual general meeting in August 1898.[24] After the corporation shut down, Nakagawa remained in Nagura to continue land reclamation with some eighty Japanese immigrants who had been dismissed from the Nagura office.[25]

In the meantime, the Japanese government tried to develop the sugar industry in colonial Taiwan. When Kodama Gentarō was appointed governor-general of colonial Taiwan in 1898, he stressed the development of industries, promoted the economic independence of the colony, and deemed sugar production to be one of the major industries. With strong support from Governor-General Kodama, the Taiwan Sugar Industry Corporation (Taiwan Seitō Kabushiki Gaisha) was founded in 1900.[26] In 1901, Nakagawa went to Taiwan to hand over the machinery used by the Yaeyama Sugar Industry Corporation to the Taiwan Sugar Industry Corporation. Thereafter, he chose to launch another sugar enterprise in Taiwan and did not return to Yaeyama.[27] Nakagawa was one of the first Japanese mainlanders to advocate the full integration of Yaeyama into Japan. However, its critical location between Japan and China meant that the Japanese government remained cautious about normalizing Yaeyama's social and political institutions. Ironically, by the time Japan's victory in the First Sino-Japanese War clarified Yaeyama's position, Nakagawa's interests had shifted from Yaeyama to colonial Taiwan. He swiftly left Yaeyama and soon inaugurated a new venture in the new "southern gate," Taiwan.

New Settlers Dominate the Imperial Network

Following Nakagawa Toranosuke's role in introducing the money economy to Yaeyama, new settlers from the main island of Okinawa and Mainland Japan came to dominate the commercial businesses and modern industries of the region. While some immigrants in the fishery industry settled in Kohama and Yonaguni Islands, others made homes on Iriomote Island, where several companies had been mining coal since the late nineteenth century.[28] Shika District, the political and economic center of Ishigaki Island since the time of the Ryukyu Kingdom, attracted more settlers than other areas did. In the commercial district of Ishigaki Island, businesses owned by settlers from Mainland Japan and the main island of Okinawa were larger than those run by the local islanders, and the new settlers' sugar retailers especially were larger than their other enterprises.[29]

New settlers not only played a leading role in Yaeyama's commercial businesses but also contributed greatly to the inauguration and development of modern fishery in the region. Although Yaeyama is surrounded by water, fishery had never been encouraged and was even regarded as a vulgar activity during the rule of the Ryukyu Kingdom. Itoman fishers, originally from the main island of Okinawa, first came to Yaeyama to gather valuable tur-

Commercial district of Ishigaki Island, ca. late 1920s–early 1930s. Source: Editorial Committee of Municipal History Books, Ishigaki-shi, Board of Education. Used with permission.

ban shells and agar weed,[30] which had not yet been commercialized by Yaeyama Islanders.[31] They found Yaeyama particularly attractive after the Koga Firm opened on Ishigaki Island in 1882. Founded in Naha by Koga Tatsushirō (1856–1918) just before Okinawa's annexation to Japan, the Koga Firm produced various marine products and dealt with international traders. Koga was particularly successful in trading turban shells, which were used for shell buttons. He sent materials from Yaeyama to the Osaka Koga Firm, which was managed by his brother, and the Osaka Firm exported marine products overseas. Itoman fishers consequently conducted business with Koga, who needed fishers capable of collecting shells and other marine products for his business.[32]

The establishment of the first sawmill on Ishigaki Island in 1916 led to the development of the timber industry by the new settlers. While some sawmills exported timber to Miyako and the main island of Okinawa, the Yamabishi Firm (Yamabishi Shōkai)—one of the largest timber companies on Ishigaki Island—exported to Taiwan. The firm was founded by Maeda Sentarō, who arrived in Taiwan in the 1910s as a migrant farmer from Kagawa Prefecture. As the colonial government of Taiwan promoted the development of infrastructure through the construction of various services and facilities such as railways, there was a huge demand for timber in Taiwan. The Yamabishi Firm, with its headquarters in Keelung and a branch

Fishers' village, Ishigaki Island, 1934. Source: Ishigaki Municipal Museum of Yaeyama. Used with permission of the museum director.

in Tokyo, provided timber for these projects. The development of the timber and commercial fishing industries was accompanied by the growth of the shipbuilding and steel industries. In fact, there were several docks and ironworks in the same vicinity as sawmills in the coastal area. The docks and ironworks worked mainly in tandem with bonito fishing boats and were likewise founded by new settlers from the main island of Okinawa or from Kagoshima and Miyazaki Prefectures.[33] In short, the transplantation of modern industries to Yaeyama at the beginning of the twentieth century made the new settlers leaders in the industrial and commercial sectors of Ishigaki Island, the commercial center of the Yaeyama Islands.

While commercial businesses were dominated largely by new settlers from the main island of Okinawa and Mainland Japan, Yaeyama became the geoeconomic node of the imperial network linking the Inner Territory and the Outer Territories of the Japanese Empire. As soon as Taiwan was ceded to Japan in 1895, the Osaka Merchant Ship Company (Osaka Shōsen) opened a shipping line between Osaka and Taiwan by way of Kobe, Kagoshima, Ōshima, Okinawa, and Yaeyama in 1896. As Taipei grew as the capital of colonial Taiwan, it became one of the nearest urban cities to Yaeyama. The Osaka Merchant Ship Company's steamships carried not only visitors to Taiwan but also various commodities between Ishigaki and Keelung. Although there is no reliable statistical data documenting the growth of long-term trade between Yaeyama and Taiwan, it is possible to assume that trade between Ishigaki and Keelung rapidly increased in the 1910s. Export items traveling from Ishigaki to Keelung numbered 18,770 in 1916, and the number increased by 65.7 percent to 31,107 in 1920.[34] Yaeyama's trade with colonial Taiwan almost equaled its trade with the main island of Okinawa in the early 1920s.

Yaeyama's local newspapers reflected the development of its commercial businesses as it was integrated into Japan's imperial network.[35] Not only did the newspapers report the news, particularly the commercial news from Taiwan; they also published commercial advertisements for several business branches with headquarters in Taiwan. A page in the June 5, 1922, edition of the *Sakishima News* (Sakishima shinbun) illustrates an aspect of Yaeyama's commercial businesses at that time. There are six large advertisements and eight smaller ones on the page. Some of the larger advertisements are for Japanese-style hotels; two are for restaurants serving Taiwanese as well as Japanese and Western cuisine; and another promotes souvenirs and handicrafts made from Yaeyama wood. The publication of these articles and advertisements in the local newspapers indicates the extent to which trade with colonial Taiwan was intrinsic to Yaeyama's commercial businesses.

Furthermore, Taiwan had become an important market for Yaeyama producers by the end of the 1920s. For example, the Association of Fresh Fish Transportation (Sengyo Yusō Kumiai), established in January 1932, shipped fresh fish to Keelung almost weekly in January, exporting 18,271 *kin* (10,962.6 kg) and making 1,087.615 yen from the month's total sales.[36] An article in another local paper, *Yaeyama People's News* (Yaeyama minpō), demonstrates that as local purchasing power declined during the economic depression, the Yaeyama fishing industry responded by establishing the Association of Fresh Fish Transportation and exporting fish to other places. The article also states realistically: "The purchasing power of Keelung cannot be compared with local purchasing power, as Taipei is behind Keelung. . . . [However,] the association is attempting to export fish to Moji by way of Taiwan as well."[37]

Yonaguni, a remote island situated west of Ishigaki Island, maintained even closer economic ties with Taiwan. According to a March 1929 newspaper article, although steamships rarely stopped in Yonaguni, three motorboats regularly went to Keelung and Ishigaki five to six times per month. About 90 percent of Yonaguni's trade was related to business with colonial Taiwan.[38] In writing about his postal worker father, Ikema Nae, who was born on Yonaguni Island in 1918, recollects the islanders asking fishers to post mail in Taiwan en route to their fishing trips in Taiwanese waters. Some mail to Yonaguni Island was delivered by way of a post office in

先嶋新聞

八重山石垣港
や
旅館

廣告
▲晝食 ▲米粉 ▲スキ焼
▲スシ 其他和洋料理仕出シ
今般左記場所ニ於テ大勉強安價ニテ
御好ニ應ズ可ク簡間御引立ノ程願上候
濱崎商店向新築二階
吾妻家

旅人宿
旅館

台湾料理御好み次第
共ノ他
すし ぜんざい
色々出來マス
來々軒

八重山郡石垣港郵便局前
旅館
石本寅次郎

八重山ヨリノ御土産ハ
八重山名木ニテ製作セル工藝品ヲ御進メ致シマス
弊工所ハ最高ニ名木ヲ準備シ出來得ル限リノ
努力ト技術ヲ以テ製作致シマス
製品ニ付テハ製品共物ガ雄辯ニ語リマス
池原挽物工所

營業案內
石垣用宗商店
天川製材所
土地測量
並ニ製圖
三島龜鶴堂
質屋
濱崎商店
川上製材所
小野商店

Advertisements in a local newspaper. Source: *Sakishima shinbun*, June 5, 1922.

Keelung. In fact, a delivery to Yonaguni Island via Keelung was faster than a delivery via Ishigaki Island.[39] In this way, Yaeyama became a commercial satellite of colonial Taipei in the 1910s, and people's everyday lives were also integrated into the imperial network. Importantly, the new settlers' dominance of commercial business in Yaeyama culminated in their commanding position in commercial trade between Ishigaki and Keelung.

Moving toward the "Civilized Colony"

While the new settlers leading Yaeyama's commercial enterprises were swiftly linked with colonial Taiwan next door, Yaeyama farmers, who accounted for the majority of the population, struggled to catch up with the ensuing radical economic and social transformations. Most local islanders remained unfamiliar with the money economy until the end of the nineteenth century. Money was used for the first time in public office in 1879, after a Japanese immigrant was installed as a public official. However, it was used only for payments and exchanges within the public office. Islanders did not have the opportunity to use money until the government allowed Yaeyama villages to pay taxes in cash in 1892.[40] Even after money was introduced by the public office and new Japanese settlers, people still more or less maintained their self-sufficient economy and did not use money in their everyday lives. This changed after the enactment of land reforms in 1903, whereupon the local farmers were obliged to pay individual land taxes and public expenses in cash. As Yaeyama communities were integrated into Japanese systems and institutions, residents bore the burden of paying for education, hygiene, and the promotion of industry.

Until the 1910s, most local farmers earned money by selling vegetables and livestock, with some making money from tobacco and sugarcane production. Farmers also commonly made money by cutting timber, carrying charcoal from the forest, and gathering firewood. As Panama hats became a Japanese export product, Yaeyama became part of the Panama hat industry in the early 1910s due to its ample supply of native *adan* plants, which provided the fiber for the hats. It consequently became popular for farmers to gather *adan* leaves from the forest or work in *adan*-processing factories. With only a small number of factories producing hats on Yaeyama and most of the fibers going to factories on the main island of Okinawa, profits for local islanders were not sizeable. Nevertheless, it was an important industry for Yaeyama Islanders until the Panama hat industry declined in the early 1920s.[41]

Yaeyama farmers began to grow more cash crops to meet their need for money. The government likewise encouraged them to turn to cash crops, and sugarcane was popular among the local farmers. The Meiji government's industrial policy in Okinawa Prefecture emphasized the importance of the sugar industry, in contrast to the Ryukyu Kingdom period when Yaeyama Islanders were forbidden to produce sugar under the government-controlled economy. The Meiji government promoted the sugar industry in Yaeyama by giving loans and distributing young sugarcane to Yaeyama communities. As a result, both migrant farmers and local farmers grew sugarcane beginning in the 1880s.[42] Unfortunately, the inexperience and lack of skills among Yaeyama local farmers meant that productivity remained lower than the average for the prefecture until the 1930s.[43]

The local farmers were mostly excluded from the commercial trade between Yaeyama and Taiwan; however, this does not mean that local farmers had no contact with Taiwan. On the contrary, their alienation from the local economy resulted in many local farmers becoming labor migrants to Taiwan, thereby underpinning Japanese development of the colony. *Biographies of Yaeyama Residents* (*Yaeyama jinji kōshinroku*) published 275 life histories of well-established Yaeyama locals in 1951, including the biographies of several of the earliest immigrants to Taiwan. One of these early migrants was born on Ishigaki Island in 1898 and entered a junior high school on the main island of Okinawa in 1912. He later left the school in Okinawa and entered Taihoku First Middle School in Taipei, where he graduated in 1917.[44] Another early migrant was born on Kohama Island in 1904; he moved to Tokyo, then to Taiwan, where he joined a Taiwan police training school in 1916 and later became a policeman.[45] The book suggests that Yaeyama Islanders had been traveling across the Japanese imperial space for education and employment since the 1910s.

According to government records, there were 156 Yaeyama immigrants in Taiwan in 1921;[46] this number grew to 241 in 1922.[47] The *Sakishima Asahi News* (*Sakishima asahi shinbun*) of June 1931 reports that the number of Yaeyama female immigrants was 843, and the majority of them resided in either Taipei or Keelung. Although the reliability of the data is

Table 2.1. Origins of Yaeyama Female Immigrants in Taiwan, June 1931

	Ishigaki Island	Taketomi Island	Yonaguni Island	Total
Number of immigrants	387	280	176	843
Female population, 1930	10,229	3,993	2,201	16,423

Sources: Sakishima asahi shinbun, June 28, 1931; Naikaku Tōkeikyoku, *Kokusei chōsa hōkoku, vol. 4, Okinawa-ken,* 2.

questionable, this suggests that the number of female immigrants from Yaeyama to Taiwan increased rapidly in the 1920s.

The immigrants' memoirs and my interviews suggest that the Yaeyama Islanders usually utilized a network of people from their hometowns who had already settled in Taiwan during the early years of Japanese colonization. Some former immigrants, originally from Taketomi Island, witnessed new migrants from their home island receiving help from Takeshima Kaoru, who had arrived in Taipei sometime between 1920 and 1921. After Takeshima opened a bicycle shop in the Shinki District in Taipei City, new migrants, sometimes more than sixty at a time, stayed at his home until they found jobs and settled down. Tsuji Hiroshi, born on Taketomi Island in 1915, describes how Takeshima helped the Taketomi Islanders begin their new lives in Taiwan: "Takeshima and his wife cooked rice porridge in a big pot to feed the islanders. Because their dining table was not big enough for so many visitors, they used a shutter as a table and fed them by dividing them into three or four groups. They offered a place to sleep by spreading mats on the earthen floor and made efforts to find jobs for the islanders."[48]

Why did Yaeyama Islanders migrate to Taiwan? In the interviews, former migrants to Taiwan revealed that many of the common Yaeyama Islanders migrated to Taiwan in search of job opportunities; others went to shop, sightsee, and visit friends. For instance, Kuroshima Nae (pseudonym), who was born on Taketomi Island in 1912, explained her reasons for going to Taiwan:

> I finished the compulsory six-year primary education, and there was a two-year advanced course. After graduating from the advanced course, everyone emigrated. There were migrants everywhere. Because it was a self-sufficient economy and everyone was a farmer, there was no income to be had. Thus, everyone became migrants.[49]

Another informant, Tsuji Hiroshi, explained that he also went to Taiwan in 1930 in search of employment:

> I decided to go to Taiwan immediately after graduating from the advanced course of primary school. Since there were no jobs on the island at that time, most of my seniors went overseas and were successful. People envied the emigrants and their families. I was no exception. We thought that it would be best for me to depart as soon as possible. As my aunt, Shiraho Sue, would take care of me, I went to Taiwan on the *Konan-maru* with one piece of luggage wrapped in cloth. I remember that I first stayed with the Shiraho family in the Shimogafu District of Taipei.[50]

A popular image is that Okinawans migrated to foreign countries to earn money so they could send remittances to their families at home. Indeed, in focusing on the income gap between rural and urban areas as an incentive for migration, previous studies of Okinawan migration often stress the significance of remittances from emigrants. For example, Kinjō Isao makes the following claim:

> People appreciated the amount of money sent home by the migrants, and their remittances were believed to have significantly contributed to the Okinawan economy, which was suffering from economic depression.... Poverty in Okinawa, especially poverty in the agricultural areas, was the primary cause of migration.[51]

My interviews, however, suggest that Yaeyama migrants did not necessarily remit money to their families on their home islands. Some only sent presents for the New Year celebrations or special occasions, and others never sent anything to their straitened families. Some migrants remitted the whole of their small incomes; others never sent goods or money and instead spent their income on their own living expenses, expensive clothes, or leisure activities in Taipei. Migration certainly reduced the number of mouths that had to be fed at home. In this way all migrants contributed financially to their families, regardless of whether or not they sent remittances. Still, there is no clear connection between the amount of money remitted, the financial straits of a migrant in Taiwan, and his or her family in Yaeyama. Mizuta Kenji, who conducted his own interviews with twenty-six Yaeyama Islanders who had worked in colonial Taiwan, also deduces that Yaeyama migrants did not always send remittances home.[52]

In short, Yaeyama Islanders' migration to colonial Taiwan cannot be assessed purely on the basis of their economic objectives, for subjective reasons also contributed to their departure from their home islands. In my conversations with Yaeyama Islanders who traveled to Taiwan for work, education, and other reasons, I discovered that they shared very similar views of their home islands as uncivilized and Taiwan as a developed, civilized land full of opportunities. Tsuji Hiroshi notes that he migrated to Taiwan seeking work:

> After graduating from primary school, most men and women traveled off the island in search of jobs. The destinations varied: Ishigaki-chō (at that time), which was the nearest; the main island of Okinawa; Tokyo; Osaka; Taiwan; or the South Sea Islands. Taiwan in particular was the most popular, as people celebrated it as a paradise island. Everything was

> convenient because many youths from the island who were older than me were already working in Taiwan.[53]

A female informant, Yamamoto Kiyoko (pseudonym), born on Ishigaki Island in 1924, detailed her reasons for migrating to Taiwan with her friend in 1940:

> Well, the thing is that everyone rushed to Taiwan. My sister was in Taiwan and worked in a university professor's house as an apprentice servant. We told my sister that we were going to Taiwan. We relied on someone who was no more than an apprentice servant, rather than someone who was established with a family. Thinking back on it, this was absurd. After all, we were simply two casual visitors who went to Taiwan by ourselves. . . . I wanted to go to Taiwan because—I wanted to go there because there was electricity and running water in Taiwan. It was very attractive to me. Well, here, we had to draw water from a well. We had to draw water and use a lamp. Thinking about it, I thought the city was great and so convenient.[54]

The contrast between Taiwan's civilized image and the uncivilized home island may have been strengthened when local islanders received fancy gifts from migrants, saw the Western attire of returnees from Taiwan, and heard rumors of the urban lifestyle in Taipei. It is possible that neighborhood rumors of Taiwan's imagined level of civilization sprang from Yaeyama's adoption of several advanced technologies from Taiwan throughout the 1920s and 1930s. Yaeyama's development projects were significantly undermined by the spread of malaria, yet neither the national nor prefectural government sought to seriously combat this problem until the 1910s. When the local government finally organized a committee for the prevention of malaria in 1921, its members learned a disease prevention method from Taiwan.[55] Moreover, several new varieties of rice introduced to Yaeyama in the 1920s came from Taiwan, including Hōrai rice.[56] The yield from Hōrai rice was three times greater than that of conventional rice, and it thus became very common in Yaeyama. Cultivation of Taiwanese rice varieties not only increased agricultural production but also transformed the technique of rice farming in Yaeyama.[57]

In short, population movement from Yaeyama to colonial Taiwan could be characterized as rural-urban migration within a colonial empire. Yaeyama's economic situation, coupled with its surplus labor force, created the conditions that made migration a popular course of action among local farmers. These objective conditions cannot fully explain the Yaeyama Islanders' reasons for working in Taiwan because some of them were not in need and did not have to provide financial support for their families. The commonly held image of "civilized Taiwan," in sharp contrast to "underdeveloped Yaeyama," was also an incentive for migration. The opening of the seaway and the strengthening of commercial ties between the two regions resulted in Taiwan becoming a reference point of modernity for Yaeyama Islanders. Additionally, some villages witnessed a surge in immigration to Taiwan because migrants tended to rely on pioneer migrants, neighbors, and relatives who were already living in the colony.

During the Ryukyu Kingdom period, Yaeyama was treated as a peripheral region by the government, and vast amounts of land were left undeveloped. Despite the Japanese government's eagerness to clarify the national border by fully integrating Yaeyama into Japan, it was reluctant to antagonize Qing China with a radical change in national policy. In the meantime, pioneer civilians such as Nakagawa Toranosuke proactively exploited the Yaeyama Islands and integrated them into the Japanese national economy. In short, Yaeyama's political status was left in limbo between Japan and China when the former transitioned from a Sinocentric to the modern nation-state system. However, once Taiwan was ceded to Japan after the First Sino-Japanese War, Yaeyama became the borderland between the Inner Territory and the Outer Territories. After Taiwan became Japan's "southern gate," Nakagawa Toranosuke, who was most passionate about developing Yaeyama, swiftly lost interest and moved to Taiwan.

Meanwhile, a significant number of new immigrants from the main island of Okinawa and Mainland Japan settled in Yaeyama, and they dominated modern industries and commercial businesses in the region. The lives of Yaeyama Islanders were further integrated in the Japanese Empire's commercial, social, and cultural networks when the Osaka Merchant Ship Company established passage between Mainland Japan and colonial Taiwan. In his study of Japanese sex workers—so-called *karayuki-san*—during the late nineteenth century, Bill Mihalopoulos illustrates how Japan's transformation into a money economy gave the Amakusa women economic and social autonomy, which led the increase of sex workers abroad.[58] Similarly, Yaeyama farmers' immigration to Taiwan increased against the background of Yaeyama's social and economic incorporation into the Japanese imperial market. While new immigrants from the main island of Okinawa and Mainland Japan achieved economic dominance in the region by means of the colonial seaway, a significant number of Yaeyama farmers migrated to colonial Taiwan by sea. It could thus be said that Yaeyama's socioeconomic transformation as well as its liminal state between the Japanese nation and the empire, effected colonial migration from Yaeyama to colonial Taiwan.

Nevertheless, we should not conclude that Yaeyama Islanders migrated to Taiwan solely for the purpose of earning money and sending remittances to their families in Yaeyama. Instead, we should acknowledge the role played by the commonly held image of a "civilized Taiwan" in attracting numerous Yaeyama youths to Taiwan, some of whom were not in urgent financial need and did not have to support their families back home.

Chapter 3

Making Distinctions in the Extension of Japan

Beginning in the early 1920s, the number of Okinawan immigrants in Taiwan rapidly increased. This coincided with Den Kenjirō becoming the first civilian governor-general of Taiwan in 1919. Den is well known for elucidating the general principle of the Japanese colonial government in Taiwan in "Gradual Extension of the Inner Territory" (Zenshinteki naichi enchō shugi), his inaugural address. In this address, he claimed that Taiwan would be completely equal to the Inner Territory in the future; however, equal systems and institutions would be gradually introduced after the gaps between the Inner Territory and Taiwan had been remedied. In short, there was a shift away from coercive power to an approach that emphasized unity between the Japanese and the Taiwanese.[1]

In the belief that ethnic unity would be possible only through the cultural integration of the two groups, the assimilation (so-called *dōka*) of Taiwanese was highly valued and systematically promoted by various educational institutions. In other words, it was supposed that Taiwanese were the one who should conform to mainstream Japanese customs and manners based on the premise that Japanese were superior to Taiwanese.[2] Until 1936, eight civilians held the position of governor-general after Den. While the colonial authorities stressed unification of the Inner Territory and Taiwan through various social and educational policies during this period of civilian governors (1919–1936), Taiwan was excluded from the rights and obligations ordained by the Japanese Constitution.[3] The life histories of male and female Okinawan immigrants in this chapter demonstrate their attempts at social advancement, urbanization, and modernization. To that end, this chapter shows how fluency in the Japanese language and mastery of Japanese traditions were entangled with social advancement in the colonial context.

Under the Gradual Extension policy, unskilled Okinawan immigrants were the most ambiguous imperial subjects because they lived in the malleable boundary between the colonizer and the colonized. For that reason,

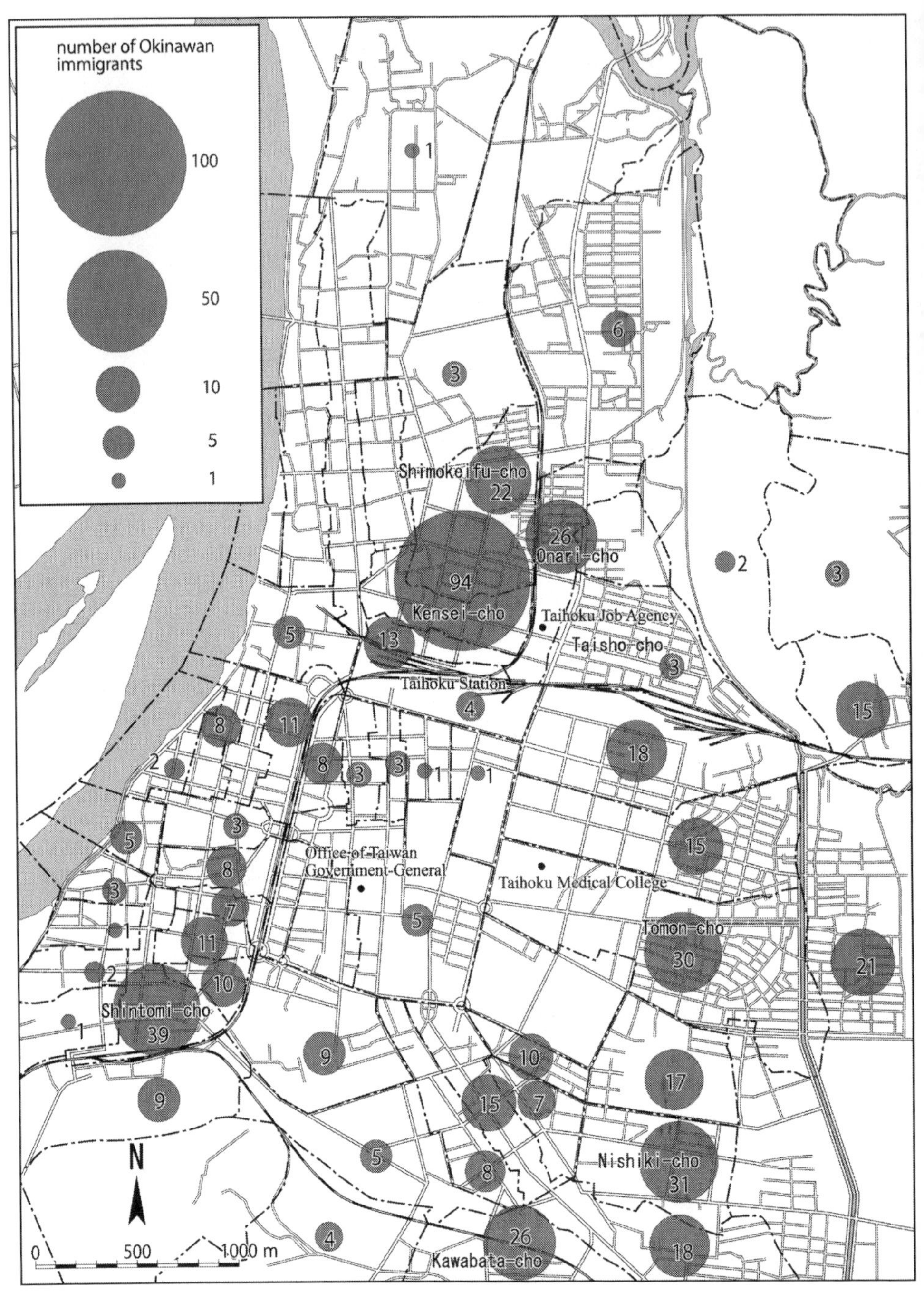

Okinawan immigrants in Taipei, 1942. Source: Arashiro Hajime, *Shōwa 17nen-ban Taihokushimin jūshoroku*. Map by Mizuta Kenji

the process of becoming Japanese was essential to the social advancement of Okinawan migrant workers. In exploring the migrants' colonial experiences, this chapter illustrates the struggles of Okinawan immigrants as they sought to become Japanese in the contact zones where Okinawans and Taiwanese met in their everyday lives. According to Mary Louise Pratt, contact zones are "social spaces where disparate cultures meet, clash, and grapple with each other, often in highly asymmetrical relations of domination and subordination."[4] While the personal experiences of Okinawan migrants did not necessarily reflect actual differences enshrined in policies and legal institutions, their everyday politics were intrinsic to the larger framework of colonial rule. The chapter also demonstrates how the struggle to become Japanese was highly gendered.

Migration as a Chance for Social Advancement

As mentioned, Okinawans usually did not go to colonial Taiwan through an intermediary. Instead, they relied on their network of family or friends. It was not unusual for Okinawan youths without work experience to arrive in Taiwan not knowing what they were going to do. Moreover, the immigrants frequently changed workplaces. It would indeed be difficult to track each immigrant's career in Taiwan because it was common to see an unskilled immigrant start out as a shop boy or factory laborer and eventually secure work as a government employee or a policeman after living in Taiwan for several years. Employers might deplore the tendency to change jobs frequently, but this shows the Okinawan immigrants' agency and willingness to advance socially in the colony. The autobiography of Takemoto Seigi (b. 1912) indicates that it was commonplace for Okinawan migrants to attend evening schools in colonial Taiwan:

> Because the last clerk (*bantō*) retired, they hired me. The first clerk went to an evening school, but once he graduated, he went back to Naha in order to go to a driving school. The second one worked for a year and then became the postal officer of Keelung. I was the third clerk. Perhaps Sōichi-san [the employer] had learned a lesson because he told me, "I will never let you go to school because Okinawans quit their jobs after further education."[5]

Takemoto was born on Ishigaki Island, arrived on Taiwan in 1926, and worked there for nearly twenty years. His anecdote suggests that it was common for Okinawan migrants to go to school while working as manual laborers. Some of my interviewees also went to evening schools in Taipei City. Pseudonymous interviewee Higa Takeshi went to an evening school for a while but dropped out because he was unable to handle both his studies and his live-in job at a pharmacy.[6] Another interviewee, Ishigaki Shincho, attended evening school while working at a printing factory and a wholesaler of marine products.[7] He may have been able to continue his studies because, unlike the preceding interviewee, he commuted to the printing factory and his working hours were relatively fixed. Enrolling in evening school was a common means of achieving social mobility for young Okinawan male migrants who could not afford a secondary education at home.

Nevertheless, for Okinawan migrants in Taiwan, becoming an apprentice was the most common method of acquiring a professional skill and advancing their careers. Japan's *decchi* system, which developed in the shogunal period, was similar to the Western apprenticeship and played an important role in the Japanese commercial world until the nineteenth century. It originally assumed a feudalistic relationship between a master and an apprentice, rather than a contractual relationship. The apprentice owed his master long-term loyalty because his master treated him like a family member. This custom persisted well into the early twentieth century. Although it became less feudalistic in the twentieth century, and an apprentice was less likely to serve a master for a long time, the practice still maintained an element of folkloric education.[8]

Through apprenticeships, Okinawan youth migrants who could not afford higher education at home acquired the knowledge and skills they needed to raise their social positions. For instance, after graduating from evening school, Ishigaki Shincho went to Kaohsiung to make a career for himself. He got a job at Ishibashi Photographic Shop, which was owned by a person from Saga Prefecture. Ishigaki spent three years as an apprentice in the shop alongside four other colleagues: one from Korea, one from Taiwan, and two from the Inner Territory. He later worked in a photographic shop in Tokyo for two years before returning to Kaohsiung and operating his own shop until he was forced to leave Taiwan after World War II.[9]

Tsuji Hiroshi, born on Taketomi Island in 1915, also learned a professional skill as an apprentice in Taiwan (discussed in chap. 2). He went to Taiwan at the age of fifteen and worked as a shop assistant at South Gate Bookstore (Nanmon Shoten) in the Kodama District. As the bookstore shared its premises with a hairdresser, the owner suggested that Tsuji become the hairdresser's apprentice.[10] In his autobiography, Tsuji recalls: "Luckily, Kurashita Tsutomu, who was originally from Hirae [a ward on East Ishigaki Island], was working at the hairdresser's as a professional. Because he also recommended that I do it, I decided to become an apprentice to a hairdresser. It was the first step toward becoming a hairdresser."[11]

In the end, he gave up becoming a hairdresser in Taiwan after passing an employment test for the public railway company in November 1935. While he was working at Keelung Station in 1936, he took another employees' certificate examination (*koin shikaku shiken*), which was equivalent to the exam taken by fourth-year junior high school students. In order to pass, he took a correspondence course known as the Waseda Lecture Series (Waseda Kōgiroku). He succeeded and was promoted. When he returned to Taketomi Island after the war, he made a living as a hairdresser until he retired.[12] Although both Ishigaki Shincho and Tsuji Hiroshi went to Taiwan as unskilled migrants, they became skilled workers while living in the Japanese migrant community.

In colonial Taiwan, it was uncommon for Japanese female migrants to have full-time jobs. The highest concentration of Japanese migrants in Taiwan was in the administrative division of Taipei Prefecture (Taihoku-shū). In 1930, 46,385 of the 101,184 Japanese migrants in Taipei Prefecture were women,[13] and only 14.5 percent of these migrants were employed.[14] Whereas women composed a sizeable part of the important labor force in rural and agricultural areas, Taiwanese and Japanese female residents in the urban areas of Taipei Prefecture were financially dependent on men. Although the exact number of Japanese female workers is unavailable, it is evident that the majority of Japanese female migrants came to Taiwan as dependent family members. In contrast, it was not unusual for Okinawan female youths to immigrate to Taiwan in search of jobs. According to the Taihoku Employment Agency, 70 percent of female job applicants in 1933 were from Okinawa Prefecture.[15] Although not every immigrant sought employment through

Table 3.1. Number of Japanese Job Seekers, 1933

	Okinawa	Japanese in total
Male	151	1,490
Female	1,099	1,569

Source: Taihoku-shi Shokugyō Shōkaijo, "Shokugyō shōkaijo jigyō gaiyō," 29–30.

Table 3.2. Age of Japanese Job Seekers, 1933

	Under 15	15–19	20–24	25–29	30–34	35–39	40–44	45–49	50–54	Over 55
Male	—	112	471	573	212	114	41	32	27	14
Female	18	511	661	159	76	63	37	29	12	11

Source: Taihoku-shi Shokugyō Shōkaijo, "Shokugyō shōkaijo jigyō gaiyō," 32–33.

Table 3.3. Educational Background of Japanese Job Seekers, 1933

	No schooling	Elementary school graduates	Secondary school dropouts	Secondary school graduates	University dropouts and graduates
Male	3	1,296	29	253	5
Female	13	1,459	28	77	—

Source: Taihoku-shi Shokugyō Shōkaijo, "Shokugyō shōkaijo jigyō gaiyō," 35.

Table 3.4. Job Vacancies by Occupation, 1933

	Commerce (%)	Domestic service (%)	Miscellaneous (%)	Industry and mining (%)
Male	71	—	19	1
Female	—	85	11	1

Source: Taihoku-shi Shokugyō Shōkaijo, "Shokugyō shōkaijo jigyō gaiyō," 37.

this public agency, the figure indicates that female Okinawan migrants formed a distinct segment of the female labor force in colonial Taiwan.

Job options were limited for Okinawan female youths, most of whom were elementary school graduates with little work experience. In 1934, domestic work represented 85 percent of the job offers made to female applicants by the Taihoku Employment Agency;[16] however, they were unlikely to consider these jobs appealing. Domestics normally were obliged to perform various household chores, including cooking, cleaning, shopping at markets, and needlework. They had days off once or twice a month on average. Although they were required to remain in the home for long hours every day, they were not well paid. Thus, some female migrants who had dreamed of colonial Taipei's modern life were disappointed with the reality of their situations. Others managed to find different jobs.

As mentioned in chapter 2, Yamamoto Kiyoko was attracted by the "civilized life of Taipei" in the stories she heard from older friends who had worked in Taiwan. Although she knew that most female Okinawan migrants became domestics, she refused to follow suit. Consequently, her sister, who worked as a domestic in Taipei, found employment for her as a laborer in a confectionery factory. However, she was unhappy with her job. While she was "running sweet bean jelly into molds and stuffing cakes with sweet beans," she "cried every day," thinking, "I did not come to Taiwan to do this!"[17]

> Young girls would have some idealized image of their lives, wouldn't they? For example, we were jealous of people who went to advanced girls' schools, wearing fine pleated skirts and putting on their white sailor's uniforms, school caps, and leather shoes, because these things could never be found in Yaeyama. Similarly, when I saw women confidently walking in high-heeled shoes in Taiwan, I was jealous and thought that I should not be a maid or a shop assistant.[18]

After working in the confectionery factory for a couple of months, Yamamoto became a domestic through the recommendation of a Yaeyama migrant from her neighborhood, serving in the household of a Taiwan Electric Power Company (Taiwan Denryoku) executive and his mistress, a former geisha. The house was located in the Taishō District, the richest suburb in Taipei City, and, unlike the average Japanese migrant household, employed two servants.[19]

> There were two maids. The newcomer was the "under maid" (*shimo jochū*), and the senior maid already with the house was the "upper maid" (*kami jochū*). Although there were only two servants, they made a hierarchy between the two! Japanese people in the colony were arrogant in the past.... Because I had to survive, I reluctantly worked there. But one rainy day, the master and mistress came back drenched. When they got back, we went to the entrance hall to welcome them. I noticed that they held out their feet towards us. The senior servant said to me, "Wipe their shoes with a cloth." I brought out a cloth and wiped their shoes at that time. But soon after, I threw away the cloth and said, "I will get out of here!" I felt so insulted. Did I have to wipe other people's feet for just a small amount of money? It would have been a human rights issue if it happened today. So I immediately left the house, saying, "I will no longer do this kind of work."[20]

She subsequently tried to find a better job with her good friend, who worked as a domestic in a medical doctor's household.

> I wanted to be an office worker with the friend, so I sent a false telegram to her master's house saying, "Your mother is in critical condition. Come back immediately." It was difficult for a maid to leave a job otherwise. Unlike today, we could not suddenly declare, "I quit." We had to have a good reason for leaving a job then. Then I sent a false telegram to her so that she could say, "I have to go back to my home island because my mother is sick." She managed to leave the job, and we rented a room together.[21]

Yamamoto and her friend rented a room in a Japanese-style townhouse (*nagaya*) in the Kensei District and began to live on their own. This time, rather than relying on her sister and acquaintances to find jobs, they went to a public employment agency and found jobs as telephone operators. Yamamoto's best friend continued to work in the job, but Yamamoto was still dissatisfied. She searched for another job by herself and eventually found employment as a telephone operator in Taihoku Imperial University Hospital. She said, "I transferred to the hospital because there were more operators and the working conditions were better."[22] When she began to earn forty yen every month at her new workplace, she was finally satisfied with her life in Taipei.

A factory worker or maid did not fit Yamamoto's idealized image of the civilized and modern life in Taipei City, which she had longed for when she was on Ishigaki Island. Indeed, telephone operator was deemed to be one of the jobs undertaken by the emerging class of "professional working women" (*shokugyō fujin*). The phenomenon of the professional working woman had attracted much social attention in Japan after World War I. Although the notion of professional working women has never been clearly defined, the term usually includes occupations like office workers, teachers, typists, shop assistants, nurses, and telephone operators. Due to the economic development of the interwar period, there were many openings in these occupations. These jobs required some educational qualifications or special skills and were distinguished from the more common occupations of factory laborers or domestics undertaken by Japanese women at the time. Professional working women were not always favorably received and were frequent targets of criticism and sources of controversy. Nonetheless, the idea of a professional working woman was new and associated with modern urban life.[23] Although most jobs for professional working women required graduation from advanced women's high schools, telephone operators did not need such educational qualifications.[24] Therefore, it can be said that Yamamoto found the best possible job, for it fit her idealized image of modern colonial life.

It should be noted that women's social advancement was not only shaped by the strong will and vitality of individual women but also fueled by a rapid increase in the female labor force in the 1930s. After the outbreak of the Second Sino-Japanese War, women entered workplaces that had hitherto been dominated by men. As the war resulted in labor shortages, women were offered more opportunities to participate in various fields of income-earning work. Although Japanese women did not go to the battlefield as soldiers, they served as a hardworking labor force during the war.[25]

The career of the pseudonymous Ōhara Yayoi clearly demonstrates the ways in which some Okinawan female migrants were involved in the Japanese military during wartime. Ōhara was born on Miyako Island in 1923. With her father chronically ill, her mother supported the family as a broker of hemp cloth. Like many girls her age, Ōhara longed to be a Red Cross nurse. In pursuit of that dream, she worked for a clinic on Miyako Island after graduating from the advanced course of her neighborhood elementary school. However, she was soon disappointed by the tiresome work at the clinic. She quit her job half a year later and moved to Taiwan in 1937 when she was fifteen or sixteen years old. She was not alone there, as two of her much older brothers were already working in Taiwan as police officers.[26] Although migration from the Yaeyama Islands was substantial (discussed in chap. 2), the Miyako Islands also sent a significant number of immigrants to Taiwan. Unfortunately, there are considerably fewer archival documents available to verify the extent of emigration, yet my field research suggests that a significant number of immigrants left Miyako Island for Taiwan after Taiwan came under Japanese rule.[27]

Upon arriving in Taiwan, Ōhara stayed in Keelung, but, unable to find interesting jobs there, she went to Taipei. Following her move to Taipei City, she immediately visited the Taihoku Employment Agency. Considering her short-term experience at the clinic on Miyako Island, the agency found her a job as a live-in nurse at the Kobayashi Clinic in the Yamato District, where another live-in nurse from Yaeyama also worked. Like most young Okinawan migrants, she initially encountered a language barrier at the hospital because she had rarely used standard Japanese in her daily life on Miyako Island. Standard Japanese, which was considered the only "correct" spoken Japanese, was standardized based on the Japanese spoken by the middle class in Tokyo. After working at the Kobayashi Clinic for two years, however, she grew accustomed to the language and culture of the Japanese settler community. She then decided to move on:

> I saved money at the clinic. There were some increases in salary. Having utilized the money I'd saved over two years, I decided to do something for myself. . . . You know, at that time, people without education were laborers. They were physical laborers under the sun. I realized that only those who graduated from schools of higher education could become office workers. Today, I wonder how I came up with the idea of going to a Japanese typewriting school near the clinic. It was a school that taught typewriting in the Japanese language. Usually, it took six months to complete the course, but I found out that students with excellent grades could graduate in four months. So I tired very hard. I memorized thirty to forty sentences from [Natsume Sōseki's] *I Am a Cat* and eventually was able to touch-type

them quickly. I got an excellent grade and completed the course in four months.[28]

After completing her course at the typewriting school, she was recruited as a typist by the airbase in Okayama (present-day Gangshan District in Kaohsiung City). Under Japanese colonial rule, Okayama rapidly grew into one of the most important transportation and military sites in the region. During World War II, Okayama was a Japanese military airbase.[29] Ōhara worked at the airbase for six years until she was repatriated to Miyako Island in 1946.[30]

Apprenticed to the Japanese Colonial Empire

It should be noted that Yamamoto and Ōhara were not representative of all female Okinawan migrants. The majority of Okinawan migrants without educational and professional backgrounds accepted the reality of their situations and continued to work as domestics, regardless of their personal feelings. According to the 1930 census, 32 of the 1,635 males and 1,514 of the 8,242 females working as domestics (*kaji shiyōnin*) in Taiwan were Japanese.[31] Of the total number of Japanese domestics in Taiwan, 27 percent came from Okinawa Prefecture.[32] The October 1924 edition of *Yaeyama News* also reported that the Yaeyama Islands were known as a "supplier of

Ishigaki female immigrants, Taipei, ca. 1940. Photo courtesy of Itosu Masa

maids" to Japanese settler communities in Taiwan: "It seems that the number of Yaeyama girls migrating to Taiwan has increased rapidly of late. Each ship carries more than ten migrants to Taiwan; many of them live as apprentice maids (*jochū bōkō*). As people associate maids (*gejo*) with Yaeyama girls, Yaeyama is now known as a supplier of maids."[33]

Domestic service has a long history in Japan. It remained one of the most popular occupations for Japanese women until the 1940s. Before the word *jochū* became common in the early twentieth century, a domestic was usually called *gejo* in Japanese, which literally means "under woman." Until the nineteenth century, a young Japanese woman did not necessarily become a domestic in order to make money. Rather, she worked for an upper-class family as an apprentice servant so that she could learn proper manners and etiquette. By practicing good manners and having a solid grounding in traditional Japanese etiquette, a young Japanese woman from a less prosperous background could prepare herself for marriage. This folk educational custom continued to be practiced even after the state introduced universal education.[34]

The nature of the female apprenticeship was transformed during the interwar period. Instead of becoming an apprentice servant, a young woman could go to technical school or advanced girls' school (*kōtō jogakkō*) and learn cooking and sewing before marriage. Domestic service was no longer the only way for a woman to earn a respectable living. She could take better-paying jobs in an office or factory. As women came to have more educational and professional options in the interwar period, domestic service lost its appeal both as an apprenticeship and as an occupation.[35]

However, the demand for domestics increased in the early twentieth century. Until the nineteenth century, domestics were employed mostly by upper-class households. With the rapid economic development and growth of the interwar period, a new middle class emerged, and its members became the employers of domestics. Of the 10,589,403 working women in Japan in 1930, 697,116 were domestics.[36] A majority of these domestic workers are supposed to have been maids (*jochū*).[37] Domestics were also in great demand in colonial Taiwan, where government officials, freelance workers, and merchants composed a large majority of the Japanese migrant population. The *Taiwan Daily News* reported in 1923 that domestics were in high demand and that the Taihoku Employment Agency was listing their average wages at fifteen to twenty-five yen.[38] This same newspaper noted on June 25, 1924, that domestics were the most sought-after employees at the employment agency, followed by shop assistants under the age of twenty.[39]

In the Yaeyama Islands, I also came across many female repatriates from colonial Taiwan who had been in domestic service in Japanese settler households. Interestingly, not all of them look back on their experiences with bitterness. For instance, Kuroshima Nae (pseudonym), who was born on Taketomi Island, arrived in Taiwan in the 1920s. Her first job was babysitting the three-year-old son of a Japanese migrant family who owned a souvenir shop and sold folk crafts from Micronesia. After working in the souvenir shop for a few months, Kuroshima was employed as a domestic by the National Railway News Agency (Kokutetsu Jihō). Her last employer was Yamaguchi Shigetaka, the educational supervisor (*shigakukan*) for the colonial government of Taiwan. Yamaguchi was originally from Niigata Prefecture. The Yamaguchi household consisted of husband and wife, one daughter, and two sons. She described her everyday life as the domestic in Yamaguchi's household:

> It was a great spacious house. The living room was almost fifteen tatami mats in size and had a grand piano.[40] There were three entrances: one for guests, another for merchants, and the other one was for taking away garbage. A piano teacher visited the Miss every Thursday. The Miss, who was one year older than me, learned to play the piano properly from the teacher. Today, I still remember some pieces of piano music that I heard from the piano lessons of that time!...I was the only maid at the house, but the family was very kind to me. As there were no electric appliances [and nearly everything had to be done by hand], they did all the housework with me. It was not like, "You must do everything because you're a maid." On the contrary, we did all the work together. They even cleaned the toilet and the house with me.[41]

When I asked if she had any problems with standard Japanese, she replied:

> I was not familiar with the language at the beginning. Later, well, the Yamaguchi family taught me things like etiquette and manners. At that time, because there was no such thing as a ready-made futon, we all had to buy cloth and cotton and make it by hand. They also taught me how to do it. They taught me so many things.[42]

In interviews in 2004 and 2005, she happily told me how she came to appreciate piano music and poems while working at the Yamaguchi household. Today, she still remembers phrases from piano pieces that she heard at Yamaguchi's house and enjoys writing poems for herself. Kuroshima's experience is not indicative of the experiences of the average Yaeyama migrant.

Needless to say, not all employers were as kind as the Yamaguchi family. Many may have been harsh, unkind, and even abusive toward their domestics. Even so, Kuroshima's narrative suggests that migration to Taiwan meant more than working for a rich family and earning money. In the late 1920s and early 1930s, some Japanese employers continued to maintain the feudalistic master-servant relationship when hiring servants. As Murakami Nobuhiko's case study of a domestic in the mid-1920s illustrates, a servant would occasionally receive pocket money instead of a monthly wage and work from early morning till night while learning to perform domestic chores.[43] If a master was humane and inclined to be instructive, like Kuroshima's, a domestic would have been able to learn a lot and would be treated as one of the family rather than a mere servant. However, if a master was abusive, a domestic would have had to work hard for very little money in the name of "apprenticeship." In other words, working as domestics in the households of wealthy Japanese migrants was more than a means of earning money to send home to their families.

An autobiography by Ōhama Eishō, who was born on Ishigaki Island in 1914, shows the local islanders' perceptions of returnees from Taiwan:

> Because there were few jobs in which we could make money, many people went to Taiwan to look for work. At that time, the locals were wearing Ryukyu-style dress, but people who came back from Taiwan wore Western-style clothes, and they looked sophisticated. Even neighborhood girls who used to be ordinary had become stylish and refined when they returned from Taiwan. People paid attention to them. "Taiwan is close, and many Yaeyama locals stay there," people would say. I decided to go to Taiwan to make money. When I talked to my mother about it, she immediately approved of my plan. It was surprising to me. It was probably because my uncle, my mother's younger brother, Kuroshima Chōshin, was also working in Taiwan.[44]

Learning standard Japanese, eating Japanese food, and watching Japanese movies were major topics in the narratives of female migrants who had worked as domestics in elite Japanese households. It is doubtful that their acquired knowledge and new experiences were useful in the everyday lives of rural Okinawan women when they returned to the rural life of their home islands.

Nevertheless, the significance of apprentice servants cannot be evaluated solely by their salaries or the practicality of the knowledge and skills they acquired. To female Okinawan migrants, apprenticeship meant more than picking up professional skills and specialized job knowledge; they had become apprentices of Japanese arts and customs. By learning standard Japanese, becoming schooled in Japanese etiquette and manners, and familiarizing themselves with Japanese middle-class culture such as piano music and poetry, Okinawan female migrants attempted to raise their symbolic status as women within the cultural system of imperial Japan. Acquisition of Japanese mainstream culture allowed Okinawan female migrants to move away from the culturally marginal rural and advance toward the culturally central urban.

In the Contact Zone of the Japanese Colonial Empire

Colonized subjects were not the only ones who sought to become Japanese by learning the Japanese language and conforming to Japanese customs. Even residents who were legally categorized as Japanese migrants had to construct themselves as "Japanese." In their interviews, Okinawan migrants who went to Taiwan in search of jobs immediately after graduating from elementary schools frequently mentioned their initial difficulty with speaking standard Japanese. For example, when Kuroshima Nae first arrived in Taiwan at the age of sixteen, her cousin, who had been working in Taiwan for some time, told her, "You must greet the master properly by saying, 'I am from Yaeyama. Nice to meet you.'" On hearing this, she burst into tears and protested, "I cannot give such a proper greeting!"[45]

Other interviewees, asked about the difficulties of working in Taiwan, frequently mentioned their struggles to remember unfamiliar Japanese words, such as the ones domestic workers would hear while shopping at the markets. Although most schools in Okinawa conducted their lessons in Japanese, Okinawan children and adults continued to use local dialects at home and in their daily lives. As a result, Okinawan teenage migrants—who had never left their home islands—found it intimidating to speak basic standard Japanese every day. This corresponds to the situation in Okinawa, where the local government and schools implemented the standard-language campaign. Kondō Ken'ichirō has studied the government's program of forcing pupils to speak standard Japanese in everyday conversations as well as in classrooms; he also described the children's struggles as they tried not to speak their mother tongue or dialect.[46] On the main island of Okinawa, the government promoted special language education for immigrants to the main islands of Japan by encouraging them to speak standard Japanese.[47] As migration to Taiwan was not mobilized by an external authority, there was no systematic education for Okinawans migrating to Taiwan. Upon their arrival, however, they soon discovered they would have to work hard to master standard Japanese if they hoped to get good jobs in the Japanese migrant community.

In colonial Taiwan, the Japanese language played a special role in constructing the imaginary social categories of "Japanese persons" and "Taiwanese persons" because the modern school system, which promoted Japanese-language education, was a vital part of colonial Taiwan. An educational system was introduced in Taiwan at the outset of Japanese rule, but Taiwanese and Japanese students were strictly segregated. After the Taiwan Educational Ordinance (Taiwan Kyōikurei) was enacted in 1919, the colonial government of Taiwan reformed the educational system in accordance with the Gradual Extension of the Inner Territory policy. Furthermore, the New Taiwan Educational Ordinance, which in principle abolished official discrimination against Taiwanese, was enacted in 1922. This led to the integration of all secondary and tertiary institutions into one system. Primary education was still divided into two systems: primary schools (*shōgakkō*), for pupils who usually spoke Japanese, and public schools (*kōgakkō*), for Taiwanese speakers. Although this assumed that Japanese migrants should go to primary schools and Taiwanese should go to public schools, the mandate permitted Taiwanese children to attend primary schools and vice versa.[48] In other words, while pupils were required to speak standard Japanese in order to go to primary school and pursue tertiary education, the Japanese language became the crucial indicator defining the imaginary categories of Japanese and Taiwanese.

Ōyama Masao's *Taketomi during the Showa Period*, which retraces memories of Taketomi Island in the early twentieth century, contains a number of anecdotes on the lives of Taketomi migrants in colonial Taiwan. In this book, the migrants' mistakes with the Japanese language are presented as "funny stories."

One such story recounts the shopping trip of two female migrants from Taketomi, Yonaguni Kaishi and Takara Mōshi, who go to a market in Taipei. Kaishi needs to buy goat meat soup but does not know the word for "goat" in standard Japanese. So she asks her companion in Taketomi dialect, "Do you know what 'goat' is called in Japanese?" As Mōshi does not know the Japanese word for "goat" either, she imitates the sound a goat makes for the Taiwanese shopkeeper, going, "m-baah, m-baah." The shopkeeper immediately understands and sells them the soup with a laugh.[49]

In another story, Sakai Hatsu, a domestic serving in the household of a Japanese military man, goes to a vegetable market. She points at a winter melon (*tōgan*), indicating to the Taiwanese shopkeeper that she wishes to buy one. The shopkeeper then says to her, "Say the name." "My name is Hatsu," she replies. The shopkeeper clarifies, "I'm not asking for a person's name. Why don't you name the vegetable?" (*Hito no namae gafu. Yasai no na, iu yoroshi.*) On hearing this, she answers, "*Shobore,* please." The Taiwanese shopkeeper falls silent but soon recovers himself and tells her, "This is not *shobore.* This is called *tōgan.*"[50]

These so-called funny stories tellingly reveal the distinction between local Taiwanese and Okinawan migrants in the contact zone of colonial Taiwan. Although the Taiwanese locals were not Japanese, they had to adapt to the language and customs of the colonizing Japanese. The Okinawan migrants, who were legally categorized as Japanese, were uncertain as to their place in this contact zone, for they were neither Japanese nor Taiwanese.

Under the Gradual Extension policy, some Taiwanese could go to schools dominated by Japanese migrant students. At the beginning of Japanese rule, many laborers were brought from the Inner Territory to start new industries and develop the economy in Taiwan. Later, however, the Taiwanese were able to meet the needs of Japanese migrant employers. They were equally capable but worked for lower wages and soon penetrated the unskilled labor market in Japanese migrant communities. In spite of always occupying lower positions, some Taiwanese nevertheless advanced in their careers. Some worked in Japanese migrant communities because they spoke fluent Japanese. While the policy gave the Taiwanese some opportunities to merge into the world of the Japanese migrants, it also enabled Japanese migrants to merge with the Taiwanese.

Most Okinawan migrants lived and worked with Japanese migrants and Taiwanese who spoke fluent Japanese in the "Little Tokyo" areas of Taipei and Keelung. In Taiwan's Little Tokyo, Okinawan migrants took on positions that were also available to local Taiwanese. On the one hand, Okinawan migrants and Taiwanese formed friendships because they often worked together. On the other, they were rivals because they competed for the same jobs, as Yanaihara Tadao explains:

> Japanese migrant technicians and miners were in demand when capitalist corporations were first established. Laborers were needed to migrate with the movement of capital. However, as the capitalist economy developed in Taiwan and the Han Taiwanese became more proficient, demand for Japanese laborers declined. Japanese migrants demanded double the wages of Han Taiwanese, and more Taiwanese ended up being hired as laborers instead. . . . So Japanese migrant artisans can stay in their jobs only as highly qualified workers, and will have the status of aristocratic laborers. In an industrial dispute, they will tend to stand with the capitalists. It is clear that these Japanese migrant laborers would unite with Japanese capitalists because they are the same ethnicity. . . . In general, the ethnic conflict between Japanese migrants and Han Taiwanese would be in line with the

conflict between the political ruler and the ruled, as well as the class conflict between capitalists, farmers, and laborers.[51]

In the context of colonial Taiwan, the difference in class translated into a difference in ethnicity. Inexperienced and unskilled Okinawan migrants were likely to be on a par with Han Taiwanese in terms of class. Hence, struggle over the distinction between "Japanese" and "Taiwanese" was an everyday matter to Okinawan migrants, who were positioned at the social and economic margins. The pseudonymous Kamei Tōru, who was born on Taketomi Island in 1920, first made his way to Taiwan at the age of fourteen. He became a deliveryman for the Onohara Store, a rice wholesaler owned by Onohara Son'ichi from Nagasaki Prefecture. Kamei's coworkers were a head clerk (*bantō*) from Taketomi Island and three Taiwanese shop boys, Wang, Ching, and Yang. Kamei and his three Taiwanese colleagues had to take orders and deliver rice to Japanese migrant customers. He described an interaction with a customer in a 2005 interview.

Onohara Store, Taipei branch, ca. 1920. Source: Yonaguni Chōshi Hensan Īnkai, *Chinmoku no dotō*. Used with permission.

Kamei: As usual, I said, "Excuse me, this is the Onohara Store. Here's the rice that you ordered. Thank you for your continued patronage." Then a maid appeared at the back door and said to me, "*Gina,* come here. Put rice into this tin container, *gina.*" I said, "I'm not a Taiwanese; I'm a Japanese." "Really? You're lying," she answered. I yelled at her, calling her "*Chabo!*" At that time, a Taiwanese girl was called *chabo,* and a guy was called *gina.*

Interviewer: So, where was this maid from?

Kamei: Some maids were from the main island of Okinawa. There were also a number of Ishigaki maids. Because I did not bother to say I was from Ishigaki or Taketomi every time, I usually didn't care when they called me *gina.* But I retorted that time because I knew that maid was from Ishigaki Island. I said to her, "Oh, you're from Ishigaki Island. You know, I'm from Taketomi Island." "Are you?" she said. "I'm sorry. Wait a moment." Then she brought out eggs and bananas for me. In the end, we became good friends."[52]

Kamei's job was categorized as "Taiwanese work," so he was misidentified as Taiwanese. In correcting his label, he identified himself as Japanese rather than Okinawan or Ryukyuan. Kamei did not reject the Han Taiwanese as human beings because he still acknowledged them as fellow unskilled workers. Rather, he rejected the label of "Taiwanese," which at the time had a series of inferior connotations such as unhygienic, backwards, and cheap labor.

Living on the fringes of the Japanese migrant community, Okinawan migrants and their children were also active agents in reproducing the boundary between Japanese and Taiwanese. Bourdieu explains the process as follows:

> Principles of division, inextricably logical and sociological, function with and for the purposes of the struggle between social groups; in producing concepts, they produce groups, the very groups which produce the principles and the groups against which they are produced. What is at stake in the struggles about the meaning of the social world is power over the classificatory schemes and systems which are the basis of the representations of the groups and therefore of their mobilization and demobilization.[53]

The colonial authorities determined and implemented discriminatory treatment toward Japan's colonized Taiwanese subjects. However, civilian Japanese migrants, including those from Okinawa, played an important role in reproducing and maintaining the classifications of Japanese and Taiwanese as well. As Kondō Masami argues, Japanese migrants were an important force in the suppression of the Taiwanese nationalist movement against Japanese rule. In 1933, Japanese migrant elites—including lawyers, dentists, medical doctors, and journalists—established the Taiwan Reform Party (Taiwan Kaishin-tō), which insisted on giving various privileges to Japanese migrants in order to protect their interests. Its members claimed that public offices should hire only Japanese migrants and demanded that the government allow Japanese migrants to transfer their registered addresses to Taiwan. As differentiating the Japanese from the Taiwanese had resulted in immense benefits for the Japanese, members of the Taiwan Reform Party strongly resisted anything that disturbed the status quo of Japanese superiority.[54]

It is clear that Okinawan youth migrants were not major actors in the Japanese migrant politics of Taiwan. Despite their existence on the periphery of the Japanese migrant community in Taiwan, the Okinawan migrants' everyday politics of distinction were underpinned by the macropolitics that prevented the Taiwanese from getting equal rights and benefits. By identifying themselves as "Japanese," the Okinawan migrant laborers differentiated themselves from the Taiwanese. In so doing, they perpetuated the distinctions between Japanese and Taiwanese.

Before World War II, Okinawan immigrants overseas were mostly in primary industries such as farming and fishing; some of their descendants moved away from such jobs and later started commercial businesses or became professionals. Few of the first-generation Okinawan immigrants overseas worked for government offices, as they were not granted citizenship in their host countries. In contrast, few Okinawans in Taiwan were engaged in agriculture because the majority resided in larger cities such as Taipei, Keelung, or Kaohsiung. Despite prevalent discrimination against Okinawan immigrants, they still had a good chance of becoming public officials. Indeed, it was not unusual for unskilled Okinawan migrants to first work as shop boys or manual laborers, and then become train conductors or postal workers. As this chapter demonstrates, some of these unskilled migrants became skilled migrants by attending evening classes or apprenticing themselves to Japanese migrants.

Unlike the majority of female Japanese who migrated to Taiwan as dependent family members, a significant number of female Okinawans went to Taiwan in search of jobs. Many Okinawan female immigrants worked as domestics, but some were professional women such as nurses, typists, and telephone operators. This kind of social advancement suggests not only the rise of social and economic status but also the acquisition of standard Japanese and other forms of upper- and middle-class Japanese culture and traditions.

The politics of becoming Japanese encompassed mastering the customs of the Japanese while simultaneously establishing a distance from the colonized Taiwanese subjects. The struggles over ethnic classification intensified on the social margins, such as in the everyday lives of unskilled laborers, people from rural areas, and minority groups like Okinawans.

Chapter 4

Imperial Schooling across the Border

In addition to the migration of Okinawan labor, it should be noted that Okinawan youths went to Taiwan to pursue higher education. In other words, imperial careering encompassed not only an immigrant's professional career in the Japanese Empire but his or her school career as well. As these youths made use of the imperial structure to pursue higher education in colonial Taiwan, they are deemed to have embarked on "imperial schooling."

Imperial schooling is one of the characteristics of Okinawan migration to colonial Taiwan. As there were no tertiary educational institutions in Okinawa Prefecture, the medical school in Taipei, in particular, became one of the most popular institutions of higher education for Okinawan youths who had completed secondary education. Under the direction of Gotō Shimpei, who was civilian administrator of Taiwan from 1898 to 1906, ideals of scientific colonialism were translated into policies. As noted by Ming-Cheng M. Lo, medical science occupied a special and important position in Taiwan under Japanese rule.[1] The Taiwan Colonial Government Medical School (Taiwan Sōtokufu Igakkō) was established in 1899 and became the top elite school in colonial Taiwan. While the medical school and its Taiwanese graduates did indeed play important roles, the significance of colonial Taiwan's medical science and medical education was not limited to Taiwan. As this chapter demonstrates, the evolution of medical science and practices in Okinawa cannot be fully appreciated without taking into account the medical development of colonial Taiwan.

Imperial schooling became popular among Okinawans after the Extension of the Inner Territory policy, which created particular educational networks across the Japanese Empire. When the New Taiwan Educational Ordinance was enacted in 1922, it abolished official discrimination between Japanese migrants and Taiwanese at institutions of secondary and higher education. These reforms were not only initiated by the colonial government's policy change but also generated by the changing relationship between the government and the Taiwanese, who became more enthusiastic about modern education. However, the reforms of 1922 did not necessarily bring equal opportunity to Japanese migrant and Taiwanese students. Rather, the Taiwanese remained at a disadvantage because they had to take the entrance examinations in Japanese under the same conditions as the Japanese migrant students.[2] Okinawan youths in Taiwan, in contrast, took advantage of this educational reform.

Previous studies have examined the critical roles played by school education in colonial Japanese rule in Taiwan, with some focusing on the government's educational policies and others analyzing teaching practices and students' experiences in classrooms.[3] Recent studies add to this research by delving into the movement of teachers and scientists around the various Japanese imperial networks of schools and scientific institutions.[4] While it is relatively well known that Chinese, Korean, and Taiwanese students were educated in Japanese schools in the late nineteenth and early twentieth centuries,[5] studies on Japanese students' use of the imperial school network in pursuit of career advancement are meager. Scholars of modern Okinawan history have examined the importance of school education in Okinawa, but few existing studies highlight the fact that Okinawan students sought professional advantage by availing themselves of the imperial school network, which provided them with educational choices beyond their home islands and Mainland Japan. This chapter examines the introduction of modern medicine and medical education to Okinawa and Taiwan alongside Japanese military intervention. It elucidates the ways in which Okinawan youths overcame their disadvantage by migrating to colonial Taiwan for higher education and thus making their imperial careers.

Modern Science and Medical Education in Japan and Okinawa

Chinese medicine was the only systematic method of treating injuries and diseases in the Ryukyu Kingdom, as it was in other parts of East Asia. The introduction of medical knowledge from foreign countries was strictly regulated under the Tokugawa Shogunate's isolationist policy, but the Ryukyu Kingdom learned advanced Chinese medicine by sending its doctors to China.[6] However, these China-educated Ryukyuan doctors worked exclusively for the royal family and high-ranking officials. As a result, most ordinary people did not have access to Chinese medicine and relied instead on folk medicine. According to the investigation the Japanese government conducted in 1873, of the forty-three Chinese medical doctors in the Ryukyu Islands, twenty-one resided in Shuri, the castle town of the Ryukyu Kingdom.[7]

Western medicine was not introduced to the Ryukyus until 1837, when the American medical doctor Peter Parker stayed on the main island of Okinawa for three months and shared a smallpox vaccination technique. During 1846–1855, an English missionary doctor, Bernard John Bettelheim, lived on the main island of Okinawa, where he conducted missionary work. Despite strict surveillance, he managed to propagate Christianity and treat the sick in his neighborhood. Unfortunately, neither doctor had a significant impact on Ryukyuan medical traditions.[8] Western medicine began to spread in the islands after the Ryukyu Kingdom was abolished in the late nineteenth century. With its annexation of the Ryukyus, the Japanese government sent the national army and a medical unit to the islands. After Okinawa Prefecture was formally established in 1879, the military medical unit became Okinawa Prefectural Hospital.[9] Thus, the introduction of Western medicine and Japanese military intervention in the Ryukyu Islands occurred in tandem.

The Meiji government learned from European medical institutions and rushed to institutionalize medical practices and education in Japan. Although Chinese medicine was practiced and medical education was conducted in various schools in early modern Japan, there was no centralized authority governing medical treatment. After Japan opened to the West, the government feared that the rapid and increased exchange with foreign countries would result in the spread of contagious diseases. In order to prevent the outbreak of a potential epidemic, it perceived an urgent need to disseminate Western medical knowledge.

In August 18, 1874, the government instituted the Medical Care Law (Isei). Under this law, only those who completed formal medical education and had clinical experience were given medical licenses and allowed to practice medicine. However, there were few doctors with formal qualifications in Western medicine and more than twenty thousand practicing doctors of Chinese medicine. Given the shortage of medical practitioners, the government allowed doctors of Chinese medicine to apply for temporary medical licenses.[10]

By 1879, however, new doctors had to pass a national examination before they could obtain licenses to practice medicine. With the exception of a small number of privileged people who received a formal education in official medical schools or universities, most aspiring medical doctors in the countryside had to join a local training school in preparation for the national medical licensing examination.[11] Many of these preparatory schools were small-scale and attached to local hospitals. In 1879, there were twenty-one public training schools with 2,058 students and twenty-five private schools with 875 students preparing for the national licensing examination.[12]

In pre–World War II Okinawa, the Okinawa Prefecture Medical Training School (Okinawa-ken Isei Kyōshūjo) (hereafter Medical Training School) was the only institution of Western medical education in Okinawa where students could prepare for the national medical licensing examination. The school was attached to Okinawa Prefectural Hospital and accepted its first class of twenty students in February 1885. The school's financial condition was far from excellent, and there was no building for students during the first six months of its existence. Not until it settled in the vacant lot that had housed the Okinawa Normal School and its attached elementary school did it have its own school compound.[13]

Many students were also poor. In an effort to attract good students, the school offered scholarships to the honor students whose registered addresses were in Okinawa Prefecture in 1889. They were granted 1.5 yen monthly on the condition that they practice medicine in Okinawa after graduation.[14] In addition, the local municipal governments in Okinawa Prefecture provided the students with financial assistance. Thus, the school was called "the savior and only gateway" for youths unable to pursue secondary education because of their families' financial situations.[15] Kinjō Kiyomatsu, a member of the eleventh graduating class who was born in Kunigami-gun in 1880, noted that he did not have any financial problems as a student because he received both a scholarship from the school and financial aid from his local government.[16] Because the Medical Training School aimed to promote Western medicine and increase the number of medical doctors in the prefecture, all its graduates were required to work in Okinawa Prefecture for the first three years after graduating and receiving their medical licenses. Failure to do so would result in a heavy financial penalty of three hundred yen that had to be repaid at once.[17]

As Western medicine was not widespread in the Ryukyu Islands in the beginning, the school initially was not recognized by Okinawans. Nevertheless, people gradually came to appreciate it as one of the few secondary schools on the main island of Okinawa that was open even to the poor. Despite this positive view, the school was commonly regarded as the last resort for students who did not do well enough to go to the Okinawa Normal School or a middle school.[18] Higashion'na Kanjun, one of the most prominent Okinawan scholars of the time, commented, "The [Okinawa] Normal School, [First and Second Okinawa] Middle Schools, and Medical Training School were the three top schools in Okinawa at that time, and the Medical Training School was least esteemed by the public."[19] In some cases, students who failed to enter other secondary schools went to the Medical Training School to prepare for the next year's secondary school entrance examination.[20] The school was not highly regarded partly because it was so poorly equipped and disorganized that most of its students dropped out without getting their medical doctors' licenses. Its substandard facilities could not provide students with sufficient opportunities for practice. Moreover, all the teachers worked in the Okinawa Prefectural Hospital and held classes during their breaks. Thus, despite the officially stated forty hours of classes per week, classes were irregular and sometimes were not held at all.[21] As a result, the school took in a total of only 565 students before it closed down after twenty-three years; of these, only 150 passed the national examination and obtained their medical licenses before graduation, and 22 received their licenses after transferring to another school.[22] In short, the Medical Training School was unable to prepare its students for the national medical licensing examination.

In 1912, the Medical Training School—Okinawa Prefecture's first and foremost medical school and one of its few secondary schools—closed down.[23] Thereafter, the government abolished the national medical licensing examination and made schooling at authorized medical colleges or university medical schools compulsory for all those who wished to become licensed doctors.[24] Hence, medical preparatory schools, like the Okinawa Medical Training School, no longer had a reason to exist. Although the school was poorly equipped and poorly financed, sixty-one of the eighty-nine medical doctors practicing in the prefecture were graduates.[25] With the school closed and the licensing examination abolished, Okinawa Islanders had no choice but to seek a medical education outside their home island.

The Establishment and Development of Medical Education in Taiwan

Meanwhile, Japan devoted itself to suppressing the numerous anti-Japanese guerrilla activities in Taiwan for the first ten years of colonial rule. As many Japanese troops and policemen fell prey to malaria and other diseases while combating the insurgents, the colonial government urgently needed to improve sanitary conditions in Taiwan. However, Gotō Shimpei, who was then head of the Home Ministry's Public Health Bureau as well as health and hygiene adviser to the colonial government of Taiwan, had great difficulty recruiting medical professionals willing to take responsibility for establishing a sanitary and medical administration in Taiwan. Few medical professionals were attracted to the newly occupied territory that was notorious for its unsafe and unhygienic conditions.[26]

Yamaguchi Hidetaka (1865–1916) rose to the challenge by accepting the unpopular post of director of Taihoku Hospital (Taihoku Iin). Ever since attending Tokyo Imperial University's Faculty of Medicine, he had maintained great interest in the development of European nations and their colonial management. In fact, he became so serious about traveling to foreign countries and making a success of colonial medicine that he planned trips to Central America and China. In the end, however, he chose to take the position of director at Okinawa Prefectural Hospital instead.[27] He likely intended to use the post as a stepping-stone to working in other countries in the future. On arriving in Okinawa in 1891, he worked aggressively to develop the Ryukyu Islands' first proper medical school, but, owing to his bungling and incompetence, the school did not materialize, and he was removed from the position in less than three years.[28] Thus, going to Taiwan was his second chance to fulfill his lifelong dream of developing colonial medicine in Asia.

Yamaguchi left Tokyo in November 1896 and joined Taihoku Hospital, which was located in an area with a high concentration of Taiwanese residents. The hospital was originally an ordinary home that had been remodeled to serve as a hospital for the Japanese army. It resembled a field hospital, and Yamaguchi turned it into a general hospital for the public. After June 1898, Taihoku Hospital came under the management of the colonial government of Taiwan. When Yamaguchi arrived, his fellow doctors were busily engaged in treating plague and other contagious diseases. Furthermore, doctors had to perform surgery almost every day because of the numerous anti-Japanese guerrilla uprisings around Taipei.[29]

Despite the ongoing sociopolitical unrest, Yamaguchi submitted a proposal for a medical school in Taiwan to the colonial government. He reportedly did so in an attempt to remedy his failure in Okinawa. Western medicine was not in wide use among ordinary Taiwanese residents, but Yamaguchi utilized it to embark on his "civilizing mission" in the Japanese colonies. Furthermore, his dream involved more than opening a medical school in Taiwan; he also hoped that the school would eventually lead to the establishment of a university. His ultimate goal was not only to develop Taiwan through Western medicine but also to civilize China so that Japan and China would be able to work together and enhance Asian civilization. As expected, the harried government officials, who had their hands full containing contagious diseases and suppressing Taiwanese resistance activities, rejected his proposal. However, Yamaguchi and the colonial government reached a compromise, and the medical training center (*igaku kōshūjo*) was established as part of Taihoku Hospital in April 1897, only two years after Japan annexed Taiwan.[30]

As the Taiwanese were largely unacquainted with the Japanese language and Western medicine, very few were willing to attend the newly opened medical training center. By recruiting students through various channels such as acquaintances of school board members, staff, and pharmacists' children, the school managed to enroll twenty first-year students. Doctors and pharmacists from Taihoku Hospital formed the teaching staff. Some students were illiterate and did not know Japanese, so the teachers had to teach in both Taiwanese and Japanese, as well as explain by gesturing and showing objects. Most of the new students dropped out within a year, and only five completed the first-year curriculum.[31] Nevertheless, Yamaguchi insisted on turning the training school into a medical school, claiming that the remaining five students had achieved excellent academic results. With the support of Gotō Shimpei, who had become the secretary of Domestic Affairs in the Colonial Government of Taiwan, the medical training center was upgraded and became the Taiwan Colonial Government Medical School on March 31, 1899, with Yamaguchi as the school's first principal.[32]

In April 1899, there were fifteen students in the school's regular course and seventy in the preparatory course. Initially, classes were conducted at Taihoku Hospital but were soon moved to the new school building when it was ready. In 1902, all students were required to live in the dormitories. Despite Yamaguchi's passion and Gotō Shimpei's support, few students completed the course. In the first year, only three students finished the program, and only one person graduated the second year. However, the situation did improve for the school. As Western medicine gained acceptance among the people and the school's graduates received their medical licenses, public opinion of the school rose.[33] Nevertheless, Yamaguchi, a born bungler, was removed from his post as principal in 1902, before the school had sent off its first batch of graduates.[34] Still, the powerful Gotō appreciated Yamaguchi's passion for medicine and colonial development, and the medical school eventually became the foremost professional school in colonial Taiwan.

Schooling and Migration

In the earlier period of colonial rule, there was a controversy about the extent to which the colonial government should promote school education among the Taiwanese. Some colonial elites favored popularizing school education, as in the Inner Territory, so that the colonized subjects would be loyal to the Japanese nation; others tried to discriminate against the colonized and were reluctant to develop school education in Taiwan. Although there were some disagreements among colonial elites, there was consensus that the Taiwanese should be obedient to the colonial government regardless of the education they received. Because the Japanese viewed education for both colonized subjects and Japanese citizens as a means of molding them into loyal and useful Japanese subjects, rather than developing critical thinking, the colonial government grew concerned with the popularity of social science studies in Japanese universities. The colonial government was indeed right to worry because the Taiwanese were increasingly frustrated with its educational policies, with some looking to the Inner Territory and beyond for their educational needs. Although large numbers of Taiwanese completed elementary education, the colonial government continued to limit the quantity and quality of secondary education available to them.[35]

Kumamoto Shigeyoshi, the sixth chief of the colonial government's educational division from 1911 to 1920, decided to increase the number of primary, secondary, and higher educational institutions, despite his initial reluctance to develop education for the Taiwanese. Rather than deprive the Taiwanese of educational opportunities, the colonial government sought to control them through educational institutions. In other words, offering more opportunities for education under the colonial government's aegis was preferable to letting the Taiwanese study overseas, beyond the control of the authorities. There were two reasons for the colonial government's educational policy change: the rapidly developing economy and industries of colonial Taiwan needed more skilled workers with advanced knowledge, and the growing number of Japanese migrants in Taiwan demanded more schools.[36]

The Taiwan Colonial Government Medical School was initially founded to educate Taiwanese students. As it was one of the few secondary educational institutions allowed to admit Taiwanese students, a significant number of its graduates came to play leading roles in nationalist movements.[37] In 1918, the newly opened Department of Medicine (Igaku Senmonbu) accepted Japanese students who had graduated from middle school. The Specialized Course of Tropical Medicine (Nettai Igaku Senkōka) was also established to allow licensed doctors to specialize in tropical medicine. From the beginning of colonial rule, Taiwan was considered a steppingstone for Japanese expansion in the Pacific and Southeast Asia. Unlike the Department of Medicine, the Specialized Course of Tropical Medicine accepted both Taiwanese and Japanese doctors, and students earned a bachelor's degree in tropical medicine by completing a one-year program. The purpose of the course was to promote tropical medicine in Taiwan and encourage Taiwanese and Japanese doctors to practice medicine in the Pacific and Southeast Asia.[38]

The New Taiwan Educational Ordinance, enacted in 1922, integrated all institutions of secondary and higher education into one system. Accordingly, the Taiwan Colonial Government Medical School conformed to the laws and ordinances of the Inner Territory's colleges and accepted both Japanese and Taiwanese students. The school was renamed Taiwan Colonial

Government Medical College (Taiwan Sōtokufu Igaku Senmon Gakkō) in 1922 and came to be known as the Taiwan Colonial Government Taihoku Medical College (Taiwan Sōtokufu Taihoku Igaku Senmon Gakkō) in 1927 (hereafter Taiwan Medical College).[39] Even though Taiwanese students could now study alongside Japanese nationals in secondary and post-secondary education, they continued to face discrimination. They were still at a huge disadvantage in examinations because they were competing directly with Japanese students who were native Japanese speakers. This is reflected in the enrollment of Taiwan Medical College. For instance, in 1933, 183 Taiwanese and 151 Japanese were enrolled at the college, although Japanese nationals accounted for less than 5 percent of Taiwan's total population.[40] Because the number of graduates varied each year, it is difficult to make a simple comparison. Still, it is clear that granting the Taiwanese access to the same secondary and post-secondary education as the Japanese in Taiwan did not contribute to a great increase in Taiwanese students at the medical college.

Although the Specialized Course of Tropical Medicine was abolished in 1923, after only twenty-three students had graduated,[41] tropical medicine was once again highlighted in the 1930s, when interest in Japanese advancement into Southeast Asia and the South Pacific Islands grew. Thus, Taihoku Imperial University (founded in 1928) established its own Faculty of Medicine in 1936. This Faculty of Medicine promoted the study of tropical sciences and other research areas deemed essential to Japan's southward advance. Taiwan Medical College was closed, and the Specialized Division for Medicine at Taihoku Imperial University (hereafter Specialized Division for Medicine) took its place. As their organization and staffs were very similar, it can be said that the Specialized Division for Medicine was the sister institution of the Taiwan Medical College.[42]

Since the Taiwan Medical College accepted Japanese students, a significant number of Okinawan students moved to Taiwan for their medical education. Of the 893 graduates from Taiwan Medical College from 1922 to 1933, 331 were Japanese, and among them, 46 were from Okinawa Prefecture.[43] Furthermore, 226 of the 444 graduates from the Specialized Division for Medicine were Japanese, 50 of whom had addresses registered in Okinawa Prefecture.[44] In contrast, only 3 of the 176 Japanese graduates from the Faculty of Medicine at Taihoku Imperial University between 1940 and 1943 were from Okinawa Prefecture.[45] In other words, the majority of Okinawan medical students went to either Taiwan Medical College or the Specialized Division for Medicine, with very few attending the Faculty of Medicine at Taihoku Imperial University. According to the Japanese Alumni Association of the College (Nanmei-kai), 574 Japanese students graduated from Taiwan Medical College and the Specialized Division for Medicine between 1922 and 1941, and 109 were supposedly from Okinawa Prefecture.[46] As shown in table 4.3, most Okinawan alumni were graduates of Okinawa First or Second Middle School, Okinawa Normal School, Miyako Middle School, or Okinawa Third Middle School. In short, most Okinawan students attending Taiwan Medical College or the Specialized Division for Medicine had graduated from a middle school in Okinawa before studying medicine in colonial Taiwan.

Why did so many graduates of Okinawa First and Second Middle Schools pursue medical education in Taiwan? As these schools were the best middle schools in Okinawa Prefecture, the most outstanding students from all over the prefecture attended them. Nevertheless, as is evident in tables 4.1 and 4.2, many of these middle school graduates did not have regular jobs and passed their time by "staying home to study." This implies that educated Okinawans in Okinawa Prefecture had difficulty finding jobs, even though they had graduated from the region's best secondary schools. Certainly, some of them worked in schools or public offices in Okinawa Prefecture, but these positions were limited in number. In order to pursue tertiary education, they had no option but to leave Okinawa, where there was neither university nor college.

During the early twentieth century, many students in Okinawa had to forgo secondary and tertiary education because of financial constraints. As mentioned, the Medical Training School attracted needy students because the school and the local municipal governments in Okinawa Prefecture offered scholarships to top students. Similarly, Taiwan Medical College was attractive to needy Okinawan youths who wished to further their education. For instance, Yoshino Kōzen (formerly Iramina Kōzen) entered Taiwan Medical College in 1919, a year after the school opened its doors to Japanese students. Yoshino was born to a farming family on Kohama Island in 1898. The family led a fairly simple life, and Yoshino went to elementary schools on Kohama Island and then on Ishigaki Island. It was uncommon for a poor farmer's son to go to a middle school in Yaeyama, regardless of the excellence of his academic performance. However, Yoshino convinced his father to allow him to continue his studies and entered Okinawa Second Middle School in 1914. Because of his excellent academic results, he was an honor student and was exempted from school fees. Yet, he was at a loss as to his future options because he knew his family was unable to finance his tertiary education. On discovering that the local government of his home island was concerned about the shortage of medical doctors and was providing scholarships to medical students, Yoshino decided to make his career in medicine. While taking the entrance examination for Taiwan Medical

Table 4.1. Status of Okinawa First and Second Middle Schools Alumni, One Year after Graduation

	Business-person	School-teacher	Public official	High school student	College student	Business college student	Self-study	Self-study in Tokyo	Unknown	Other	Total
1919	4	25	11	2	5	0	34	—	18	8	107
1920	10	23	6	9	8	3	39	—	11	6	115
1921	9	18	3	1	8	4	37	—	2	20	102
1922	5	33	5	4	6	3	55	0	13	17	141
1923	2	33	1	4	5	4	31	0	23	15	118
1924	2	44	2	7	23	5	29	0	54	12	178
1925	4	50	2	8	7	2	21	16	52	5	167
1926	9	46	8	5	16	4	17	13	48	16	182
1927	28	34	19	4	25	10	18	10	47	10	205
1928	18	26	18	9	18	4	28	34	50	19	224
1929	9	9	12	2	20	0	100	34	6	34	226
1930	11	3	15	3	13	5	101	44	5	46	246
1931	15	0	16	3	24	3	126	12	10	27	236
1932	21	0	27	7	21	8	112	8	12	30	246

Sources: Okinawa-ken, *Okinawa-ken tōkeisho, Taishō 12-nen,* 58–59; Okinawa-ken, *Okinawa-ken tōkeisho, Shōwa 2-nen,* 48–49; Okinawa-ken Chiji Kanbō, *Okinawa-ken tōkeisho, Shōwa 7-nen,* 48–49.

Table 4.2. Status of Okinawa First, Second, and Third Middle Schools and Miyako Middle School Alumni, One Year after Graduation

	Business-person	School-teacher	Public official	University prep	High school student	University student (specialist program)	College student	Business college student	Normal school student (evening division)	Self-study	Self-study in Tokyo	Family business	Other	Total
1933	53	1	17	3	5	0	31	18	22	87	42	0	34	313
1934	63	1	19	6	5	5	17	28	18	105	20	20	41	348
1935	61	0	16	9	1	4	23	18	19	141	20	30	13	355
1936	55	4	20	8	2	3	24	12	23	121	26	61	11	370
1937	53	10	24	11	1	1	33	6	25	111	23	20	20	338

Source: Okinawa-ken Sōmu-bu Tōkei-ka, *Okinawa-ken tōkeisho, Shōwa 12-nen,* 44–45.

Table 4.3. Profiles of Okinawan Graduates of Taihoku Medical College

No.	School attended	Year graduated	Status in 1941
1	Okinawa First Middle School	1922	Deceased
2	Okinawa Second Middle School	1923	Practicing on Ishigaki Island
3	Okinawa Second Middle School	1924	Residing in Tokyo
4	Okinawa First Middle School	1925	—
5	Okinawa First Middle School	1925	Practicing as an ophthalmologist at Taichū Clinic
6	Okinawa Second Middle School	1925	Practicing in the Republic of China
7	Okinawa First Middle School	1926	Practicing at the Matsuyama Railway Factory infirmary, Taipei City
8	Okinawa First Middle School	1926	Deceased
9	Okinawa First Middle School	1927	—
10	Okinawa First Middle School	1927	Practicing in Osaka City
11	Okinawa First Middle School	1928	—
12	Okinawa Second Middle School	1928	Practicing in Saipan
13	Okinawa First Middle School	1928	Practicing on Kume Island, Okinawa Prefecture
14	Okinawa First Middle School	1928	Practicing in Nakagami-gun, Okinawa Prefecture
15	Okinawa Second Middle School	1928	—
16	Okinawa Second Middle School	1928	Practicing in Heitō City, Taiwan
17	Okinawa First Middle School	1928	Practicing in Shuri City, Okinawa Prefecture
18	Okinawa Second Middle School	1928	Practicing in Miyako-gun, Okinawa Prefecture
19	Okinawa First Middle School	1928	Practice in Ishigaki Town, Okinawa Prefecture
20	Okinawa Second Middle School	1928	Residing in Kumamoto City
21	Okinawa Second Middle School	1929	Residing in Nakagami-gun, Okinawa Prefecture
22	Okinawa First Middle School	1929	—
23	Okinawa First Middle School	1929	Deceased
24	Okinawa Second Middle School	1930	Residing in Miyazaki Prefecture
25	Okinawa First Middle School	1930	—
26	Okinawa Second Middle School	1930	Deceased
27	Okinawa Second Middle School	1930	Deceased
28	Okinawa First Middle School	1931	Practicing in Shimajiri-gun, Okinawa Prefecture
29	Okinawa First Middle School	1931	Practicing as an ophthalmologist at Takao Clinic
30	Okinawa First Middle School	1931	Residing in Singapore

(continued)

Table 4.3. Profiles of Okinawan Graduates of Taihoku Medical College *(continued)*

No.	School attended	Year graduated	Status in 1941
31	Okinawa Second Middle School	1931	
32	Okinawa Second Middle School	1931	Working at Tokyo City Contagious Disease Research Institute
33	Okinawa Second Middle School	1931	Working at Īzuka City Mitsubishi Miner Hospital
34	Okinawa First Middle School	1931	Practicing in Tainan City
35	Okinawa Second Middle School	1931	—
36	Okinawa First Middle School	1931	Practicing in Taiwan City
37	Okinawa First Middle School	1932	Working at Naha City Zenkōdō Hospital
38	Okinawa First Middle School	1932	Working in Taihoku City Clinic
39	Okinawa Second Middle School	1932	Residing in Yonaguni Village, Okinawa Prefecture
40	Okinawa Second Middle School	1932	Residing in Kunigami-gun, Okinawa Prefecture
41	Okinawa Second Middle School	1932	—
42	Okinawa Normal School	1932	Residing on Kume Island, Okinawa Prefecture
43	Okinawa Normal School	1932	Working at Dōjindō Clinic, Taiwan
44	Takao Middle School	1932	Deceased
45	Okinawa Second Middle School	1933	Working as a surgeon at Sakai Municipal Hospital
46	Okinawa Second Middle School	1933	Residing in Nago Town, Okinawa Prefecture
47	Okinawa First Middle School	1933	—
48	Tainan First Middle School	1933	—
49	Okinawa First Middle School	1933	Working as a police medical officer for the state Taichū
50	Okinawa First Middle School	1933	Residing in Miyako-gun, Okinawa Prefecture
51	Okinawa Second School	1934	Working as an otolaryngologist at Taipei City Railway Clinic
52	Okinawa Second School	1934	Practicing in Naha City, Okinawa Prefecture
53	Okinawa First Middle School	1934	Working at Masuko Hospital, Tokyo City
54	Okinawa Second School	1934	Working in Naha City, Okinawa Prefecture
55	Okinawa Second School	1934	Working at the Department of Telecommunications, Taipei City
56	Okinawa Second School	1934	—
57	Okinawa Second School	1935	—

No.	School attended	Year graduated	Status in 1941
58	Okinawa Second School	1935	Working at Kohagura Clinic, Naha City, Okinawa Prefecture
59	Okinawa First Middle School	1935	Working at Fukumoto Clinic, Saipan Island
60	Okinawa Normal School	1935	—
61	Okinawa Second School	1935	Working at Okinawa Prefectural Hospital
62	Okinawa First Middle School	1935	—
63	Taipei Second School	1935	—
64	Okinawa First Middle School	1935	Working at the Taipei Prison infirmary
65	Okinawa Second School	1935	Deceased
66	Takao Middle School	1936	Working at the Japan Sugar Refinery infirmary, Torao Town, Tainan
67	Okinawa First Middle School	1936	—
68	Okinawa Second Middle School	1936	—
69	Okinawa Second Middle School	1937	—
70	Okinawa Second Middle School	1937	—
71	Okinawa First Middle School	1937	Working in gynecology at Taipei City Railway Clinic
72	Okinawa Second Middle School	1937	Working at Hakuaikai, Japanese Navy, Hainan Island
73	Okinawa First Middle School	1937	Working at the Department of Health, Saga Prefecture
74	Okinawa Second Middle School	1937	Working at Saipan Clinic, Saipan Island
75	Miyako Middle School	1937	Residing in Hirara Town, Okinawa Prefecture
76	Okinawa Second Middle School	1937	
77	Okinawa Second Middle School	1937	
78	Okinawa First Middle School	1937	Residing in Miyako-gun, Okinawa Prefecture
79	Okinawa Second Middle School	1937	Working at the Laboratory of Anatomy, Taipei Imperial University
80	Okinawa First Middle School	1937	Residing in Taketomi Village, Okinawa Prefecture
81	Okinawa Second Middle School	1937	Residing in Naha City, Okinawa Prefecture
82	Okinawa Second Middle School	1937	Working as an internist at Taitō Clinic
83	Okinawa Second Middle School	1937	Deceased

(continued)

Table 4.3. Profiles of Okinawan Graduates of Taihoku Medical College *(continued)*

No.	School attended	Year graduated	Status in 1941
84	Okinawa First Middle School	1938	—
85	Okinawa Second Middle School	1938	Working at the Chiyoda Life Insurance Company, Taipei City
86	Okinawa First Middle School	1938	—
87	Okinawa First Middle School	1938	—
88	Okinawa First Middle School	1938	—
89	Okinawa First Middle School	1938	Working as an otolaryngologist at Taihoku Imperial University
90	Okinawa First Middle School	1938	—
91	Okinawa Second Middle School	1938	Residing in Naha City, Okinawa Prefecture
92	Ikubunkan Middle School	1939	—
93	Okinawa Second Middle School	1939	Working at Okayama Medical University
94	Okinawa Second Middle School	1939	—
95	Okinawa First Middle School	1939	—
96	Okinawa Normal School	1939	Practicing in Miyako-gun, Okinawa Prefecture
97	Okinawa First Middle School	1939	Working at Taihoku City Clinic
98	Okinawa Second Middle School	1939	Residing in Kunigami-gun, Okinawa Prefecture
99	Miyako Middle School	1940	—
100	Okinawa Second Middle School	1940	—
101	Okinawa Second Middle School	1940	—
102	Miyako Middle School	1941	—
103	Okinawa First Middle School	1941	—
104	Okinawa First Middle School	1941	—
105	Okinawa Third Middle School	1941	—
106	Okinawa Third Middle School	1941	—
107	Okinawa First Middle School	1941	—
108	Okinawa Third Middle School	1941	—
109	Okinawa Second Middle School	1941	—

Source: Kan'no Hisao, *Nanmeikai Kaiin meibo.*

College, he also applied to Lushun Technical College (Ryojun Kōka Gakudō) in Dalian as a backup.[47]

Yoshino's experience is not unusual. The memoirs of Okinawan alumni of Taiwan Medical College and the Specialized Division for Medicine indicate that the availability of scholarships was a factor in their choice of institutions. Additionally, a medical doctor's license was seen as highly advantageous because doctors could easily find work in Okinawa Prefecture. Inafuku Zenshi, born in 1909, graduated from Okinawa First Middle School before enrolling in Taiwan Medical College in Taipei. He explains his reasons for studying medicine in colonial Taiwan in his memoirs: "I graduated from the First Middle School [present-day Shuri High School] in 1932. Having been a precocious and ambitious boy, I was disappointed when my relatives encouraged me to go to Taiwan Medical College. I had never imagined that I would end up as a humble town doctor. However, my family was poor, and my father was already dead. I had no choice but to rely on relatives to go to a school."[48]

Genga Chōkō, who was born in Yomitan Village in 1910, had wanted to be a medical doctor ever since he was a student at Okinawa Second Middle School. He initially planned to major in civil, construction, or electrical engineering at a university. However, jobs in these fields were scarce in Okinawa Prefecture, and graduates had to migrate to either Mainland Japan or Manchuria for employment, which worried his family. As a doctor, he could work in Okinawa and be near his parents, in accordance with their wishes.[49]

After the Medical Training School was abolished in 1912, Okinawa Islanders had no choice but to look beyond the prefecture for post-secondary educational opportunities. Under these circumstances, many Okinawans preferred Taiwan to Mainland Japan because of the relatively low school fees. For instance, Tanaka Kōei, who was born in Tomari Village in Okinawa Prefecture in 1918, dreamed of going to an art school to study painting while he was attending Okinawa First Middle School. But when some of his close relatives and family members, including his father, died of tuberculosis, he changed his mind and worked toward becoming a medical doctor.[50] However, after his father's death, his family could not afford to send him to medical school. Thus, Tanaka applied to the Specialized Division for Medicine at Taihoku Imperial University and the Chōsen Colonial Government Keijō Medical College (Keijō Igaku Senmon Gakkō), which both were notably more affordable than other medical schools in Mainland Japan. Tanaka's decision may have been influenced by the fact that school seniors in his neighborhood also attended Taihoku Imperial University. He was admitted to the Specialized Division for Medicine in 1937 and paid his school fees with public student loans and his earnings from teaching part-time.[51] He also applied to Taikyū Medical College (Taikyū Igaku Senmon Gakkō) (in present-day Daegu) and Heijō Medical College (Heijō Igaku Senmon Gakkō) (in present-day Pyongyang) in colonial Korea. As these schools accepted Japanese and local students, some Okinawan students went to medical colleges in Korea instead of Taiwan.[52]

Ishimine Genki, who was born on Miyako Island in 1924, aspired to be a doctor because when he was a young boy, he had been successfully treated for typhoid by a local doctor. He applied to Taikyū Medical College and the Specialized Division at Taihoku Imperial University.[53] This suggests that it was not unusual for students from Miyako Island to take entrance examinations for medical colleges in Korea, Manchuria, and Taiwan. Before World War II, forty students from the Miyako Islands went to medical schools or colleges; twenty-one studied at Taiwan Medical College, two went to the Faculty of Medicine at Taihoku Imperial University, four went to Heijō Medical College, two attended Taikyū Medical College, and another went to Manshū Medical University (Manshū Ika Daigaku).[54] While studying medicine in Taipei under the sponsorship of his home village on Miyako Island, Ishimine Genki was called to join the Japanese navy in 1944. He returned to the school after the war, only to find that circumstances had changed and there was no way for students to continue their studies. He graduated from the Specialized Division for Medicine in December 1946, just before repatriating to Miyako Island.[55]

These life stories suggest that students from Okinawa middle schools were likely to go to Taiwan Medical College or the Specialized Division for Medicine at Taihoku Imperial University, which were more affordable than other medical schools in Mainland Japan. Graduates of Okinawa middle schools were also attracted to Taiwan Medical College and the Specialized Division for Medicine because they accepted Japanese students who had only completed middle school. While there used to be a number of public medical colleges, most were upgraded to medical universities in the 1920s and 1930s. There were still a significant number of private colleges teaching medicine, but tuition was expensive. For instance, annual tuition at Shōwa Medical College (Shōwa Igaku Senmon Gakkō), a major private medical college, was 150 yen, and students were required to pay 50 yen for their graduation examination.[56] Tuition at public medical universities was slightly more affordable; Kanazawa Medical University (Kanazawa Ika Daigaku), for example, charged 120 yen for tuition in 1932.[57] Public universities, however, required applicants to have graduated from high school. This was a considerable hurdle for Okinawan students, as there were no high schools in the prefecture until World War II. Okinawan youths could bypass the high school graduation requirement by taking the entrance examinations for Taiwan Medical College and the Specialized Division for Medicine immediately after graduating from middle school. Furthermore, tuition fees in colonial Taiwan were much cheaper, at 60 yen in 1932, and the student dormitory cost only 1 yen per month.[58] Similarly, other colleges and schools in colonial Korea were more affordable than those in the Inner Territory. It is difficult to compare all colonial tertiary institutions because the cost of living varied among territories and each school had different scholarship systems and honor student programs. Nevertheless, these circumstances help explain why Okinawan middle school students preferred to continue their education in the colonies rather than the Inner Territory.

Okinawans Making Careers in Medicine

Many of the Okinawan students at Taiwan Medical College and the Specialized Division for Medicine were sponsored by their local municipal governments, which expected them to return home and practice medicine on their home islands. Although it is beyond the scope of this book to uncover the career of every Okinawan medical graduate, the list of names from the Nanmei Alumni Association reveals the status of some Okinawan students in 1941. As expected, those who had graduated earlier tended to open their own independent clinics. Interestingly, the graduates practiced medicine not only in Okinawa and Mainland Japan but also in places within Japanese imperial territories, including colonial Taiwan, the Republic of China, the South Sea Islands, and Singapore. Graduates also worked at hospitals in various locations across the Japanese Empire.

Graduates of Taiwan Medical College and the Specialized Division for Medicine also moved frequently across Japanese territory. For instance, Yoshino Kōzen, who graduated from Taiwan Medical College in 1923, became a research student immediately after graduation. While majoring in internal medicine, he worked part-time as a doctor at the Taiwanese branch of the Japanese Red Cross Hospital. After completing his graduate studies in 1925, he was a practice instructor at Taiwan Medical College for two months and eventually accepted a position as head of internal medicine at the Taiwan Colonial Government Karenkō Clinic (Taiwan Sōtokufu Karenkō Iin) in eastern Taiwan. Most of his patients were residents of the Japanese community in the neighborhood. Two years later, in 1927, he returned to Ishigaki Island and opened his own clinic. With the success of his clinic, Yoshino was finally able to repay the money his home village had loaned him for his tuition at Taiwan Medical College.[59]

Genga Chōkō, who initially set his sights on becoming a doctor in order to practice medicine in Okinawa Prefecture, graduated from Taiwan Medical College in 1933. Instead of returning immediately to Okinawa, he worked for the Japan Sugar Refining Factory (Nihon Seitō Kōjō). Intending to further his studies in surgery, he moved to Osaka and entered the Faculty of Medicine at Osaka Imperial University. While juggling his studies at the university with his job at Sakai Municipal Hospital in Osaka's Sakai City, he was called to Dōjin Hospital (Dōjin Byōin) in Shanghai, where there was a shortage of doctors. He later served as a military doctor in China.[60]

Genga's experiences were not exceptional. Tanaka Kōei graduated from the Specialized Division for Medicine in 1941 and took his first job at Okinawa Prefectural Hospital. Soon after, he was called up to join the military and serve as a doctor in Toyohashi City, Aichi Prefecture. There, he contracted pleurisy and was admitted to the Toyohashi Army Hospital. Upon recovery, he remained at the hospital and worked as a military doctor. In 1943, he was drafted into the Japanese army in Manchuria and stayed in China until the end of World War II.[61] Like Genga and Tanaka, most Okinawan doctors were drafted into the Japanese armed forces as military doctors and were stationed at various battlefields when the war ended.

Some Okinawan doctors in Taiwan were ordered to join the military in Okinawa and were dragged into ground warfare. After graduating from the Specialized Division for Medicine in 1941, Shinzato Kōtoku worked at Taihoku Imperial University and Hakuai-kai Guangdong Clinic (Hakuai-kai Kanton Iin) in China. While serving the colonial government of Taiwan as a part-time ophthalmologist, he was conscripted into the army on the main island of Okinawa. During the war, Okinawan doctors, who were supposedly familiar with local conditions, were specifically drafted into the army in Okinawa. However, the battleship that carried Shinzato to Okinawa was hit and sunk by the US military. As a result, 4,000 of the 4,600 soldiers and nine of the ten Okinawan military doctors lost their lives; Shinzato was the only Okinawan doctor to survive. After his injuries were treated, he joined the military on the main island of Okinawa.[62] Although he survived the war, many of his fellow doctors and nurses perished in the fierce land battle.

Okinawa's local municipal governments encouraged youths to attend Taiwan Medical College or the Specialized Division for Medicine because Okinawa desperately needed doctors, but most Okinawan graduates did not return to their home islands and practice medicine. While quite a few Okinawan graduates did plan to set up their own clinics in the prefecture, their status and locations before World War II suggest that many remained outside Okinawa in case Japan held on to the Outer Territories. In reality, the shortage of medical doctors in Okinawa was overshadowed by the demand for military doctors when World War II broke out in the 1930s. Okinawan doctors who had graduated from Taiwan Medical College and the Specialized Division for Medicine were drafted and sent to battlefields, from which they were repatriated to Okinawa under US military occupation.

The imperial schooling of Okinawan youths in Taiwan reflects Okinawa's liminal position in the Japanese colonial empire. Taiwan had benefited from heavy Japanese investment in colonial development, whereas Okinawa was left behind and marginalized within the Japanese Inner Territory. The Medical Training School was the first and most eminent medical school in Okinawa before World War II, but it was poorly equipped and had insufficient human resources. In contrast, the support the colonial government of Taiwan provided for medical education enabled Taiwan Medical College to quickly become the top educational institution for the Taiwanese. Nevertheless, Okinawan youths were able to take advantage of their "Japanese" status in obtaining imperial schooling. Taiwan Medical College opened its doors to Japanese students in 1919 and allowed Taiwanese students to enroll alongside them in 1922. Bringing the Taiwanese into tertiary institutions with Japanese students reinforced the fact that they were in direct competition with the Japanese and at a disadvantage because they were not native speakers of Japanese. Instead, Okinawan youths gained the most from the policy allowing Taiwanese students to attend medical school alongside their Japanese peers. Taiwan Medical College and the Specialized Division for Medicine paved the way for Okinawans to become medical doctors without incurring great debt. Indeed, Okinawa's medical development cannot be understood without understanding the circulation of people and knowledge beyond the metropole-colonies divide. Modern medicine in Okinawa was, on the one hand, marginalized within the scientific network of the Japanese Empire; on the other, Okinawans' liminality allowed them to gain the greatest benefit from the imperial school network.

Chapter 5

Between Japanese and Okinawan

Okinawan immigrants were often subjected to prejudice and discrimination in colonial Taiwan and nearly all their host countries (discussed in chap. 1). As a way of coping with severe ethnic discrimination from the Japanese, Okinawan immigrants established prefectural associations in cities with large migrant populations. Ben Kobashigawa points out that *issei* (first generation) Okinawans in the US mainland formed two organizations in the 1920s: the Okinawa Overseas Association (Okinawa Kaigai Kyōkai), which promoted assimilation into mainstream Japanese culture and ways; and the Okinawan Young People's Association of America (Zaibei Okinawa Seinenkai), renamed the Okinawan Prefectural Association of America (Zaibei Okinawa Kenjinkai). The leaders of the Okinawa Overseas Association believed assimilation was the only means of tempering negative Japanese attitudes toward Okinawan immigrants and promoted a policy of doing things "the Japanese way." The Okinawa Prefectural Association of America challenged this assimilationist stance by encouraging pride in Okinawan culture and insisting that Okinawans should consider their distinctive culture an asset in the fight against American racism alongside fellow Japanese immigrants. Kobashigawa argues that Okinawan identity in Southern California evolved through rivalry and negotiation between these two organizations.[1]

In actuality, however, the position of the Okinawan Prefectural Association of America was the exception rather than the norm. In his study of Okinawan migrant labor in the greater Osaka area, Tomiyama Ichirō argues that the Kansai Okinawa Prefectural Association simultaneously shaped ethnic identity among Okinawan immigrant laborers and encouraged these Okinawans to become more "Japanese."[2] In discussing the circumstances of Okinawan immigrants in Taiwan and Osaka, Alan S. Christy notes, "The examples from both Taiwan and Osaka remind us that Okinawan struggles to deal with discrimination from Japanese and improve their economic lot must be understood within the context of the Japanese Empire, in which being Japanese was the only way to access power."[3] Though I agree with Christy's main general argument, I nonetheless reconsider the discourses in previous studies on the immigrants' ethnic identity and assimilation into Japanese mainstream culture.

First, although Okinawan immigrants living in the Japanese settler community in Taiwan tended to assimilate into mainstream Japanese culture, this form of assimilation—conscious efforts to conform to Japanese customs and manners—should be distinguished from the creolization that was prevalent among second- and third-generation Okinawan immigrants. In questioning the assumption that assimilation was the only way for Okinawan immigrants to access power in Taiwan, this chapter contends that some Okinawans resisted assimilation and assertively fostered pride in Okinawan culture in Taiwan during World War II. The movement was promoted by Japanese scholars who took a special interest in Okinawan folklore, anthropology, and archeology. These scholars were so passionate about Okinawan culture that they wanted to make Taipei the center of Okinawan studies. Yet the rise of "Okinawan consciousness" did not result in the establishment of a powerful, ethnicity-based organization capable of uniting Okinawan immigrants from diverse social and regional backgrounds.

Creoles in the Japanese Colony

While numerous younger immigrants came to Taiwan soon after graduating from school, a significant number of Okinawans with dependent families journeyed to Taiwan in search of better lives. In 1930, there were 7,442 Japanese nationals in Taiwan with addresses registered in Okinawa Prefecture. Okinawans born in Taiwan accounted for approximately 22 percent of the total Okinawan population in Taiwan, and 45 percent of the Okinawan population were under the age of nineteen.[4] The considerable number of children with Okinawan backgrounds born or raised in Taiwan in the 1930s suggests that many Okinawan migrants settled there with their families. These second- and third-generation Okinawans shaped their identities quite differently from their parents, who had been born and raised in Okinawa. My informants' life histories suggest that Okinawan immigrants were a diverse group of people who led liminal lives in colonial Taiwan.

Noda Yoshiko, a Descendant of the Chinese

The grandparents of the pseudonymous Noda Yoshiko were among the earliest Okinawan migrants to Taiwan. Originally from Kume Village in Naha

City, they migrated to Taiwan at the turn of the twentieth century.[5] Kume Village was a distinctive district, founded by Chinese immigrants and commonly called the "Thirty-Six Families of Fukien." It is traditionally believed that the first Chinese immigrants came to the Ryukyu Islands in the late fourteenth century when each of the three kingdoms established tributary trade with China.[6] The majority of the villagers either had been officially dispatched to Okinawa by the Ming dynasty or were Chinese immigrants who had traded privately with Southeast Asian countries. When the population of Kume Village declined in the late sixteenth century, the Ryukyu government ordered some native Ryukyuans to join the Kume Village registry. Thus, Kume Village was not a "purely Chinese enclave" but a district of professionals who handed down their knowledge and skills in traditional Chinese arts and crafts. Their literacy and fluency in the Chinese language, and their familiarity with Chinese traditions and administrative methods, enabled them to play distinguished roles in the Ryukyu Kingdom's maintenance of formal and informal trading networks.[7]

Born in the transitional period when the Ryukyu Kingdom came under Japanese rule, Yoshiko's maternal grandfather, Kina Chōfu (pseudonym), was also well educated and proficient in the Chinese language.[8] After Japanese annexation, however, he was no longer entitled to receive the economic and social privileges granted by the government of the Ryukyu Kingdom. Moreover, there were very few professional positions for educated Okinawans under the new Japanese government. Thus, like many other Okinawan *shizoku* families, members of the former ruling class, who had lost their privileges, Chōfu decided to leave his home island and start a new business. He was particularly interested in Taiwan because he mistakenly believed that he could utilize his Chinese-language ability in the former Chinese territory. Upon his arrival in Taiwan, he was disappointed to learn that the Taiwanese dialect of Min Chinese was the common language of the locals, and few residents understood Mandarin.[9] Chōfu worked as an engine driver for the Taiwan Railway Company for nearly thirty years. His name appears on the list of Taiwan Colonial Government personnel nearly every year from 1905 to 1934. Throughout this time, he was at the colonial government's Railway Department.[10]

Thus, Yoshiko's mother, Shizuko (pseudonym), was born in Kaohsiung and attended Shinchiku Advanced Girls' School and Tainan Normal School in Taiwan. Her parents arranged her marriage to an Okinawan immigrant, even though she knew very little about her parents' home island. Yoshiko's father, Higa Tomonori (pseudonym), was born on Okinawa Island, but his mother came from Kagoshima Prefecture. He dropped out of Naha Commercial High School (Naha Shōgyō Kōtō Gakkō), moved to

Amoy (present-day Xiamen), and migrated in the early 1920s to Taiwan, where he passed the examination to join the colonial Taiwan police force.[11] His reasons for migrating and becoming a policeman in Taiwan are unknown, but Yoshiko assumed her father did so because he could not find a suitable job in Okinawa.

Yoshiko's parents were married in 1938, and Yoshiko, their first daughter, was born the following year in Tainan, where Tomonori was working as a police officer. Although the family's official registered address was Okinawa Prefecture, Yoshiko was unfamiliar with Okinawan traditions. Her family communicated in standard Japanese at home because Shizuko did not understand the Okinawan dialect.[12] During our interview, Yoshiko recalled that their home cooking did not have much traditional Okinawan flavor: "The food of Okinawan repatriates from Taiwan differs from local Okinawan food. Ours certainly was influenced by cuisine from mainland Japan. We use a lot of sweet sake [*mirin*] and sugar as seasoning in dishes. Okinawans today use *mirin* as seasoning, but they rarely used it in the past. . . . During the Meiji period, *mirin* was uncommon in Okinawa. I don't know where she purchased it. In any case, Father told me that she used a lot of *mirin* at home."[13] I asked if her father, who had immigrated from Okinawa Prefecture, was comfortable with the flavor of *mirin*. She replied that he was familiar with the taste of *mirin* because his mother was from Kagoshima Prefecture. In short, Yoshiko's mother was a descendant of the so-called Thirty-Six Families of Fukien, and her father had been born to Okinawan and Japanese parents.

Yoshiko had a unique childhood under the direction of her mother, who was a teacher in a public school.[14] In the late 1930s, following the change in official policy, the secondary and tertiary schools in Taiwan began accepting Taiwanese students along with Japanese students, allowing them equal access to secondary and post-secondary education. However, elementary education was divided into two types of schools: primary schools, for native or near-native Japanese speakers, and public schools, for native Taiwanese speakers. Although the official language was Japanese during the colonial period, only a small number of Taiwanese children spoke fluent Japanese. Thus, only a few Taiwanese children—usually from very wealthy families with close ties to Japanese settlers—were allowed to enter a primary school and study alongside the children of Japanese settlers. In addition, Japanese children went to kindergartens for the Japanese and were segregated from Taiwanese children. However, Yoshiko joined the Taiwanese children's kindergarten as part of her mother's "experiment." Shizuko expected the Taiwanese children to be linguistically influenced by Yoshiko and learn to speak fluent Japanese before they started elementary school, but her experiment failed. Instead, because most of the children were Taiwanese, Yoshiko became fluent in Taiwanese and did not contribute much to the Taiwanese children's Japanese-language learning.[15]

It can be said that Yoshiko's kindergarten life was a microcosm of the Japanese settlers' lives in colonial Taiwan. The government encouraged Japanese migrants to settle in Taiwan from the beginning because it was considered the most effective method of assimilating the Taiwanese into Japanese sociocultural norms and integrating Taiwan into the Japanese Empire. Nonetheless, very few Japanese actually settled down in Taiwan in the early days of Japanese colonial rule because of the poor infrastructure, political and social instability, and fear of tropical diseases. Later, as living conditions improved and more Japanese immigrants settled in Taiwan, the Japanese settlers' attitudes toward Taiwan and Japan changed. As Gan Kyōju (Yan Xinru) observed, Japanese settlers who had lived in Taiwan for decades increasingly viewed Taiwan, not Japan proper, as their "homeland."[16]

There was also growing public concern that Japanese children born and raised in Taiwan did not know the "real Japan" and were becoming "Taiwanized." For instance, some Japanese children who grew up in Taiwan's tropical climate found it difficult to imagine the four seasons and could not appreciate seasonal events with the proper "Japanese sensitivity." In the late 1910s, primary schools in Taiwan conducted trips to the Inner Territory in an attempt to nurture this Japanese sensitivity and prevent the Taiwanization of Japanese children. In sum, a growing number of Japanese migrants settled in Taiwan with their families in the 1920s and 1930s. Although they were expected to be model "authentic Japanese imperial subjects," the Japanese who had been born and raised in Taiwan were instead influenced by local Taiwanese culture and developed a unique "Taiwan-born [*wan-sei*] Japanese" identity.[17]

Yoshiko also stated that her father could speak Taiwanese, not because of the influence of local Taiwanese, but because the skill was necessary for his job as a policeman.[18] Indeed, Japanese police officers in Taiwan were strongly encouraged to master local languages, including the Han Taiwanese variants of Min Chinese (Hokkien), the Guangdong dialect of Hakka, and the aboriginal languages. There were language certificate examinations for police officers, who could receive allowances and promotions based on linguistic proficiency.[19]

The life stories of Yoshiko's family suggest that the category of "Okinawans" in Taiwan cannot be identified as the homogeneous ethnic group with a coherent cultural identity. Okinawans included those from the Naha-centered Chinese community of Kume Village, as well as those who married Japanese mainlanders. Furthermore, it was fairly common for Okinawans born and raised in Taiwan to rarely visit Okinawa. Their upbringing in the Japanese settler community in colonial Taiwan also meant that they mostly did not identify themselves as ethnic Okinawans. In particular, Okinawans whose parents were also raised in Taiwan normally assimilated into Japanese mainland culture in colonial Taiwan. Despite their official registered addresses in Okinawa Prefecture, these Okinawans in Taiwan are properly called "creole Japanese." However, they could still be the target of prejudice and discrimination due to their ancestral roots.

Shimoji Yasuo, Son of the Wushe Policeman

Shimoji Yasuo's father, Shimoji Keikō, was also a policeman in colonial Taiwan. Keikō was born on Miyako Island in 1906. He graduated from the advanced course of Miyakojima Elementary School in 1921 and got by on temporary jobs because he could not find suitable employment. He was married in 1929, when he was a mountain gatekeeper, but was soon laid off. During this period of unemployment, his first daughter was born, on July 12, 1930. To help him out, Shimoji's cousin called him to Taiwan, alerting him to the urgent need for policemen there. In response, he went to Taiwan and began working as an assistant policeman in November of that year.[20]

Indeed, Okinawans joined the Taiwan police force very early in the period of Japanese colonial rule. Okinawan local newspapers periodically ran advertisements for policemen in Taiwan. According to government records, there were 106 Okinawans in the colonial Taiwan police force in 1931, including one assistant inspector, sixty-seven police officers (*junsa*), and thirty-eight assistant policemen (*keishu*).[21] It is possible there were more inspectors, police officers, and policemen from Okinawa Prefecture, but some may have transferred their registered addresses to other prefectures.

Police work was a popular occupation for Okinawan immigrants in Taiwan partly because recruits were not required to have much educational background. In 1931, there were 5,336 Japanese, 1,208 Han Taiwanese, and 110 aboriginal police officers working in Taiwan. It was clear that the colonial Taiwanese police force hired Japanese staff, irrespective of educational background—64.8 percent of Japanese policemen had only graduated from the advanced course of elementary school (*kōtō shōgakkō*), and 23.4 percent were either attending or had graduated from middle school (*chūgakkō*).[22] The Japanese recruits were equally diverse in terms of occupational background, with 51 percent being former farmers and 19.2 percent having been employed as public officials.[23] Previous studies have stressed that the police played unique and vital roles in the Japanese colonial rule of Taiwan.[24] It should be noted that the Taiwan police force was, in fact, sustained by a number of Japanese and Okinawan migrants who were mostly from agricultural regions and did not have much educational background.

Although Okinawans had consistently joined the Taiwan police force from the beginning of Japanese colonial rule, Shimoji Keikō's migration likely corresponded to Taiwan's urgent need for more Japanese policemen to quell the anti-Japanese uprising known as the Musha Incident (also called the "Wushe Uprising"). The insurrection occurred in Wushe (Japanese, Musha), Taizhong County, home of the Seediq indigenous group.[25] On the early morning of October 27, 1930, groups of Seediq warriors led by the chief, Mouna Rudao, attacked neighborhood police stations and killed Japanese policemen. That day, the biggest community event, the School Sports Festival, took place at the Musha Public School athletic field. Approximately 350 pupils, including Japanese and Taiwanese aborigine children, participated in the festival, and their families and neighbors thronged the field. When the event was just about to start, more than a hundred Seediq warriors attacked the site and indiscriminately murdered the Japanese.[26]

As a result of this guerrilla attack, 134 Japanese, including women and children, and two Han Chinese wearing Japanese kimonos were killed.[27] Several Okinawan policemen and their families fell victim to this attack as well. A police officer named Maeda Seishirō was killed, and the second son of another police officer was murdered, even though the officer and his family managed to escape, as did two Okinawan police assistants.[28] Immediately after this attack, 1,303 soldiers and military officers along with more than a thousand police officers and police assistants were called to Wushe. The armed conflict continued until the Seediq leaders committed suicide in mid-December 1930.[29] According to the colonial government's records, 564 Seediq warriors had surrendered by December 17, 1930, and 644 were either killed or committed suicide to avoid being taken alive.[30] Today, the Musha Incident is known as the largest anti-Japanese insurrection by Taiwanese aborigines since the colonial government seized control of their residential area in 1915.

In the aftermath of the uprising, the Taiwan police force increased the number of assistant policemen in Taizhong County from 512 to 712 in January 1931.[31] While it is unknown if Keikō took part in the action against the Seediq, he is nonetheless associated with it because he began his career as an assistant policeman in the middle of Japanese military action in Wushe. Two years later, he was formally appointed a police officer at Musha Station, the very target of the uprising. From then on, he worked at several police stations in the indigenous Taiwanese residential areas of Taizhong. Thus, his son, Shimoji Yasuo, was born in Shuitou (Japanese, Suitō), the indigenous district in the mountainous area of Taizhong.[32]

With his elder sister, Yōko, being raised by their grandmother on Miyako Island, Yasuo grew up as an only child in this remote village: "It was a place deep in the mountains. It is quite nostalgic to remember the place and the indigenous people occasionally dancing with fire. It was so peaceful. I was the only son of a police officer, and my sister lived with my grandmother on Miyako Island. Thus, I was raised as if I were a prince of that place. It was the best time of my life."[33] When he was of school age, he went to live with his sister and grandmother on Miyako Island. It was necessary to send him to Miyako Island because there was no primary school for Japanese children in that area of Taizhong. Thus, he spent the first two years of elementary school on Miyako Island.[34]

In 1941, Shimoji Yasuo, his sister, and his grandmother moved to Taiwan because his father, Keikō, left the indigenous residential area in the mountains and went to work at a police station in downtown Puli. In the remote mountain village, Yasuo hardly ever met other Japanese settlers, except the family of his father's colleague from the same police station. In Puli Town, however, the Shimoji family stayed at the police official residence in the Japanese settler community.[35]

> Our school was located near the residence. Every day, I commuted between school and home and didn't have many chances to look around other places. There was a Taiwanese community in the neighborhood, but I never had any exchanges with them. Thus, I don't know their language. I knew only a couple of slang words and could not have a proper conversation in the Taiwanese language. I can recall only three Taiwanese students in our primary school, but they never spoke Taiwanese in school. I visited their houses, but even their families spoke Japanese at home.[36]

Born in Taiwan and growing up as the son of a Japanese policeman, Shimoji Yasuo did not experience any difficulty living in the Japanese settler community in downtown Puli. However, his grandmother, who had spent her whole life on Miyako Island, could not assimilate into Japanese culture in the colony.

> When I moved into the official residence with Grandmother, my mother told her, "Don't show the tattoos on your hands. We're now living with Japanese from the other prefectures. It will be embarrassing. Japanese mainlanders will laugh at the tattoos and look down on us Okinawans." So Grandmother covered her hands with cloths and moved into the official residence quietly. Because Grandmother spoke only the Miyako dialect, we sometimes had conversations in the dialect. She could not go outside and

socialize with the neighbors, even if she wanted to. Mother socialized with the neighbors and the families of Father's colleagues. But Grandmother always stayed at home. And do you know what she was doing? She was spinning thread all day at home. Today, I feel so sorry for her. For five years, she stayed indoors, and I guess she made a small amount of money from spinning thread to sell on Miyako Island.[37]

In the course of my research, I came across a number of Taiwan-born Okinawans. Most had no trouble assimilating into mainstream Japanese culture, as they had been born and raised in Taiwan's Japanese community. Whereas their parents, first-generation immigrants, had to make conscious efforts to assimilate, members of the second generation tended to identify themselves as "Japanese" rather than "Okinawans." Their imperial Japanese identity was not naturally constructed but shaped by their parents' concealment of their Okinawan heritage and active assimilation into the culture of Mainland Japan. In other words, the assimilation and creolization of Okinawan migrants are both distinct and entangled.

Struggling with Multiple Identities

The hybridity and flexibility of Okinawan migrants' identities in Taiwan are most visible through the life histories of the Sakiyama family, originally from Ishigaki Island in the Yaeyama Islands. Sakiyama Masa's father, Sakiyama Hiroshi, was one of many Okinawans to transfer his household's official registered address to Kagoshima Prefecture upon his migration to Taiwan. Born on Ishigaki Island in 1901, Hiroshi taught at elementary schools both there and in Naha, the capital of Okinawa Prefecture. In April 1925, Masa, his first daughter, was born on Ishigaki Island. Soon after, the family moved to the main island of Okinawa, and she spent her early childhood in Naha, where Hiroshi taught music at Kōshin Elementary School. Then, just before Masa reached school age, Hiroshi decided to migrate to Taiwan.

Several reasons contributed to his decision. On the one hand, Masa disclosed that her parents were attracted by the fact that Okinawan teachers would be granted a "colonial allowance" in addition to their regular salaries in Taiwan.[38] Indeed, Japanese schoolteachers in Taiwan were granted colonial service allowances amounting to approximately 60 percent of their regular salaries.[39] Moreover, schoolteachers whose salaries exceeded fifty-five yen were offered twenty yen as a monthly housing allowance.[40] On the other hand, Masa's mother, Toshi, explained that she encouraged Hiroshi to move away from Okinawa because he was very popular with local women,

Sakiyama family, Taipei, ca. 1944. Photo courtesy of Itosu Masa

and she wanted to keep him away from temptation.[41] Very likely, both accounts present partial and real reasons for the Sakiyama family's immigration to Taiwan.

Hiroshi left his family behind in 1931 and moved to Keelung, where his relative Sakiyama Yōkyō was teaching at Kiryū Advanced Girls' School. Yōkyō was five years older than Hiroshi and had migrated to Taiwan in 1923. He had transferred his official registered address to Hiroshima Prefecture, where he attended Hiroshima Higher Normal School.[42] Following Yōkyō's course of action, Hiroshi changed his registered address to Kagoshima Prefecture in the hope of improving his employment prospects.[43] Eventually, in 1932, he got a job at Gilan Public School (in present-day Yilan County). According to the book celebrating the school's fortieth anniversary, there were 1,351 pupils in 1933, most of whom were supposedly male Taiwanese.[44] There were twenty teachers (*kundō*), including nine instructors of Taiwanese and four assistant teachers (*kyōin kokoroe*).[45] Because

Hiroshi had not obtained the teacher's license as stipulated in Taiwanese educational legislation, he first worked as an assistant teacher and became a proper teacher in 1934.

Masa went to a primary school on Ishigaki Island and transferred to Gilan Primary School when the rest of her family joined her father in Taiwan in 1933. Unlike Gilan Public School, where Hiroshi was teaching, Gilan Primary School accommodated only 459 pupils, most of whom were female and male children of Japanese settlers. From the time it opened in 1899, all the teachers were Japanese and Taiwanese were never employed. Pupils came from the city of Yilan and neighboring districts that had no primary schools for Japanese children. Many of the pupils' parents were public servants. In 1940, police officers and prison guards accounted for 16 percent of the parents' occupations, public officials made up 15 percent, and schoolteachers composed another 9 percent.[46] Indeed, Gilan Primary School was typical of the Japanese colonial settler community.

Although the Sakiyama family, including Masa's two younger sisters, settled in Yilan, Hiroshi's mother, Nabema, chose to remain on Ishigaki Island by herself. Toshi later explained, "I suspect Mother refused to emigrate not only because of the language barrier but also because of the tattoos on her hands."[47] Evidently, the Japanese language and Okinawan women's tattoos were the biggest obstacles to the migration of Okinawan women to Taiwan.

After living in Yilan for a year, Masa acceded to her beloved grandmother's wishes and moved back to Ishigaki Island to live with her. Traveling between Ishigaki Island and Yilan, Masa spent almost an equal amount of time at the two primary schools.

> I told you that I also went to the primary school in Yaeyama, didn't I? I went to the fourth and fifth grades. . . . We were from Taiwan. I put a white hat on, even though I was treated like a servant at home [*laughs*]. I wore a white hat as if I were a daughter of the aristocracy and wore Western clothes with a pair of white shoes. People would look at me enviously and say, "Folks from Taiwan are great." Because we came back from Taiwan, there were some differences.[48]

According to interviews and autobiographies, Yaeyama people regarded returnees from Taiwan as sophisticated or wealthy. These feelings may have turned into jealousy or antipathy toward the returnees' styles and tastes. Regardless of the nature of their perceptions and feelings, Yaeyama locals saw long-term residents of Taiwan, like Masa, as different. Living with her family in the Japanese migrant community in Taiwan, Masa developed an identity that was different from the identities of those who grew up in Yaeyama. In the Japanese migrant community, however, she was also regarded as different because she was from "Ryukyu," which had a negative connotation at the time. Although Masa identified herself as a "Japanese migrant" rather than an "Okinawan," she was set apart from the Japanese mainlanders. She recalled her experiences at Gilan Primary School this way:

> When we moved to Taiwan, our registered address was changed from Okinawa to Kagoshima Prefecture. . . . When my uncle graduated from the higher normal school (*kōtō shihan gakkō*) in Hiroshima, he changed his registered address from Okinawa to Hiroshima. Thus, during the recession, my father thought of changing our registered Okinawa address to improve our situation and minimize discrimination. As his sister's husband was from Kagoshima Prefecture, I suppose he spoke with her. So we changed the registered address to Sendai-shi in Kagoshima Prefecture.
>
> Because there was a recession, some people changed their names, and others changed official registered addresses. . . . But because I moved back and forth between Taiwan and Ishigaki, my classmates found out that I was actually from Okinawa Prefecture. They said to me, "You, you're from Ryukyu, aren't you?"
>
> I was only a second-grade pupil at the primary school and didn't know what "Ryukyu" was. I asked them, "What's Ryukyu?"
>
> They said, "Ryukyuans walk barefoot, don't they?"
>
> "No, some were barefoot, but I wore shoes to school."
>
> They also said, "What language do you use? Speak to us."
>
> "I don't know. I use this language at home as well as at school. I use only this language."
>
> "Do you take a bath?"
>
> "I do!"
>
> They said these things during break every day.

Then, she continued, "One day, they brought a small knife and said to me, 'Cut your finger. Let's see what color blood will come out.' I was bullied."[49]

Masa's difficult experience was not unique. The pseudonymous Arakawa Kiku was born on Taketomi Island in 1926. She also told me that her primary school classmates in Keelung discriminated against her because of her regional background, and Taketomi Islanders regarded her as different because she wore different clothes.[50] Children of Okinawan migrants in Taiwan, like Sakiyama Masa and Arakawa Kiku, embodied the liminal status of Okinawan migrants' self-identities. As discussed in chapter 1, the terms "Ryukyu" and "Okinawa" had connotations of backwardness or oth-

Keelung Advanced Girls' School, ca. 1942. Source: Editorial Committee of Municipal History Books, Ishigaki-shi, Board of Education. Used with permission.

erness vis-à-vis "Japanese." Yet, as chapters 2 and 3 demonstrate, Yaeyama locals thought of colonial Taiwan as the "other" because it was urbanized and advanced compared to rural Yaeyama. Moving between Okinawa and the Japanese settler community in Taiwan, children of Okinawa migrants had to confront their liminal status in the Japanese colonial empire.

Sakiyama Masa entered an advanced girls' school in Yilan in 1937. Most of the students were daughters of Japanese migrants, and Sakiyama generally enjoyed school life there. Things changed when her father decided to resign from the public school in Yilan and accept a job with an automobile company in Taipei. The Sakiyama family moved to Taipei City in 1937. Unlike the smaller city of Yilan, there were three advanced girls' schools in Taipei City. While most of the daughters of Japanese migrants attended Taihoku First Advanced Girls' School and Taihoku Second Advanced Girls' School, Taihoku Third Advanced Girls' School—established for Taiwanese girls—was dominated by Han Taiwanese students. Officially, there was no discrimination in secondary education after 1922; however, in practice, there was a clear distinction, justified by reason of tradition. Although there were no official regulations on eligibility for entrance examinations, both Japanese migrants and Taiwanese chose different schools by self-assessing their ethnic backgrounds and capabilities.

Taihoku First Advanced Girls' School was famous for being the top elite school. The Sakiyama family decided that Masa should apply to the Second Advanced Girls' School. When Masa did not pass the competitive entrance examination, her name was put on the waiting list for admission.

> As many people applied to the school, my name was put first or second on the waiting list. Because we were unsure whether I'd be admitted to the school if there were vacancies, my father asked a teacher at the Third Advanced Girls' School to let me take its entrance exam. I was admitted to the Third School but was reluctant to go. I said, "Dad, people say that it's a school for Taiwanese."
>
> But my father tried to convince me by saying, "Don't worry. After graduating from the advanced girls' school, you'll go to normal school anyway. It doesn't matter which school you attend at the secondary level as long as the school is a public one."
>
> My parents decided to send me to Taihoku Third Advanced Girls' School. A couple of days later, the Second Advanced Girls' School called us and said I was admitted to the school.[51]

According to Masa, her parents declined the offer from Taihoku Second Advanced Girls' School because they had already paid the fees for the Third Advanced Girls' School. In 1940, when she was in her final year at the school, Japanese migrants accounted for 9.8 percent of students and Han Taiwanese accounted for 89.2 percent.[52] After graduating from the Third Advanced Girls' School, she attended a special teachers' training course. In 1941, she became a teacher at Hōrai National School (Hōrai Kokumin Gakkō), which provided elementary education mainly to female Taiwanese pupils.

In my two interviews with her, Sakiyama Masa frequently mentioned that she did not study hard and did "bad things" at Taihoku Third Advanced Girls' School.

> Author: Why didn't you study hard in Taipei?
>
> Sakiyama Masa: Oh well, I was angry! My parents made me enter such a school. They made me go to a school for Taiwanese. It was my best way of resisting.
>
> Author: Was it resistance against your mother?
>
> Sakiyama Masa: Against my father, too. Resistance against my parents. Although I was admitted to the other school, they made me go to that school because they did not want to spend money.
>
> Author: Yes, it was said that the Second and Third [Advanced Girls'] Schools were different. But did they teach different subjects?

Sakiyama Masa: No, no. They should have been the same. The teachers at both schools were all Japanese.[53]
Author: So, what was the difference?
Sakiyama Masa: The students were different.[54]

It would be erroneous to simply identify her as a racist who refused to integrate with Taiwanese students. In fact, she stated that she enjoyed school life and made many Taiwanese friends.

Author: It seems you had a lot of fun in Taiwan. Didn't you have bad experiences?
Sakiyama Masa: Of course, I had many. I told you my mom did not take good care of me, didn't I? But the girls' school was fun. People discriminated against the Taiwanese, but I didn't discriminate against them. My family was also poor. Because our living standard was not so different from theirs, I didn't discriminate against them. I enjoyed school life very much.[55]

Living with the colonial elite in the Japanese migrant community and studying with the daughters of well-off Taiwanese at Taihoku Third Advanced Girls' School, Masa did not recognize her family as particularly privileged. In reflecting on her family's financial struggle, she expressed solidarity with the Taiwanese, who were also socially underprivileged in the colonial context. Her desire not to attend a "school for Taiwanese" did not contradict her feelings of solidarity with them. While she refused the label of "Taiwanese," which had connotations of inferiority, she had no trouble making Taiwanese friends. She was not unhappy to be with actual Taiwanese but was angry with her parents for reconciling her to the imaginary social construct that presented a negative representation of "Taiwanese."

Struggles over classifications were not mere representational or psychological matters; they produced and reproduced physical boundaries in residential areas and social institutions such as schools. The notions of "Japanese" and "Taiwanese" were not neutral classifications but were constructed in a power relationship. Living as liminal subjects of the Japanese Empire, Okinawan migrants and their children were active agents in reproducing the boundary between "Japanese" and "Taiwanese."

Okinawan Pride

As Okinawans experienced severe prejudice and discrimination, any indication of their origin was considered disadvantageous to an imperial career. Hence, passing for Japanese and changing their names and the prefecture of their official registered addresses were fairly common practices among Okinawan migrants in Taiwan.[56] Some Okinawans refused to admit their ethnic background and even distanced themselves from other Okinawans. The majority, however, generally maintained family and neighborhood ties with those from their home islands, even though they had changed their names and registered addresses. As observed in the life histories of Sakiyama Hiroshi and others, networking with family and friends from their home islands was vitally important for job hunting and settling down in Taiwan.

Apart from numerous informal networks among Okinawan migrants, there was also a prefectural association that was supposedly open to all migrants from Okinawa Prefecture. The prefectural association was not unique to Okinawans in Taiwan, as most Japanese prefectures established their own associations for migrants from similar regions, usually in bigger cities where Japanese settlers were concentrated. In addition to prefectural associations, there were associations based on smaller geographical units. According to Gan Kyōju's study, prefectural associations were mainly societies for male adults.[57] In 1925, the *Taiwan Daily News* reported the existence of forty-four prefectural associations across Taiwan and approximately four thousand participants in Taipei City.[58] As there were approximately twenty thousand Japanese males over the age of sixteen in Taipei City in 1925, this suggests that about one-fifth of these men joined prefectural associations. Generally speaking, the associations promoted friendship and provided comfort to those living in a strange land. Common activities included taking care of funerals, giving support to the poor of the same regional origin, and periodically holding social gatherings. By examining newspaper articles and association bulletins, Gan demonstrates that prefectural associations held various social gatherings, such as New Year celebration parties, as well as farewell and welcome parties, where they served dishes from the homeland and entertained members with traditional songs and dances.[59]

The studies of Tomiyama Ichirō and Steve Rabson indicate that prefectural associations in Osaka played vital roles in promoting the welfare of Okinawan migrants and shaping their political identity.[60] In contrast, Okinawan prefectural associations in Taiwan functioned more as friendship associations and were not politically oriented. Is it possible that Okinawan settlers in Taiwan were politically inactive, and assimilation into Japanese mainstream culture was the only way they could survive in the Japanese settler community? It should be noted that some Okinawan migrants were highly conscious of their Okinawan identity to the extent that they made conscious efforts to promote Okinawan culture in Taiwan.

Kabira Chōshin was one of the few Okinawan migrants actively promoting Okinawan culture in Taiwan during World War II. He was born in

1908 and spent his early childhood on Izena and Iheya Islands, where his father, Chōhei, was a police officer. He, his parents, and two younger brothers immigrated to Taiwan in 1924. His grandfather Kabira Chōhin was one of the highest-ranking government officials in the Ryukyu Kingdom and was in the service of the last Ryukyu king when Japan annexed the kingdom in the 1870s.[61] Chōshin's father, Chōhei, initially worked as a police officer but quit and started a business in Naha City. However, his business failed during the Great Depression that followed World War I. Chōshin was still a student at Okinawa Second Middle School at the time. He left and entered a school for engine drivers in Keelung, Taiwan, but he and his family then moved to Taizhong, where he entered Taichū First Middle School in 1925.[62]

After graduating from middle school in 1926, he worked at several jobs, including postal officer, news reporter, and editor. When the Taihoku Broadcasting Station was established in 1931, Chōshin found employment there and began to produce some of its children's programs. He also drew up a special program of Ryukyuan classical music.[63] As his father, Chōhei, was a master of Ryukyuan classical music, Chōshin played the three-stringed Okinawan banjo (*sanshin*) and sang. In the program, Chōhei's pupil accompanied him on a koto, a long zither with thirteen strings, and Chōshin explained the performance.[64] The program provoked a strong reaction. Some listeners were happy to hear familiar Okinawan songs and sent him letters of gratitude; others vociferously attacked the program: "The program on Ryukyuan classical music yesterday is an affront to Okinawans. Ryukyuans in Taiwan are always seen as Japanese aborigines. Other Japanese are doubtful of our status as pure Japanese. Thus, the radio station in Taipei has done us a great disservice by broadcasting enigmatic Ryukyuan music. By broadcasting music that is incomprehensible to other Japanese, the radio station proves that we Okinawans are indeed Japanese aborigines. You should not do this anymore."[65]

Although Chōshin did not garner much support from his fellow Okinawan migrants, he was not alone. While working in Taipei City, he audited anthropology classes at Taihoku Imperial University and studied archeology, anthropology, and linguistics under Utsushikawa Nenozō, the pioneer of Taiwanese Aboriginal Studies and the first director of the anthropology division at the university.[66] He also enjoyed a close friendship with Sudō Riichi, a teacher at Taihoku High School and a scholar of mathematical history and maritime affairs. Sudō became interested in Okinawan traditions while investigating Okinawan quipu as part of his studies in mathematical history. As he frequently visited nearby islands, his interest went beyond mathematical history and eventually culminated in his translation of *Account of a Voyage of Discovery to the West Coast of Corea and the Great Loo-Choo Island in the Japan Sea,* written by Basil Hall, a British naval officer from Scotland.[67] It was not unusual for Japanese scholars to take a special interest in Okinawan history and culture. As documented in previous studies, Yanagita Kunio, the so-called founder of Japanese Folklore Studies, had been especially interested in Okinawa since the 1920s. He claimed that the Japanese were originally from the south and that there are traces of ancient Japanese language and culture in present-day Okinawa.[68] Thus, the study of Okinawa was essential to students of Japanese folklore, a subject on which Yanagita Kunio was the greatest influence at the time.

In the 1930s, Sudō was indeed one of the key persons promoting Okinawan cultural studies in Taipei City. He frequently joined Okinawan gatherings in the city and networked with others who were interested in Okinawan culture and traditions. Chōshin maintained excellent access to the Ryukyu Kingdom's cultural assets and asserted his Okinawan identity, which made him a favorite among Japanese scholars interested in Okinawan history and culture. The grassroots development of Okinawa Studies eventually led to the launch of the journal *Nantō* (Southern islands), in August 1940. In the inaugural issue, Sudō elucidated the reasons for founding the journal, writing in an editorial that he and his fellow local researchers on Ishigaki Island planned a serial publication focusing particularly on the Yaeyama region with the purpose of recording old documents and preserving unique traditions that were vanishing. They initially intended to title the publication *Yaema*, meaning "Yaeyama," but changed the title to *Nantō* when they decided to cover the Ryukyu Islands as a whole.[69]

The editors of the first issue, which highlighted the Yaeyama Islands, were Higa Seishō, Miyara Kentei, Kabira Chōshin, and Sudō Riichi.[70] Higa and Miyara were both teaching at schools in Yaeyama when Sudō met them while exploring and conducting research around the region. In 1940, they both moved to Taipei and joined the editorial group after Sudō arranged for their employment in Taiwan.[71] The editorial board comprised sixteen members, based mostly in Taiwan or Okinawa.[72] The inaugural issue of *Nantō* was well received by scholars interested in the histories and cultures of Okinawa and Taiwan, and the second issue boasted a greater number of editorial board members, including leading scholars of Japanese Folklore Studies and Okinawa Studies such as Yanagita Kunio, Ifa Fuyū, Higashion'na Kanjun, Higa Shunchō, Shimabukuro Gen'ichirō, and Shimabukuro Genpatsu.[73] The journal attracted a wide readership across the Japanese Empire. In January 1941, nearly half of its 523 members were in Okinawa and Taiwan: 285 in Okinawa Prefecture, 137 in Taiwan, and the rest in Korea, Manchuria, and Japan proper, including Hokkaido.[74]

The second issue was published in May 1942 and included "Discussion on Okinawan Culture," a transcript of the roundtable broadcast by Taihoku Broadcasting Station. The speakers included Taihoku Imperial University professors Kobata Atsushi and Kinzeki Takeo as well as four other members of *Nantō*. Sudō chaired the discussion, while Kabira Chōshin took notes. The roundtable covered a variety of topics, including historical exchanges between Taiwan and the Ryukyu Islands, the Japanese expedition to Taiwan in 1874, and Okinawan ethnicity and language.[75] In the later part of the conversation, the participants complained about Okinawa's ill-furbished public library. It was then that Higa Seishō declared: "While we're speaking of the study of Okinawan culture, Tokyo is too distant from Okinawa, and the people in Kyoto and Fukuoka are uninterested [in the Ryukyu Islands]. I believe Taipei should be the center of Okinawan cultural studies. Let's put our best efforts into it."[76] The program was more than an academic dialogue among specialists of Okinawan history and culture. While Okinawans and Ryukyu culture were unfairly despised to the point that a number of Okinawan settlers tried to mask their identities by changing names and transferring registered prefectural addresses, Okinawans in Taiwan were pleased to hear that Okinawan culture was held in high regard by authorities.[77]

The third issue, specializing on the Miyako Islands, was published in September 1944. Before it came out, the chief editor Sudō Riichi moved to Tokyo to take up a teaching position at the First Higher School (Daiichi Kōtō Gakkō). The editors planned to publish a fourth issue on Kume Island,[78] but it never materialized because Okinawa was in the midst of battle in 1945. The journal *Nantō* was, in many ways, similar to another journal, *Minzoku Taiwan* (Taiwan folklore), which was published in Taiwan between 1941 and 1945. Sudō Riichi was listed as one of its founding members, and some of its frequent contributors were either editors or editorial board members of *Nantō*. Whereas *Nantō* is little known to present-day scholars, *Minzoku Taiwan*, which published forty-four issues altogether, is very well known to both general readers and scholars of Taiwan and Japan. The founding editors recall that they were critical of the imperialization movement of the time and aimed to preserve and record the unique customs and traditions of local Taiwanese, in particular, those of the Han Chinese. After the Second Sino-Japanese War broke out in 1937, the colonial government viewed local Taiwanese customs and traditions inherited from the Chinese mainland with suspicion and forced the Taiwanese to worship the Japanese emperor and practice Japanese customs. Although it was very difficult to oppose the military government's policies, the *Minzoku Taiwan* editors challenged the government's cultural policies by shedding light on the everyday life of the common Taiwanese.

Kabira Chōshin was not involved with *Minzoku Taiwan*, but he shared the views of the *Minzoku Taiwan* editors. On the recommendation of Professors Utsushikawa and Kinzeki, Chōshin started work at the colonial government in 1939. According to his own memoirs, the professors hoped Chōshin would somehow be a good, moderating influence on the colonial government, which they thought was "overdoing imperialization."[79] One of his colleagues was Ikeda Toshio, chief editor of *Minzoku Taiwan*.[80] It is possible that Kabira Chōshin had frequent exchanges with not only *Nantō* members but also *Minzoku Taiwan* members and was inspired by them. In his memoirs, he criticizes the imperialization movement: "At that time, the colonial government rigorously promoted the imperialization movement. In Okinawa, there was a heated debate between the prefectural government and the Folklore Association [Mingei Kyōkai]. The spirit of the imperialization movement in Taiwan was on a par with the zealous promotion of 'standard Japanese' in Okinawa."[81]

Indeed, the so-called dialect debate (*hōgen ronsō*) occurred in 1940 when members of the Japanese Folklore Association, including Yanagi Muneyoshi, leading scholar of the Japanese folklore movement of the day, attended the roundtable on Okinawan tourism and culture organized by the Okinawan Tourism Association. During the discussion, Yanagi criticized the local government's promotion of "standard Japanese" for going too far and demanded respect for the Okinawan dialect. The roundtable triggered an argument over how to preserve the Okinawan dialect and promote standard Japanese in Okinawa.[82] Having been greatly influenced by the Japanese scholars in Taipei, Kabira Chōshin called for the preservation of Okinawan traditions and local dialect.

As assimilation was the Okinawan migrants' primary strategy for survival in the Japanese settler community in Taiwan, it is difficult to trace their collective assertion of their cultural identity. However, this does not mean that Okinawan migrants sought only to disguise their identity and assimilate into Japanese mainstream culture. In the late 1930s and early 1940s, Kabira Chōshin and a small number of Okinawan migrants in Taiwan actively worked to recover their ethnic pride in opposition to assimilation and imperialization, even though they lacked strong support from their fellow Okinawans. Kabira Chōshin, who inherited the very essence of Ryukyuan dynastic tradition, had an exceptional background. As mentioned, many Okinawan families in Taiwan hid their identities, and the Okinawan elderly had a particularly trying time because of the linguistic barrier and the old Okinawan tradition of inscribing tattoos on their bodies. In contrast, Chōshin's father, Chōhei, a master of Ryukyuan classical music, proudly played Ryukyuan music at the Kabira family's official residence.

The movement was, ironically, supported mostly by Japanese from the other prefectures who had a special interest in Okinawan history and culture.

Besides, it is possible that they failed to gain popular support from their fellow immigrants partly because some immigrants did not maintain an Okinawan ethnic identity. As discussed in previous chapters, Taiwan received a considerable number of immigrants from the Yaeyama and Miyako Islands as well as the main island of Okinawa. Although Yaeyama Islanders were identified as "Okinawans" in colonial Taiwan, they shaped their own Yaeyama and Miyako identities, separate from Okinawa.

Indeed, Taipei residents originally from Yaeyama established their own Yaeyama association. *Yaeyama News,* published on Ishigaki Island, reported that the Taihoku Yaeyama Association held its inaugural New Year gathering on January 22, 1933. The article notes that Yaeyama migrants had already established their own associations in Keelung and Kaohsiung. Although there was an Okinawa prefectural association in Taipei, few Yaeyama migrants attended its gatherings because "Yaeyama migrants don't really get along with migrants from the rest of Okinawa."[83] According to the report, more than 150 migrants attended the inaugural Taihoku Yaeyama Association gathering at a teahouse, where they were entertained by geishas playing traditional songs and performing dances of the Yaeyama region.[84] Yaeyama Islanders shaped their own Yaeyama identity not simply because Yaeyama is geographically remote from the main island of Okinawa. Rather, Yaeyama's regional identity was shaped through the recognition that Yaeyama Islanders had collectively suffered from the Ryukyu Kingdom's discriminatory policies during the early modern period. Thus, the claim of Yaeyama identity suggests resistance against the dominance of Okinawa over Yaeyama, the periphery of the Ryukyu Islands.[85] Hence, it is not surprising that Yaeyama immigrants did not support the cultural movement of Kabira Chōshin, who was the proud descendant of a high-ranking government official in the Ryukyu Kingdom.

Okinawan migrants in Taiwan came from diverse and mixed backgrounds; some were descendants of Chinese immigrants, and others were of Okinawan and Japanese ancestry. Furthermore, increasing numbers of second- and third-generation Okinawans grew up in the Japanese settler community in Taiwan as more and more Okinawan immigrants settled in the colony. They were creole Japanese who did not really possess a strong Okinawan ethnic identity. Some of these second- and third-generation immigrants had never visited their parents' home islands, while others moved frequently between Taiwan and Okinawa. Nevertheless, they were collectively identified as "Okinawans" and had to endure negative racial stereotyping and prejudice in Taiwan. To survive discrimination, many Okinawan migrants sought to pass for Japanese by changing their names and transferring their registered addresses to other prefectures. The majority of Okinawan migrants considered assimilation mandatory for success in their imperial careers in Taiwan.

Yet there was also a conscious effort to recover Okinawan pride in Taipei. In the 1940s, the journal *Nantō* was published through the collaborative efforts of Japanese and Okinawan residents in both Okinawa and Taiwan. The Taihoku Broadcasting Station broadcast a roundtable in which prominent scholars and Okinawan migrants discussed Okinawan history and culture. Kabira Chōshin, a proud Okinawan and one of the editors of *Nantō,* conceived the idea for this radio program after his Okinawan classical music program met with disapprobation from fellow Okinawan migrants. The Okinawan cultural movement in Taipei, which was supported by some Japanese, did not find many adherents among Okinawan migrants, but it did provide the impetus for another movement that developed after World War II.

Chapter 6

Going Home?

After the fall of the Japanese Empire, more than 6.25 million Japanese nationals, including civilians and military personnel, repatriated to Mainland Japan between 1945 and 1950.[1] Despite the large-scale mass migration that took place within such a short period of time, there were few serious scholarly studies on the subject until the 1990s. Instead, images of and discourses on Japanese repatriations after World War II were reproduced in novels, films, and the repatriates' testimonies. As repatriation from Manchuria was the largest in scale and involved numerous tragic stories, discourses on postwar repatriations have been constructed predominantly by returnees from Manchuria. In contrast, repatriation from Taiwan has rarely aroused public interest in postwar Japanese society because it was carried out relatively peacefully in a short period of time. Since the beginning of the 2000s, there has been a surge of scholarly books and articles exploring the sequences and circumstances of these mass migrations.[2] Some of these recently published works examine repatriation from Taiwan.[3] It should be noted, however, that the circumstances of Okinawan repatriations greatly differed from those experienced by Japanese mainlanders.[4]

Before the ground battle on Okinawa, the majority of those originally from Mainland Japan, who had dominated local politics and the industries, left the Ryukyu Islands. Young children, women, and the elderly were ordered to evacuate. Numerous lives were also lost in the Okinawan ground battle. After the war ended, Okinawa received a great number of repatriates from abroad and from Mainland Japan. Some repatriates from former Japanese overseas territories landed directly in Okinawa, while others stopped at one of the Japanese ports before traveling to Okinawa. War evacuees and former Japanese soldiers also returned either directly or indirectly via Mainland Japan. Although the exact numbers involved in these movements are unknown, it is clear that repatriation caused a sharp increase in the islands' population. For instance, Okinawa's residential population of 773,818 in 1944 increased to 917,875 in 1950.[5]

Previous studies by historians have examined the ways in which repatriates (*hikiagesha*) were controlled by the authorities and their experiences in reintegrating into postwar Japanese society. However, little scholarly attention has been paid to the views on repatriation held by Okinawans residing in the former Japanese colonies. While historians focused on governmental policies and the sequence of events in repatriations, contemporary anthropologists are increasingly interested in "return migrations," the changing ethnic identities of the migrants, and their subjective interpretations of the notions "return" and "home."[6] In other words, recent studies of return migrations address the impact of the migrants' subjective constructions of "home" and "homeland" in their choice of destinations and their views on resettlement. This chapter borrows the anthropological methodology used in return migration studies to explore Okinawan repatriates' ethnic identities and their subjective understanding of resettlement in the Ryukyu Islands under US military rule.

Unlike repatriates from the South Sea Islands or the Philippines, where the majority had been engaged in agriculture and farming, Okinawan repatriates from Taiwan were composed of a significant number of former policemen, teachers, public officials, doctors, and lawyers, as well as students and graduates of middle schools or advanced girls' school. Moreover, whereas the Japanese population in the South Sea Islands and the Philippines were made up mostly of Okinawans, the Okinawan population in Taiwan was relatively smaller, and many had culturally assimilated into the Japanese settler community. The second- and third-generation Okinawan immigrants raised in Taiwan were creolized and had shaped identities as Japanese settlers rather than Okinawan immigrants. Following the fall of the Japanese Empire and the US occupation of the Ryukyu Islands, they were compelled by necessity to re-form their ethnic identities. After arriving in the Ryukyu Islands, repatriates from Taiwan soon discovered a great gulf between themselves and those who had survived the Okinawan ground battle. Previous studies have already analyzed the stigmatization and categorization of repatriates as the "other" in postwar Japan.[7] This chapter will elucidate the different ways in which repatriates from Taiwan were also categorized as the "other" in postwar Okinawa under US military rule and examine the manner in which they lived their "postcolonial" careers in postwar Okinawan society.

Taiwan during the War

In contrast to the Taiwanese, who were excluded from conscription until 1945 whether they resided in the Inner Territory or Outer Territories, all males listed in the Japanese family registry (*koseki*) underwent a compulsory physical examination at the age of twenty in readiness for conscription.[8] Most of the male Okinawan immigrants described in the previous chapters were thus conscripted into the Japanese military. Takemoto Seigi, who arrived in Taiwan in 1926 and initially worked at a pawnshop before securing a job with the post office, was conscripted into a Japanese military unit in Guangdong.[9] The pseudonymous interviewee Higa Takeshi worked at a pharmacy in Taipei for about six years before he was hired by the Taipei branch of the Shimizu Corporation, one of the leading architectural, civil engineering, and contracting companies in Japan. He was transferred to the company's Guangdong branch but was reluctant to join the military. Fortunately for him, he was exempted from conscription and continued working for the company due to its successful negotiations with the military. He married a Chinese woman in Guangdong and remained there until the war ended.[10] Tsuji Hiroshi, who worked at a bookstore, barbershop, and, eventually, the Taiwan Railway Company, was assigned to the Taiwan Army in January 1944. He lost his wife to malaria while serving in the military unit in Pingtung.[11] Some of the female immigrants featured in the previous chapters got married before the war began. Those who were in Taiwan with their families remained there, with some choosing to evacuate to rural areas. Others, who had not married in Taiwan, returned to their home islands because they felt safer close to their parents.

Although some immigrants moved back to their home islands, others continued to migrate to Taiwan for education and work, even after the Pacific War began in 1941. Additionally, some Okinawans voluntarily evacuated to Taiwan, expecting that Taiwan would be safer. Furthermore, the Extraordinary Cabinet Meeting on July 7, 1944, concluded that a total of one hundred thousand women, children, and elderly from the islands of Amami-Ōshima, Tokunoshima, Ishigaki, and Miyako, as well as the main island of Okinawa, should evacuate as intense bombing and ground battles were expected in the near future.[12] While residents of Miyako and Ishigaki Islands were ordered to go to Taiwan, the rest were directed to leave for Mainland Japan, specifically, Kyushu. Residents were reluctant to leave their home islands and embark on a dangerous voyage.[13] These fears were well founded, as one of the evacuation vessels, the *Tsushimamaru*, which departed from Naha on August 21, 1944, carrying nearly 1,700 evacuees, including approximately seven hundred schoolchildren, was attacked by a

US submarine and sank south of Kagoshima Prefecture. Only 227 evacuees, including fifty-nine students, survived the attack. This tragedy further discouraged reluctant residents from evacuating.[14] Nonetheless, due to social pressure and promotions from local authorities, more than eighty thousand Okinawan Islanders—mostly women, children, and the elderly—evacuated their home islands, with approximately ten thousand to thirteen thousand departing for Taiwan between July 1944 and August 1945.[15]

The evacuation program was proposed partly in response to the fall of Saipan in June 1944. Until the tragic battle, the government office of the South Sea Islands encouraged Japanese immigrant elderly, women, and children to leave for Japan proper in anticipation of forthcoming US attacks. As the majority of Japanese immigrants were originally from the main island of Okinawa, many repatriates from the South Sea Islands left for Okinawa between late 1943 and early 1944. However, the war had rendered sea travel riskier, and a number of ships carrying the repatriates were attacked and shipwrecked.[16] Ships that could not reach Okinawa stopped at Taiwan. Much like the war evacuees from Okinawa Prefecture, repatriates from the South Sea Islands had to survive the war in an unfamiliar environment without any means of making a living. These evacuees in Taiwan faced circumstances that were very different from those of immigrants who had settled there for education and work. Most were taken to rural areas far from the Japanese community that had established itself in urban areas. Many did not have close friends or families on whom they could rely and were almost entirely dependent on government support and rations. Unfamiliar with the new environment, many suffered from starvation and tropical diseases in their places of refuge.[17]

Crossing the New Border

In August 1945, Japan accepted the Potsdam Declaration and surrendered. This meant that Japan lost control of Taiwan and that the Republic of China (ROC) had sovereignty over the main island of Taiwan and the Penghu Islands. Although the exact number is uncertain, it is estimated that nearly 350,000 Japanese civilians, including nearly thirty thousand Okinawans, were left in Taiwan when Japan surrendered.[18] Some were desperate to go back to Okinawa, and others hoped to remain in Taiwan, where they had already established themselves. The Japanese Ministry of Foreign Affairs later noted, "After hearing the news of the Japanese surrender on the radio, everyone, regardless of ethnic differences—Japanese settlers, Han Taiwanese, and Taiwanese aborigines—was at a loss and dumbstruck with amazement for a short while."[19] Some Han Taiwanese and Taiwanese aborigines were genuinely saddened by Japan's loss; others appeared relieved and delighted but were concerned about their uncertain futures.[20]

Changes in Taiwanese attitudes toward the Japanese were soon observed. Repatriates recalled that policemen and teachers, particularly those who had harshly discriminated against the Taiwanese, were the main targets of violent revenge. Nevertheless, these were individual and isolated cases, for the Japanese as a group rarely became the target of attacks resulting in death.[21] Due to the unexpectedly peaceful postwar conditions and the friendliness of the Taiwanese, the majority of Japanese settlers hoped they would be allowed to stay in Taiwan and maintain some of their existing interests, rather than be repatriated to Mainland Japan, where cities were in ruins and people were starving to death.[22]

On October 25, Andō Rikichi, the governor-general of Taiwan, and Chen Yi signed the instrument of surrender. The Taiwan Province Administrative Office began to formally requisition the administrative offices of the colonial government. The provincial administrative office then took over local governments, educational institutions, and semiofficial enterprises, including the Taiwan Developing Company, Taiwan Bank, and Taiwan Electric Company.[23] On New Year's Eve 1945, the KMT announced its official policy toward the Japanese in Taiwan, stating that all public and private properties owned by the Japanese would be requisitioned in the coming year. It also proclaimed that all Japanese, except those who were directed to remain in Taiwan for the maintenance of administration functions and industries, must be repatriated to Japan by the end of 1946.[24] As their social conditions deteriorated and futures became uncertain, the majority of Japanese longed to leave Taiwan and resettle in Mainland Japan.[25]

As soon as the KMT announced its official policy on Japanese repatriation, the Administrative Committee for Japanese Overseas was established in order to coordinate the mass migration of approximately 456,000 Japanese, civilians as well as demobilized military personnel and their family members. At the end of December, the first group of demobilized military personnel and their families was transported to Mainland Japan. The first mass transfer took place between March and May 1946, and approximately 172,000 demobilized military personnel and 284,000 civilian Japanese were shipped to Mainland Japan. During this period, nearly 90 percent of Japanese nationals were safely repatriated. The remaining Japanese nationals had been ordered to stay and maintain Taiwan's public services and industries in good working order during the transitional period; their families were also allowed to stay until their duties were completed.[26] The majority of these requisitioned Japanese had left Taiwan by early May

1947, although some professionals, such as university professors and highly skilled technicians, were asked to stay until the 1950s.[27]

Before the KMT's formal announcement of Japanese repatriation at the end of 1945, some Okinawans were already setting sail for the Yaeyama or Miyako Islands. Although the official seaways between Taiwan, Okinawa, and Mainland Japan were under KMT and US control, the people of Yaeyama and Miyako continued to sail between the islands in their fishing boats as they had done before the war. As discussed in chapter 2, Yaeyama Islanders had established strong social and economic ties with Taiwan during the fifty years of Japanese colonial rule. In particular, the Yonaguni Islanders, only 111 kilometers away from the eastern coast of Taiwan, never ceased sailing to and from Taiwan in their small fishing boats. In fact, demand for trade increased after the war. Along with the elimination of public sea transport, the Ryukyu Islands' agriculture and industries had been severely damaged during the war. Thus, islanders had no choice but to secretly import necessities from Taiwan, which had sustained less damage. Yonaguni fishing vessels evaded KMT coastal patrols and traded for provisions and daily necessities with the Taiwanese.[28]

These Yonaguni fishing vessels carried not only merchandise but also people who were willing to leave for the Yaeyama and Miyako Islands. Indeed, many of my informants from Yaeyama had left Taiwan on private vessels before official repatriation was coordinated in 1946. Most of the fishing boats gathered either in Keelung or South Su'ao (Mandarin, Nan fang'ao), where Okinawan fishers had established their bases under Japanese colonial rule. South Su'ao is located on the eastern coast of Yilan County and is closest to Yonaguni Island. Yaeyama and Miyako Islanders who wished to return home went to either Keelung or South Su'ao to find a captain willing to travel illegally to Yaeyama; then they had to wait for days or weeks until the boat had a sufficient number of passengers. Even if a boat full of passengers left port, there was no guarantee that it could sail straight to Yaeyama; it might have to turn back to Taiwan if it was caught by a patrol boat.[29]

Having lost his wife, Tsuji Hiroshi was desperate to return to his home island. He gave the following account of illegally leaving Keelung and arriving at Taketomi Island:

> Perhaps because it was soon after the war, sea transport was severely restricted. I managed to get on the *Kihonmaru,* a fourteen- to fifteen-ton small motorboat, which was carrying the luggage of twenty to thirty passengers. However, the boat was captured three times and was moored in front of the marine police. The captain and crew were severely questioned by the police.

> On January 20, 1946, I received news that someone had planned a secret passage. The boat left Sharyō Island in a hurry and was seen by a patrolman. The patrolman tried to catch us and shouted loudly in anger, but our boat ignored him and sped up to Yaeyama. Luckily, in spite of the winter season, the sea was very calm, and we arrived safely in Ishigaki Port.[30]

There is a popular belief that official repatriations from Taiwan to Mainland Japan were the most peaceful. However, as indicated in Tsuji's memoirs, repatriations by private vessels could be a matter of life and death. Indeed, some repatriates lost their lives during the risky sea voyage. One of the worst accidents occurred on November 1, 1945, when the small boat *Sakaemaru* was carrying more than one hundred people to Miyako Island. The exact number of passengers is unknown, but the survivors testified that it carried approximately 180 passengers; of these, only 20 or 30 were saved from the sea.[31]

Okinawans Left Behind

While many Yaeyama and Miyako migrants and war evacuees managed to leave Taiwan on private vessels, there were still significant numbers of Okinawans who did not know what to do, in particular, those who had arrived as war evacuees and relied on the Japanese government. These war evacuees did not have any means of making a living in Taiwan and were surviving in devastating conditions. Long-term Okinawan residents of Taiwan who had observed the war evacuees—mostly women, children, and the elderly—suffering from starvation and tropical diseases organized a mutual aid association, the Association for People from Okinawa (Okinawa Dōkyōkai Rengō-kai) (APO). The president was Yogi Kisen, who used to be the head of the Taiwan Colonial Government Fisheries' Experimental Station, and the APO office was located in the clinic owned by the vice president, Haebaru Chōho. Asato Tsumichiyo, a lawyer and former Tainan City councilor, also served as vice president. The board consisted of four directors, including Kabira Chōshin, who had been very active in promoting Okinawan traditions.[32] As discussed in previous chapters, Okinawan immigrants in colonial Taiwan had eschewed the formation of any powerful ethnic organization and established only small-scale friendship associations. Thus, this was the first time Okinawan immigrants called for fellow Okinawans to come together and cooperate as "people from Okinawa."

The association first tried to grasp the living conditions of fellow Okinawans across Taiwan. On October 31, 1945, it called for fellow Okinawans to register their names and contact details with regional Okinawan associations through *Reborn Taiwan News* (*Taiwan xinsheng bao*), which had been launched on October 25, 1945.[33] APO board members also organized a charity event in order to collect donations for Okinawan exiles in Taiwan. "Evenings of Ryukyuan Performing Arts" was staged on February 25 and 26, 1946, in Zhongshan Hall (Zhongshan-tang), formerly Taihoku Public Hall, where the formal ceremony of Japanese surrender had taken place the previous year. The program featured performances of Ryukyuan classical dance and music, choral music by Okinawan youths, and opera music performed by Japanese musicians who were still in Taiwan.[34] After the shows, Kabira Chōshin, who had taken the leading role in managing the event gave a speech at the celebratory dinner party:

> Thank you very much for helping us present the event successfully this evening. Because this public hall is already under Chinese military control, we Japanese were not allowed to use the venue. But the Chinese understood our intention and allowed us to use it as the final stage for the Japanese here. This has been a historic event for Taihoku Public Hall. I am especially grateful that Ms. Miura, Mr. Shibata, and Mr. and Mrs. Tamura kindly took the stage as guest performers. Okinawa became the shield to protect our country, Japan, and was victimized. We Okinawans are the brothers of Mainland Japan but will be under US control for some time. Your kindness as guest performers today has given me great encouragement from all in Japan, our country. I thank you on behalf of all fellow Okinawans.[35]

In addition to founding the charity for Okinawan exiles, the association sent a formal letter to the Taiwan Provincial Government and the US military controlling the sea around the Ryukyu Islands. The letter specifically addressed Chen Yi, the chief executive of the Taiwan Province Executive Office of Administrations, requesting that Okinawan exiles who had arrived as war evacuees be sent home with all due haste. The letter noted that 14,044 Okinawans had evacuated to Taiwan during the war; 12,447 were from the Ryukyu Islands, and 1,597 had been redirected from the South Sea Islands. By mid-December, 3,297 of them had either died or returned home on private vessels. The letter warned that those who had no friends or relatives in Taiwan were in particularly difficult positions, as they had been left behind in remote mountainous areas, and added that many suffered from malaria and had no one on whom they could rely. Hence, the association requested that Chen Yi send these troubled exiles home as soon as possible, emphasizing that first priority should be given to war evacuees from the Miyako and Yaeyama Islands who had no relatives in Taiwan.

Highlighting the current conditions of Miyako and Yaeyama, the letter sought permission for repatriates to take some food and necessities with them. It also demanded that those who could not immediately set sail for home be given support in Taiwan.[36]

In fact, both the Japanese government and the Taiwan Province Administrative Office had been aware of the problems faced by Okinawan exiles since early November. In December, representatives of the Administrative Office, the US military, and the association met to come up with a concrete plan to send Okinawan exiles home from Keelung.[37] Accordingly, on January 25, 1946, four vessels carrying 526 former war evacuees departed from Keelung. Two of the vessels headed directly to Miyako Island, and the others stopped at South Su'ao before traveling to Ishigaki Island. Despite the initial plan to ship nearly two thousand people to these islands, only a little more than five hundred gathered at the port. The head of the Administrative Office assumed that the rest had already left Taiwan on private vessels. It is estimated that most of the former war evacuees from the Miyako and Ishigaki Islands left Taiwan by the end of January.[38]

Although many Okinawans from the Miyako and Yaeyama Islands were repatriated by January 1946, those who were willing to repatriate to the main island of Okinawa had not been allowed to do so because the US military government strictly regulated entry there. During and after the Okinawan ground battle, civilians were gathered into refugee camps set up by the US military. The great majority of land on the main island of Okinawa had become unusable, and, with nearly 95 percent of housing destroyed, there was a serious shortage of adequate shelter and provisions. Food production capacity was limited because there was no fertilizer available, livestock were wounded, and the fishing fleet had been destroyed.[39] Moreover, when Japan accepted the Potsdam Declaration, the US government's policy toward the Ryukyu Islands was still undetermined. Even though the US government maintained an interest in the Ryukyu Islands as a potentially important strategic military site, they were a secondary priority until 1948, when Cold War tensions mounted in East Asia. The lack of interest from Washington, DC, and the supreme commander for the Allied Powers resulted in reduced manpower and funding in the Ryukyus, which made it more difficult for the military government to build shelters and feed the refugees and the displaced.[40]

In addition to evacuating Okinawans from their home islands during the war, Okinawa Prefecture had sent numerous migrants to Mainland Japan, overseas territories including Taiwan and the South Sea Islands, the US territory of Hawai'i, and foreign countries such Brazil. As a result, the United States expected more than 115,000 Okinawans to return from

Mainland Japan and former overseas territories. Okinawa had surely lost almost an equal number of lives during the great ground battle. Yet because of the enormous material losses and devastation of the land, even those already on the island suffered from lack of shelter, basic provisions, and daily necessities. Hence, in May 1946, the US naval military government in Okinawa concluded that it was not ready to receive repatriates: "The repatriation from Japan of 105,000 Ryukyuans, at least 80,000 of whom are Okinawans, should be postponed until land and house building material on Okinawa are adequate to receive them without intensifying present unsatisfactory housing conditions on Okinawa. This at best is a temporary expedient and undesirable and should be avoided by provision of shelter materials and land, frankly recognizing, however, that each repatriate brought to the Ryukyus adds a direct burden on the United States in the form of import requirements."[41]

While the US military government refused to receive repatriates from Taiwan, the Taiwan Province Administrative Office initially planned to send Okinawans back to Mainland Japan because the "Republic of China considered Ryukyu to be part of Japan."[42] APO board members requested permission for Okinawans to remain in Taiwan until they were allowed to land on Okinawa because "Okinawans in Taiwan will not have anywhere to stay in Mainland Japan; in addition, they will suffer enormously from the unfamiliar cold winter if they are sent back too soon."[43]

The Taiwan Province Administrative Office eventually granted Okinawans permission to remain in Taiwan on condition that the APO distinguish Okinawans from Japanese mainlanders, concerned that Japanese mainlanders would hide their identities so as to remain in Taiwan as "Okinawans." In response, the APO office charged itself with the task of issuing certificates of Liuqiao (in Mandarin) (Japanese, Ryūkyō), denoting the Okinawans as separate and distinct from Riqiao (in Mandarin) (Japanese, Nikkyō). APO board members were vexed that Okinawans who had transferred their registered addresses to other prefectures out of personal interest were importuning their office for Liuqiao certificates. Some Japanese mainlanders who wished to remain in Taiwan pretended to be Okinawans and requested the certificates as well.[44] As explained in previous chapters, it was not unusual for Okinawan immigrants to hide their ethnic identities in order to survive in the Japanese settler community. Consequently, second- or third-generation Okinawans raised in Taiwan self-identified as Japanese settlers rather than as Okinawans from their parents' or grandparents' home islands. However, with the fall of the Japanese Empire, they had to accept the ethnic identity of Liuqiao for the sake of survival.

BECOMING "RYUKYUANS"

In addition to civilian settlers and war evacuees from Okinawa, there were more than two thousand Okinawan soldiers mobilized in military units in Taiwan. At the end of December, these soldiers gathered in Keelung, where official repatriation vessels had been arranged to transport them to Mainland Japan. The vessels transferred Japanese soldiers to Mainland Japan, but Okinawan soldiers were not permitted to land on the main island of Okinawa. In addition, they were neither informed of the situation on their home island nor told whether or not their loved ones were safe. Instead, they learned to their indignation that Japanese soldiers suspected Okinawans of spying for the US military and had murdered quite a few suspected "spies" during and after the ground battle on Okinawa.[45] Thus, Sublieutenant Higa Atsuo was initially reluctant when a Japanese colonel requested help from Okinawan soldiers in Keelung with repatriating civilian Japanese to Mainland Japan:

> At first, I did not respond quickly because I was quite angry about the rumor that Okinawans were suspected of being spies in the war. I wondered if I should flatly refuse to help the Japanese military or work for them as my last service to the country. I said, "Sir, there are many Japanese soldiers here. How dare you ask to use Okinawan soldiers for this service?"
>
> He answered, "You're right. I initially planned to order Japanese soldiers to do it. However, while we were preparing for repatriation, the soldiers in service started to complain, and a riot broke out before civilian repatriations had even started. So we changed our plan and dispatched the soldiers by unit. Not many Japanese soldiers are now left in Taiwan. I'm afraid that we've stopped transporting civilian repatriates. Please help me. Don't you ever need pocket money?" he implored me frantically.[46]

Consequently, Okinawan soldiers who had gathered in Keelung for their demobilization performed almost all the tasks involved in sending off the Japanese , including serving food to those who were waiting to board a vessel and helping Chinese officials examine the repatriates' luggage.[47] Indeed, this experience in Taiwan reshaped the ethnic identity of these Okinawan soldiers. They were convinced that Okinawans were indeed different from their fellow Japanese soldiers who were swiftly shipped to Mainland Japan.

Okinawan soldiers were never told when official repatriation vessels would be sent to take them back to the main island of Okinawa. Nearly half the Okinawan soldiers and their families thus gave up returning directly to the main island of Okinawa and either headed to the Japanese mainland or made private arrangements for traveling to the Miyako and Yaeyama Islands. In the end, approximately eight hundred Okinawan soldiers remained in Keelung. In early May, they were transferred to the building of the former colonial government's office in Taipei and came under the control of the General Headquarters of the ROC Police. This group of Okinawan soldiers was named the "Ryukyu Governmental Army Unit" (Japanese, Ryūkyū Kanpei) and were initially housed in the building of the former Taiwan Colonial Government building. Under the direction of the General Headquarters of the ROC Police, they were mobilized for public works such as cleaning the streets and parks across Taipei City. The ROC Police offered them Mandarin lessons, ROC anthem lessons, and classes on the Three Principles of the People, the San-min Doctrine or Tridemism. However, uncertain of their future and longing for their home island, it was likely that they did not take this Chinese assimilative instruction very seriously.[48]

In the meantime, civilians, including long-term residents of Taiwan and war evacuees, who intended to return to the main island of Okinawa were scattered across Taiwan. Although the Okinawans were told to leave Taiwan soon and were directed to gather at several meeting points in major cities, they soon realized that no official vessel had been arranged to take them to the main island of Okinawa. They were indeed in exile, for many lost not only one or some family members but also their means of livelihood, yet neither the ROC, US, nor Japanese government took care of them in Taiwan. They had no idea when repatriation vessels would be ready to return them to Okinawa, were running out of food, and did not know what to do.[49]

In May 1946, having learned of the desperate plight of Okinawans scattered across Taiwan, the APO and the Ryukyu Governmental Army Unit called for Okinawan exiles to gather in camps under their management. As a result, nearly 2,200 Okinawans traveled from regional cities, many of them war evacuees from the main island of Okinawa or the South Sea Islands. Most were women, children, or the elderly, and many had been weakened by starvation and tropical diseases. The APO and the Ryukyu Governmental Army established rescue camps in Taipei and Keelung that could accommodate the exiles. They supplied food and necessities to everyone in the camps and granted small amounts of cash to those who were particularly in need.[50] In Taipei, the rescue camps were set up in the former colonial government building and the public accommodations located in the city's southeast. The former colonial government building had been half destroyed during the war, and the roof leaked badly.[51] Naturally, the spread of contagious diseases was a great concern, and some of the Okinawan medical doctors who had studied and worked in Taiwan strove to maintain hygiene in the camps. Indeed, nearly forty medical doctors were still in Taiwan, waiting for repatriation vessels to take them to the main island of Okinawa. As a result of the well-organized mutual help system the Okinawans themselves had created, the refugee camps remained functional until the departure date for repatriation to Okinawa was finally announced.[52]

In addition to supporting the remaining Okinawans and handling the day-to-day management of the refugee camps, APO leaders prepared for returning to and rebuilding the ravaged Ryukyu Islands. For instance, knowing that the public library had burned down and that Okinawa had lost most of its books and documents during the war, Kabira Chōshin and other APO members initiated a campaign to collect books to donate to the new government of Okinawa. Taihoku Imperial University held numerous books related to the history and traditions of the Ryukyu Islands, some of which were historical and extremely valuable. Kabira, who had audited classes at the university, was desperate to bring them back to Okinawa and establish the new public library. However, the university, which had already been ceded to the KMT government, did not allow him to do so.

Nevertheless, he did not give up on the most precious historical book held by the university, *Previous Documents of Successive Generations* (*Rekidai hōan*), an official compilation of diplomatic documents of the Ryukyu Kingdom Government.[53] Even though this book is one of the most historically important records of the Ryukyu Kingdom, an original copy had been transferred to Tokyo when Okinawa Prefecture was established and was subsequently destroyed in the Great Kantō Earthquake in 1923. Another copy kept in Okinawa had been destroyed by fire when the public library burned down during the war. The copy held by Taihoku Imperial University was based on the original copy that had been in the Okinawa Prefectural Library. Kabira asked a fellow Okinawan to transcribe it while he was waiting for a repatriation vessel and managed to bring it back to Okinawa. Furthermore, Kabira requested that Japanese professors donate their privately owned books upon their repatriation. Because each Japanese repatriate was not allowed to bring more than two bags on boarding the LSTs (landing ships, tank), many professors reacted positively to Kabira's request and gave away numerous books on Okinawa-related subjects. In that way, Kabira and other APO members collected thousands of books. Kabira received special permission from the KMT government to bring these tens of thousands of books to Okinawa when he repatriated in December 1946. These books composed a major part of the Okinawa Central Library, which was reestablished in 1947.[54] Although Kabira's cultural activity (explored in chap. 5) did not gain popular support from his fellow Okinawans, he made a great contribution to the reconstruction of Okinawa's cultural life by transferring colonial Taiwan's cultural assets to his home islands.

Returning "Home" under US Military Rule

In June 1946, the Supreme Commander for the Allied Powers finally revealed a plan to repatriate some 150,000 Okinawans to the Ryukyu Islands from Japan, Taiwan, China, and the Mariana Islands. Accordingly, the US military government set up two camps for this great multitude of repatriates: Camp Kuba-saki and Camp Costello, commonly known as Camp Yin'numi. On August 17, Camp Kuba-saki officially received a total of 556 repatriates from Kumamoto, Kagoshima, and Miyazaki Prefectures on Kyushu.[55] From that time onward, ships began to travel more frequently from Mainland Japan to Okinawa and Amami-Ōshima in the northern archipelago of the Ryukyus. Between August and December 1946, a total of 139,536 repatriates from Mainland Japan arrived in Okinawa, Amami-Ōshima, and the Miyako Islands.[56]

Repatriation from Taiwan to the main island of Okinawa began in late October. By then, there were more than 10,000 Okinawans, including approximately a thousand Ryukyu Government Army soldiers detained for service. More than half of them were in the greater Taipei area, and the rest were scattered in Hsinchu, Taichung, Tainan, Kaohsiung, Taitung, and Hualien; approximately 2,400 were accommodated in the Taipei rescue camp under APO care. More than 90 percent of the repatriates had been waiting to return to the main island of Okinawa since the United States restricted entry at the end of war.[57] Between October and December 1946, two LSTs carried 8,655 repatriates from Keelung Port to the main island of Okinawa, Amami-Ōshima, and the Miyako Islands.[58]

On arriving at the designated ports, all the repatriates were met by US water transportation and medical personnel before being cleared for unloading. They were then accommodated in camps organized and supervised by US Army personnel. On the main island of Okinawa, most of the repatriates disembarked at the Port of Kubasaki and underwent physical examinations, DDT applications, and medical treatment if necessary before being guided to either Camp Kuba-saki or Camp Costello. There, repatriates were segregated by their village (*mura*) or origins and supplied with food and blankets. Repatriates stayed at the camp for a couple of days on average before returning to their home villages, if those villages still existed. However, some of their homes had been entirely destroyed during the war or were otherwise occupied by US forces for the purpose of building new military facilities. In the event that their home villages had not been released for resettlement, they were to be sent to the next-nearest available village and housed with relatives or friends. Those without places to stay were housed in tents or other forms of shelter arranged by the military government, town leaders, or village chiefs.[59]

Unlike the main island of Okinawa, where the United States had built new military facilities, the movement and resettlement of people were less controlled in the Miyako and Yaeyama Islands. Nonetheless, villages, such as those on Taketomi Island in Yaeyama, which had sent many emigrants to the former colonies, were overwhelmed by the return of massive numbers of repatriates within a short period of time. Some people did not dare return to their home villages simply because they did not want to burden their families and relatives. For instance, knowing the situation in his birthplace on Taketomi Island, the pseudonymous Higa Takeshi, who had a Chinese wife and a baby, resettled on Ishigaki Island instead of going back to Taketomi Island.[60]

Indeed, some Okinawans had been desperate to go home and were relieved to finally land in Okinawa. Yet there were also second- and third-generation Okinawans who had never been to these islands before. The pseudonymous Noda Yoshiko, whose mother was born in Taiwan and father was born in Okinawa, was only seven years old when she repatriated to Okinawa. She had never been to Okinawa and had never seriously considered her own ethnic identity. She recalled seeing traditional Okinawan dance performances before repatriating, possibly at one of the cultural events held for Okinawans who had been left behind in Taiwan. Being very unfamiliar with Okinawan traditions, she observed, "The dance looked like a performance of exotic foreigners. I wondered what Okinawa looked like."[61]

One of my pseudonymous informants, Nakamura Tameo, was about ten years old when he and his family members repatriated to Kagosima Prefecture, the location of his mother's parental home. Several months later, his father decided to move to northern Okinawa, where his own parental home was located. At that time, Tameo, who had been born and raised in Taiwan, was informed that his father was originally from Okinawa Prefecture but had transferred the family's registered address to Kagosima Prefecture in order to avoid ethnic discrimination in colonial Taiwan.[62]

Mature second- and third-generation Okinawan repatriates displayed more complicated reactions. Sakiyama Masa, who became a public school teacher during World War II, lived in Taipei City during the war. Although her parents went back to their home on Ishigaki Island in December 1946, Masa and her sister, Kazuko, refused to leave with their parents; instead, they took an official repatriation ship to Mainland Japan in April 1946. In her memoirs, she explains her reasons for migrating to Japan: "At that time, we thought there would be no way our large family could survive on such a small island. Japan is far bigger than Ishigaki Island. We assumed that we could somehow manage to survive somewhere in Japan."[63] Although the sisters' true motives cannot be ascertained, it may be that they were reluctant to go back to Ishigaki Island after living in the Japanese settler community for so many years. In other words, their refusal to go to Ishigaki Island may not have been because it was too small but because they felt Japanese rather than Okinawan. In her interview, she also spoke of her reason for going to Japan: "When I eventually die, I would rather die after seeing cherry blossoms and Mount Fuji."[64]

Determined to live in Japan rather than Okinawa, Sakiyama Masa and her sister intended to get on the LST and travel to Tanabe Port in Wakayama Prefecture, close to the home of their acquaintance. However, they got on the wrong LST and arrived at Otake Port in Hiroshima Prefecture. They managed to reach Tanabe by train, but their acquaintance declined their request for support. Alone and without support, the sisters went to the repatriates' camp in Tanabe. Luckily, Kazuko was offered a job as a nurse, and Masa took a position as a primary-school teacher, but they suffered severe hunger and loneliness in an unfamiliar environment. In the aftermath of the war, few people could afford to pay attention to these two young women, who had no connection to the place. In December 1946, Masa and Kazuko decided to go to Ishigaki Island and went to Kagoshima Port, where repatriation ships were departing for Okinawa.[65]

Postwar/Colonial Okinawa

Creolized second- and third-generation immigrants raised in Taiwan were not the only ones who felt alienated in Okinawa, as even some members of the first generation, who maintained their Okinawan identities, also noticed the gulf between repatriates from Taiwan, returnees from other former Japanese colonies, and locals who had never left. Kabira Chōshin, the passionate promoter of Okinawan culture in colonial Taiwan who organized the Association for People from Okinawa after the war, was one of them. In his bibliographic essays, he relates some of his experiences of alienation as a Taiwan repatriate.

His capability and broad knowledge of Okinawa's history and traditions was highly regarded by the leaders of the newly established Okinawa Civil Government. Thus, upon his repatriation, he was immediately recruited as the chief of the art section at the Department of Culture. Before

Kabira's appointment, Lieutenant Governor Matayoshi Kōwa advised him "not to push himself forward too much" because he had not been through the Battle of Okinawa.[66] Kabira's account of his first day at work in the Department of Culture demonstrates the contrast between those who had experienced the Okinawan ground battle and the repatriates and war evacuees who had not:

> My first day of work was January 15. I went to the office by Mr. Tōyama's car and greeted all the members of the Department of Culture. They had gone through the ground battle in Okinawa. I went up to them and said hesitantly, "I didn't experience the war in Okinawa. But I'll do my best to fulfill my duties by getting instructions from you, who had noble experiences in Okinawa." In any military unit and workplace on earth, newcomers need to take heed of existing members. The repatriates needed to be extra careful in the Okinawa Civil Government, because many of the staff had lost close family members in the Battle of Okinawa.[67]

As Kabira was outspoken and innovative and proposed a variety of new ideas, he sometimes made enemies and was harshly criticized. Some attacked him by stating, "He is too romantic and naïve because he did not survive the Okinawan ground battle and had an easy life in colonial Taiwan."[68] Although Kabira's experiences cannot be overgeneralized, his recollections are indicative of the Okinawa war survivors' perception of repatriates from Taiwan. On the one hand, Okinawa war survivors did not regard repatriates from Mainland Japan, the Philippines, the South Sea Islands, and Manchuria in the same light as repatriates from Taiwan because they believed these other repatriates had survived battle and extreme conditions in those other places. Repatriates from Taiwan, on the hand, were viewed as "lucky" people who had experienced the least suffering during the war.

The silence of Taiwan repatriates in the private sphere seems to be correlated to the dearth of public discourse on Okinawans' migration to colonial Taiwan.[69] After Okinawa's reversion to Japan in 1972, publications on modern Okinawan history have been dominated by people's memories of the Okinawan ground battle in World War II. Local governments and academic historians have gone to great lengths to uncover ordinary people's experiences of the ground battle on Okinawa, as these works have been overshadowed by the battlefield experiences of Japanese militants. Moreover, descriptions of the Okinawan ground battle in Japanese textbooks have become frequent targets of political debates in both Okinawa and Mainland Japan. Local Okinawans objected to Japanese revisionist descriptions of the war and took great pains to record the war experiences of ordinary Okinawans.[70] This focus on war memories in Okinawan public history has given rise to an unexpected discursive climate in which the colonial experiences of Okinawan migrants are rarely highlighted in public.[71] Certainly, people are aware that many Okinawans migrated to colonial Taiwan before and during the war. However, in combating Japanese revisionist discourses on the Battle of Okinawa, public historians tend to neglect Taiwan's relatively peaceful wartime circumstances. As a result, the migration of Okinawans to the nearest colony and their involvement in Japanese colonial rule have not been critically evaluated.

Underrepresentation of repatriates from Taiwan might be due to the absence of powerful associations. Whereas Okinawan repatriates from the South Sea Islands and the Philippines established active organizations early on in Japanese rule, repatriates from Taiwan did not organize a formal association until 1994, when they established the Taiwan Association in Okinawa for the purpose of enjoying "friendship and exchanges" and "a sense of nostalgia" with other repatriates from Taiwan and "people who are associated with Taiwan."[72] Repatriates from the South Sea Islands founded several organizations, such as the Association for Returnees from the South Sea Islands (Nan'yō Guntō Kikanshakai), and provided support for members who were reestablishing themselves after repatriation. For instance, the association vigorously petitioned the US government to allow the repatriates to return to Micronesia (formerly the South Sea Islands) in the late 1940s.[73] Similarly, repatriates from the Philippines founded the Davao Association in 1964 and organized a tour to visit the graves in Davao in 1968. The Davao Association also established regional branches across Japan and Okinawa, but by 2000, the Okinawa branch was the only active branch left, and the group was renamed the Okinawa Davao Association.[74]

As discussed in chapter 1, Okinawan migrants in the South Sea Islands and the Philippines had several qualities in common. First, they accounted for the majority of Japanese settler populations in these places, although they were regarded as "second-class Japanese." Second, the majority of Okinawan immigrants in the South Sea Islands and the Philippines were concentrated in particular industries, the sugarcane industry and fishery in the South Sea Islands and the abaca industry in the Philippines. Due to regional concentration and similar circumstances, immigrants in both locations established ethnic organizations that occasionally facilitated political actions. Moreover, both groups of immigrants suffered enormously during World War II, and a great number of people lost their lives and never returned to Okinawa.

In contrast, Okinawans in Taiwan had diverse regional origins and social backgrounds and were the minority in the Japanese settler community.

They did not establish any politically oriented ethnic organizations under Japanese colonial rule. In order to survive the turmoil immediately after World War II, they organized a mutual aid association, which soon came to a natural end after they left Taiwan. Unlike repatriates from the South Sea Islands, the circumstances of repatriates from Taiwan were too diverse for them to be united by a single common interest. Similarly, they were unable to unite for the commemoration of war victims, because their war experiences were so varied that they did not share collective war memories.

Despite their different circumstances and war experiences, repatriates from Taiwan in Okinawa Prefecture were inspired by the Taiwan repatriates' movement in Mainland Japan and established the Union for the Acquisition of Compensation for the Loss of Assets Overseas (Okinawa Zaigai Shisan Hoshō Kakutoku Kiseikai) in 1948.[75] This movement sought compensation for the assets and properties that Japanese settlers had accumulated in colonial Taiwan but were forbidden to bring back to Japan after the war. Indeed, the repatriates were allowed to bring only one thousand yen and two pieces of luggage when they returned to Japan. In Mainland Japan, Taiwan repatriates' associations demanded compensation from the Japanese government for private properties that had been seized by the KMT government. Repatriates from Taiwan argued that they should be compensated for these losses because their private assets were taken as a substitute for war indemnities that should have been paid by the government. This movement spread across Japan and led to the establishment of the branch in Okinawa Prefecture. Consequently, the government gave small amounts as solatia, but no formal compensation, to repatriates from Taiwan.[76]

It is doubtful that the Union for the Acquisition of Compensation contributed to the development of solidarity among Taiwan repatriates in Okinawa Prefecture. The demand for compensation was a double-edged sword because more compensation would have been paid to those who had held larger assets. In other words, those who did not have much property and money had little incentive to participate in the compensation movement. Besides, as Kabira Chōshin's experience suggests, it was likely that repatriates from Taiwan found it difficult to share their discontent with others when so many Okinawans had been lost in the tragic battles of World War II.

Although the repatriates from Taiwan did not form a unified political group, they established a number of informal circles among themselves, including school alumni groups and regional associations such as the Taihoku Association and the Keelung Association. While these fairly informal groups were organized without political incentives, they played vital roles in enabling returnees from Taiwan to maintain their particular identities as "Taiwan repatriates" and share memories of their unique experiences.[77]

Due to the paucity of public discourse, the legacies of Japanese colonialism in postwar Okinawan society are not immediately apparent, giving rise to the impression that a large gulf lay between postwar and prewar Okinawa under the Japanese imperial government. However, postwar Okinawan society is far from irrelevant to Japan's colonial past. On the contrary, the life histories of repatriates from Taiwan demonstrate the extent to which postwar Okinawan society was built on Japanese colonial rule in Taiwan. For instance, many of the repatriates from Taiwan took leading roles in politics and industries in Okinawa. One of the vice presidents of the Association for People from Okinawa, Asato Tsumichiyo, formerly a member of the Tainan Municipal Assembly, was elected governor of the Yaeyama Archipelago Government in 1950 and was later chairperson of the Legislative Assembly of the Government of the Ryukyu Islands. Another vice president, Haebaru Chōho, who had run his own clinic in Taipei, became the first president of the Okinawa Archipelago Medical Association (Okinawa Guntō Igakukai), which was reestablished in 1951. In the same year, Inafuku Zenshi, who had graduated from Taihoku Medical College and acted as a medical doctor in the repatriates' camp, became the first president of the Okinawa Archipelago Medical Doctors' Association (Okinawa Guntō Ishikai) and served as president again in 1963–1965.[78] Kabira Chōshin, who brought back numerous books from Taiwan, was soon appointed chief of the art section at the Department of Culture in the Okinawa Civil Government. In 1952, he became the head of the Ryukyu Broadcasting Corporation, the first broadcasting company in Okinawa, founded by the US military government.[79]

These people stood out from the nearly thirty thousand Okinawans repatriated from Taiwan. It was not unusual for repatriates to apply the education and work experiences they had obtained in Taiwan, which were unavailable in prewar Okinawa, to their new careers when they returned to Okinawa. For instance, Ishigaki Shincho was born into a farming family, but he managed to become an apprentice photographer after working as a shop assistant and factory laborer. Although he had to close his studio in Kaohsiung upon repatriation, he later opened a studio on Ishigaki Island. Shimoji Keikō, who was desperate for a proper job on Miyako Island, joined the Taiwan police force immediately after the notorious Musha Incident. Soon after returning from Taiwan in October 1946, he was appointed a police officer in the Miyako police force, a career he maintained until his retirement in 1967.[80] His first son, Shimoji Yasuo, who attended Taichū Middle School, became a junior high school teacher on Miyako Island.[81]

In analyzing the repatriates' postcolonial careers, it should be noted that not all of them obtained work in the same industries in which they had been employed in colonial Taiwan. Tsubota-Nakanishi Miki went over the Japanese newspaper that had circulated among repatriates from Taiwan and examined the postcolonial careers of 224 Okinawan males. According to her study, the majority of Okinawans who had worked as public officials in Taiwan, including schoolteachers, found jobs in the private sector in postwar Okinawa. Although skilled and experienced workers were in demand in the public sector, the salaries were much lower than those offered in the private sector.[82]

Many young Okinawan girls who had settled in Taiwan with their parents attended advanced girls' schools in colonial Taiwan. On the one hand, female repatriates who had received their secondary education in Taiwan had a professional advantage because girls rarely received a secondary education in prewar Okinawa. On the other hand, having been brought up in the Japanese settler community, they found it particularly difficult to adapt to their new environment after repatriation.

Tomioka Mieko (pseudonym) was born in Taiwan in 1926. Her parents were originally from Miyako Island and migrated to Chiayi (Japanese, Kagi) in central Taiwan soon after their marriage. As her father was employed by the Meiji Sugar Manufacturing Company (Meiji Seitō), one of Taiwan's major sugar manufacturing companies, her family resided amid sugarcane farms cultivated by Taiwanese farmers. After attending the company's on-site primary school for employees' children and Kagi Advanced Girls' School, she got her first job at Shōka Bank (present-day Chang Hwa Bank). After the war, she repatriated to her parents' home on Miyako Island. In colonial Taiwan, her father supervised the Taiwanese farmers, and her mother took care of domestic chores. However, on Miyako Island, her parents had no choice but to cultivate their small farm by themselves. Mieko said, "[I] was saddened to see my mother laboring on the farm when our lives in Taiwan were so easy and comfortable."[83] She felt bored and lonely on Miyako Island because she missed her friends who had returned to Mainland Japan. Because Mieko was unfamiliar with rural life and unable to help her parents with farmwork, they let her move to the island's downtown area. She subsequently found a job in the office of a food company and married one of her colleagues, who had repatriated from China. Later, Mieko and her husband moved to the main island of Okinawa, where she worked at a customs office.[84] After her parents' death, she hardly ever visited Miyako Island because, she said, "Miyako Island is not my home; my home country is Taiwan."[85]

Female repatriates who grew up in colonial Taiwan usually remarked that it was hard to adapt to life in Okinawa. Because many of them had lived in an urban district in Taiwan, those who repatriated to one of the remote islands found Okinawa's rural life particularly difficult. Nevertheless, like Tomioka Mieko, female repatriates who had received a secondary school education in Taiwan were at an advantage in finding white-collar jobs. It should also be noted that it was uncommon for female repatriates from Taiwan to find white-collar jobs and full-time work in Mainland Japan. In postwar Okinawan society, it was hard for male Okinawans to find well-paid employment as well. Thus, few Okinawan female repatriates could afford the luxury of being housewives. Most female repatriates to Mainland Japan who had graduated from advanced high schools became housewives, but female Okinawan repatriates had to utilize their educational and work experiences in colonial Taiwan in their postwar careers.[86] Although they are rarely mentioned in histories of modern Okinawa, it is undeniable that these postcolonial careers were an integral part of Okinawa's postwar development.

Okinawan immigrants in Taiwan were a highly diverse people in terms of geographical origins and social backgrounds. Some were from the main island of Okinawa, and others were from remote areas such as the Miyako and Yaeyama Islands. During Japanese colonial rule, these people were derisively assigned to the downgraded category of "Okinawans" or "Ryukyuans." In response to discrimination and prejudice, some tried to hide their regional identities, and some went so far as to transfer their registered addresses to prefectures in Mainland Japan; others preserved their ethnic pride and maintained strong ties with fellow Okinawans.

With the fall of the Japanese Empire, the liminal status of Okinawans was once again vulnerable to international politics. When the Ryukyu Islands came under US military control, people who were willing to repatriate to the Ryukyu Islands were segregated from those who intended to go to Mainland Japan. Even though a new border was drawn between Taiwan and the Ryukyu Islands, many secretly left Taiwan on small fishing boats and returned to the Miyako and Yaeyama Islands. However, those from the main island of Okinawa were temporarily stranded because the US military strictly forbade repatriates from landing there while residents were detained in camps. Thus, nearly ten thousand Okinawans were left in Taiwan at the end of World War II. In contrast, most former Japanese soldiers and civilian settlers had returned to Mainland Japan by April 1946. This clearly shows that Okinawa once again fell into liminality within Japan, as the country shrank from an empire to a nation-state.

While awaiting official repatriation to the main island of Okinawa, Okinawan migrants demonstrated excellent leadership skills by initiating a mutual aid organization. The period between the end of the war and official repatriation was crucial in reshaping the ethnic identity of Okinawans in Taiwan. Although the great majority of Okinawans were assimilated into the Japanese settler community, Okinawans were forcibly separated from the Japanese. Instead of letting this discourage them, they joined forces and organized an ethnicity-based mutual aid organization for the first time.

On resettling in postwar Okinawa, many repatriates from Taiwan played leadership roles in various fields. Nevertheless, they felt alienated in Okinawa, not only because they had spent several years outside Okinawa, but also because they had not experienced the fierce ground battle in Okinawa. As historians such as Lori Watt, Abe Yasunari, and Katō Kiyofumi have pointed out, there was a sharp divide between the Japanese who survived the war in Mainland Japan and those who had been repatriated from former Japanese territories. Unlike the Japanese in the homeland, the repatriates, especially those from China and Korea, personally experienced the hatred of other Asians and the turmoil of East Asia in the transitional period. Experiences of repatriation are told only to the limited audience of the repatriate community and have not been shared with or evaluated by a wider Japanese audience.[87] Those who repatriated to Okinawa share a similar experience, as there is a deep divide between the repatriates and islanders who did not evacuate during the war. Public memories of colonial Taiwan are also scant, overwhelmed by memories of the Battle of Okinawa. Nevertheless, colonial legacies are evident, as postwar Okinawan society was built by Okinawans whose lives were deeply embedded in the legacies of Japanese colonial rule in Taiwan.

Epilogue

At the beginning of the US occupation of the Ryukyu Islands, the money economy and commercial trade were frozen, and people had to live in an informal economy and on rations from the US military. In addition to the population increase, the Yaeyama Islands, which had enjoyed strong social and economic ties with colonial Taiwan, suffered a shortage of material goods when official ties with Taiwan were cut after the fall of the Japanese Empire. Before returning to his home island of Ishigaki, Hazama Rihō, who graduated from Taiwan Medical College in 1931 and opened his own gynecology clinic in Tainan in 1940, drew up a petition to George H. Kerr, US vice-consul in the American consulate in Taipei.[1] In it, he requested permission to bring a variety of medical instruments and drugs to Ishigaki Island upon his return.

> By this time, it is after all settled that I should go back to Yaeyama; therefore I should like very much to request for your special protection so that through you becoming my power, I may be permitted to bring back with me instruments, machineries, drugs and other materials. Yaeyama is a far away off island both from the main islands of Japan and that of Okinawa and is a place where there is not a single gynaecological specialist. Therefore, a person with my training, if he should go back without these technical medical instruments, machineries, drugs and other materials, he would not be able to look after the poor Yaeyama villagers nor the women; and in that case I will not be at cooperative in the work of constructing a new Okinawa slightly. Hence I will be most sorriest with reluctance. In this respect, Yaeyama is entirely different from anywhere in the main islands of Japan where medical instruments, machineries and etc are easily available. Therefore, I do request that you pass your wise judgement there in and interest yourself particularily in this matter.[2]

The letter was written in Japanese and translated into English for submission, accompanied by an itemized list of nearly a hundred medical instruments, equipment, drugs, and other medical paraphernalia, including an electric radiator and an electric lamp.[3] His petition clearly reveals the extent to which Yaeyama Islanders had been materially reliant on colonial Taiwan. To Yaeyama Islanders, the fall of the Japanese Empire meant separation from Taiwan, which in turn created a radical change in their cultural, material, and social lives.

Hazama Rihō might have been exceptional in his initiative in petitioning the American authorities directly. Most Yaeyama Islanders did not take such formal and direct action, preferring the informal alternative of maintaining social and commercial ties with the Taiwanese and secretly continuing to trade with them. Although public sea transport had ceased between Okinawa and Taiwan, fishers still fished and sold their wares in markets in Taiwan. On their return trips, they carried Yaeyama and Miyako Islanders back to their home islands. They also purchased food and necessities in markets in Taiwan and brought them back to Okinawa for sale. That period in the late 1940s and early 1950s is considered the "smuggling age" in Okinawa.[4] Smuggling rings soon mushroomed across the Ryukyu Islands to compensate for the lack of a regular economy, as well as the scarcity of food and daily necessities, and Yonaguni Island quickly became the transit point for the smuggling network. People on the main island of Okinawa gathered leftover Japanese military arms, pilfered a variety of foodstuffs, daily goods, and weapons from the US base, and traded food and everyday goods from Taiwan and Hong Kong. Ironically, nonmetallic and metallic items, including weapons and cartridges, were transferred to the Chinese Communist Party military by way of informal trade across the East China Sea when the civil war in China intensified. Such activities were apparently illegal and came under the purview of law enforcement. However, local police knew that smuggling was the only means of survival for people on the devastated islands, rarely probed too deeply into smuggling activities, and often overlooked them.[5]

Ishigaki Shincho, originally from Ishigaki Island, became a professional photographer in Taiwan and opened his own studio in Kaohsiung in 1944 (described in chaps. 3 and 6). After the war, he had no choice but to close his studio and move back to Ishigaki Island. He managed to bring some equipment with him but did not have sufficient materials for printing photographs. There were four photography studios on Ishigaki Island, but they had all gone out of business because photo-developing supplies were unavailable. Ishigaki temporarily gave up his photography business and turned to farming for survival. Owing to the increasing demand for a photography studio, however, he secretly went to Taiwan and picked up materials for taking souvenir pictures for Ishigaki Islanders.[6] The informal networks between Okinawa and Taiwan, created as a result of Japanese colonization of Taiwan, certainly continued after the fall of the Japanese Empire.

Informal exchanges were especially active among fishers. In September 1946, the US military government conducted a survey to investigate Okinawans' living conditions, their destinations in Okinawa, and their opinion of repatriation. Of the 10,132 individuals questioned in this survey, 9,748 looked forward to moving back to Okinawa, and 384 wished to remain in Taiwan; the survey notes that those who preferred to remain in Taiwan were mostly fishers and their family members.[7] In fact, Okinawan fishers continued to conduct their business as before. Some played crucial roles in smuggling across the sea; others were officially retained at the government's request. After official repatriation to the main island of Okinawa, which occurred between October and December 1946, only a small number of Okinawans, retained for service, were permitted to stay in Taiwan. According to the records of the Japanese Controlling Commission (Nikkyō kanri īnkai), 108 Okinawans were still retained for service in February 1947. With the exception of technicians working in Taipei, nearly 90 percent of retained Okinawans were either employees of marine products companies, part of the companies' fishing crews, captains, or fishers.[8] Okinawan fishers' techniques were indeed highly regarded in Taiwan, and present-day Taiwanese believe that Okinawans played a vital role in developing Taiwanese fishery.[9]

Some Okinawan fishers even began to work in Taiwan after official repatriation was completed. The pseudonymous Kudaka Takao was born in 1931, when Taiwan was under Japanese colonial rule, and raised on Yonaguni Island. While he attended an elementary school on Yonaguni, Kudaka's brothers and sisters were living and working in Taiwan. Thus, he frequently visited Taiwan and sometimes stayed in South Su'ao for the whole of his summer holiday. After graduating from primary school on Yonaguni Island, he responded to the call for crew members on a fishing boat. From August 1947 to May 1948, he worked as a cook on a Taiwanese-owned fishing boat, living on the boat along with other crew members, including three Taiwanese and six Yonaguni Islanders.[10] As indicated in his account, it was common for Taiwanese and Okinawan fishers to work together on the same fishing boat even after the majority of Japanese settlers had left Taiwan.

Hence, it is not surprising that a significant number of Okinawan fishers remained in Keelung when the notorious 228 Incident occurred in 1947. The 228 Incident was the culmination of growing frustration toward the new government among Taiwanese residents, the so-called Bengshenren Taiwanese. On February 27, 1947, a policeman beat up a woman who sold cigarettes on the black market, triggering a mass riot against the police. During the confrontation, a policeman shot a person dead on the street, which brought about a protest movement the following day. On February 28, the police shot at the people who had gathered to protest against the government, causing numerous deaths and injuries. A large-scale uprising ensued. It swiftly spread across Taiwan, and a number of violent confrontations and riots occurred. Chen Yi, the chief executive of the Taiwan Province Executive Office of Administrations, asked Chiang Kai-shek to send reinforcements from the mainland and forcefully suppressed the uprising. The exact death toll is still unknown, but it is estimated that approximately ten thousand to twenty thousand people lost their lives.[11]

Four Okinawans are officially recognized as victims of the 228 Incident. One was a long-term resident of the Okinawan community in Keelung who was engaged in smuggling between Okinawa and Taiwan after the war; two others were residents of Yonaguni Island who were killed when they visited Keelung during the uprising; the fourth was a former employee of the colonial government who had been repatriated to Ishigaki Island and was killed when he visited Taiwan and got involved in the incident.[12] Taiwan reinforced its security after the 228 Incident, making it much harder for Okinawans to land in Taiwan. Nevertheless, smuggling continued until Okinawa's regular economy and administration recovered. It was likely that a significant number of Okinawan fishers remained even after most of the Japanese and Okinawan colonial settlers, who had become deeply apprehensive about security in Taiwan after the 228 Incident, left Taiwan in 1947.

Kiyuna Tsugumasa (1926?–1989) is well known as the founder of the Association for Ryukyu Revolution and Independence (Ryūkyū Kakumei Dōshikai). He is, however, less known for establishing the Association for Ryukyuan People in Taiwan Province (Taiwanshō Ryūkyū Jinmin Kyōkai), an Okinawan mutual aid organization, in July 1948. He was born in Okinawa and joined the KMT in China during the Second Sino-Japanese War. After migrating to Taiwan along with other KMT members, he discovered the miserable conditions his fellow Okinawans had to endure without any government support. In his essay, he recollects the ways in which he helped fellow Okinawans in Taiwan:

> At that time, I founded another people's association, called "Association for Ryukyuan People in Taiwan Province," and organized nearly eight hundred Okinawans across Taiwan, who were displaced without any protection. Following rules of self-governance, we initiated a variety of mutual aid activities that covered many diverse areas. As the head of the association, I

> not only played a consul-like role but also arranged employment for the members; sometimes, I helped members with ceremonial occasions and administrative issues. I also supported people who had lost their means of making a living in Okinawa and had secretly migrated to Taiwan; occasionally, I saved and protected Okinawan fishers who were shipwrecked near Taiwan.[13]

The office of the Association for Ryukyuan People in Taiwan Province was on Heping Island in Keelung, where the Okinawan fishers' community had been located since the beginning of the Japanese colonial era. Kiyuna's memoirs suggest that hundreds of Okinawans (both long-term and temporary residents) gathered around Keelung without authorization from any government, even after official repatriations were completed. Okinawan fishers needed to continue doing business as they had before, and Taiwan's fishery industry required their skills and techniques in order to develop. Yet they were unlikely to receive protection and support from the US, Japanese, or KMT governments. Thus, Kiyuna offered his support to these unauthorized migrants in Taiwan. The number of Okinawans in Taiwan dropped around 1953 as irregular trade and movement between the islands declined after formal trade relations were renewed with Japan and established with the Ryukyu government in 1952. Additionally, the Taiwan Fishery Company, the major employer of Okinawan fishers, went bankrupt, and Taiwan's longshore fishing declined in the 1960s.[14] The Okinawan community on Heping Island was likely scaled back during that time.

Despite evidence of Japanese colonial legacies in postwar Taiwan under KMT rule, people were unable to talk freely about the Japanese colonial period until martial law was lifted in 1987. With the end of the long-term suppression of free speech, collective memories of Japanese colonial rule have emerged in scholarly works, school textbooks, and popular culture, as people have tried to recover this "lost memory."[15] In July 2004, I saw the documentary *Viva Tonal: Dance Age* (*Tiaowu shidai*) at a small theatre in Taipei City. The film, which won the Golden Horse Award in 2003, is about the history of Taiwanese popular music, mainly of the 1920s and 1930s, while Taiwan was under Japanese rule. The documentary features old photos and the recollections of elderly Taiwanese. In a striking scene midway through the film, a Taiwanese man who appears to be in his eighties sings "Tokyo-ondo" (Tokyo dance song) in Japanese. "Tokyo-ondo" was such a popular song in Mainland Japan during the 1930s that it was also marketed in the colonies.

The scene immediately brought to mind Kuroshima Nae (pseudonym), whom I interviewed just before coming to Taipei. In the interview, she remembered entertaining herself by singing and dancing "Tokyo-ondo" in Shinkōen (present-day 228 Peace Memorial Park) in central Taipei. She also recalled that a group of Taketomi Islanders performed it while holding artificial cherry blossoms in the Tanedori Festival some years ago.[16] When I mentioned this story to a person currently working at the Taketomi Island Visitor Center, he told me, "It was a long time ago. Since the festival was designated a cultural asset, we can no longer do such things." The Tanedori Festival, originally a locally oriented festival held in supplication for a good harvest, is the biggest festival on Taketomi Island and can be traced back to the eighteenth century.[17] After it was designated an intangible folk cultural asset in 1977, however, Taketomi Islanders were no longer allowed to share their experience of the song and cherry blossoms in the festival's "authentic" and "traditional" program, even though it formed a significant part of their group memory of colonial Taiwan.

Both *Viva Tonal* and the Tanedori Festival reveal the shared historical experiences of the people of Taiwan and Okinawa and the ways in which memories of Japanese colonialism have been incorporated into both Okinawan and Taiwanese history. While this book does not sufficiently explore the interrelationships between personal and collective memories of the colonial past, the subjective documents it employs have been socially constructed in the contexts of both Taiwan and Okinawa for past seventy years.

In spite of its apparent focus on border construction and border crossings from Okinawa at the edge of the Inner Territory, this book does not examine the Taiwanese construction and crossing of the Taiwan-Okinawa border. In fact, Okinawa also has a distinctive history of accepting Taiwanese migrants. The Yaeyama Islands, in particular, received a significant number of Taiwanese migrant farmers early in the Japanese colonial period. These migrants played important roles in the development of the Yaeyama economy and industries, as a group of Taiwanese farmers established a corporation and inaugurated the pineapple industry on Ishigaki Island in the 1930s. Initially, local farmers strongly opposed the influx of Taiwanese farmers and interrupted their development projects.[18] However, local farmers came to recognize the Taiwanese farmers' great contributions to their island's industries and economy when the Taiwanese introduced many advanced agricultural technologies and developed the pineapple industry into Yaeyama's biggest postwar industry. Indeed, the Taiwanese in Okinawa formed another group of the Japanese Empire's liminal subjects, but that is a subject for future study.[19]

Japanese continental imperialism created the liminal zone between the metropole and the colony. The Ryukyu Islands in the late nineteenth and early twentieth centuries should be identified neither as the periphery nor the internal colony but as the liminal zone of the Japanese Empire. The concept of liminality illustrates the dynamic process in which the boundaries of the Japanese Empire were drawn and redrawn through negotiations between multiple agencies. Liminality defined the Okinawan experience of migration and career making in the Japanese colonial empire. Okinawa was culturally, financially, and politically marginalized in the Japanese national space, and Okinawan migrants suffered enormously from Japanese mainlanders' prejudice and discrimination. However, they were never the passive victims of Japanese nationalist imperialism. Liminality created the space for the common people of Okinawa to exercise their agency and enabled them to make their careers in the Japanese colonial empire.

Appendix

Oral History Informants

	Gender	Year of birth	Place of birth	Approximate year of first arrival in Taiwan
1	F	1908	Taketomi Island	1926
2	F	1909	Naha (Okinawa)	1944
3	F	1912	Taketomi Island	1928
4	F	1913	Taketomi Island	1928
5	M	1915	Taketomi Island	1930
6	M	1915	Ishigaki Island	1929
7	M	1915	Taketomi Island	1930
8	M	1917	Taketomi Island	1937
9	M	1917	Taketomi Island	1934
10	M	1918	Naha (Okinawa)	1936
11	M	1918	Ishigaki Island	1938
12	M	1919	Taketomi Island	1941
13	M	1920	Taketomi Island	1935
14	F	1922	Taketomi Island	1937
15	M	1922	Miyako Island	1939
16	F	1923	Miyako Island	1938
17	F	1924	Ishigaki Island	1940
18	F	1924	Ishigaki Island	1940
19	F	1924	Ishigaki Island	1944
20	F	1924	Ishigaki Island	1944

(continued)

	Gender	Year of birth	Place of birth	Approximate year of first arrival in Taiwan
21	M	1924	Miyako Island	1942
22	F	1925	Ishigaki Island	1939
23	F	1925	Ishigaki Island	1944
24	F	1925	Ishigaki Island	1933
25	F	1925	Ishigaki Island	1940
26	M	1926	Miyako Island	1939
27	F	1926	Taketomi Island	1929
28	F	1926	Taiwan	—
29	M	1927	Taiwan	—
30	M	1929	Taiwan	—
31	M	1929	Taiwan	—
32	M	1930	Taiwan	—
33	F	1930	Taiwan	—
34	F	1931	Taiwan	—
35	F	1931	Taiwan	—
36	F	1932	Miyako Island	1935
37	M	1933	Taiwan	—
38	F	1934	Taiwan	—
39	M	1935	Taiwan	—
40	M	1936	Taiwan	—
41	M	1936	Taiwan	—
42	M	1936	Miyako Island	1944
43	M	1938	Shimajiri (Okinawa)	1939
44	F	1939	Taiwan	—

Abbreviations

CNT Itosu Masa, ed. *Chichi no nukumori toki wo koete*. Okinawa: privately printed, 1994.

OKK Zaidan Hōjin Okinawa-ken Bunka Shinkōkai Shiryō Henshūshitsu, ed. *Okinawa-kenshi, Kakuron-hen*. Vol. 5, *Kindai*. Okinawa: Okinawa-ken Kyōiku Īnkai, 2011.

RKT Taiwan Hikiage Kankō Kiseikai, ed. *Ryūkyū kanpei tenmatsuki*. Okinawa: Taiwan Hikiageki Kankō Kiseikai, 1986.

TSKE Taiwan Sōtokufu Keimukyoku. *Taiwan sōtokufu keisatsu enkakushi*. Vol. 2. Taihoku-shi: Taiwan Sōtokufu Keimukyoku, 1938. Reprint, Tokyo: Ryokuin Shobō, 1986.

TZZ *Taiwan zongdufu ziyuan xitong* (Taiwan sōtokufu shokuinroku keitō). Institute of Taiwan History, Academia Sinica, Taiwan. http://who.ith.sinica.edu.tw/mpView.action.

Notes

Introduction

1. Duara Prasenjit, *Sovereignty and Authenticity: Manchukuo and the East Asian Modern* (Lanham, MD: Rowman & Littlefield, 2003), 9.

2. Ibid., 18.

3. Ibid.

4. Benedict Anderson, *Imagined Communities: Reflections on the Origin and Spread of Nationalism*, 2nd ed. (London: Verso, 2006), 86.

5. Arnold van Gennep, *The Rites of Passage* (Chicago: University of Chicago Press, 1960), 11.

6. Victor W. Turner, *The Ritual Process: Structure and Anti-Structure* (Chicago: Aldine Publishing Company, 1969), 95.

7. Ibid.

8. Bjørn Thomassen, *Liminality and the Modern: Living through the In-Between* (London: Routledge, 2014), 89–90.

9. See, for example, Timothy S. Forest, "Defenders of Empire or Agents of Ruin? Hebridean Scot Colonies in British Columbia in the 1920s," *Canadian Historical Review* 96, no. 2 (2015): 194–222; Malvern van Wyk Smith, "Misfits in the Margins: Transgression and Transformation on the (South) African Frontier," *English in Africa* 43, no. 1 (2016): 9–30; Matthew P. Fitzpatrick, "The Threat of 'Woolly-Haired Grandchildren': Race, the Colonial Family and German Nationalism," *History of the Family* 14, no. 4 (2009): 356–368; Kristen L. Ziomek, "The Possibility of Liminal Colonial Subjecthood: Yayutz Bleyh and the Search for Subaltern Histories in the Japanese Empire," *Critical Asian Studies* 47, no. 1 (2015): 123–150.

10. Frederick Cooper and Ann Laura Stoler, eds., *Tensions of Empire: Colonial Cultures in a Bourgeois World* (Berkeley: University of California Press, 1997); Ann Laura Stoler, *Carnal Knowledge and Imperial Power* (Berkeley: University of California Press, 2002).

11. See, for example, Jun Uchida, *Brokers of Empire: Japanese Settler Colonialism in Korea, 1876–1945* (Cambridge, MA: Harvard University Asia Center, 2011); Tseng Lin-yi, "A Cross-Boundary People: The Commercial Activities, Social Networks, and Travel Writings of Japanese and Taiwanese Sekimin in the Shantou Treaty Port (1895–1937)" (PhD diss., City University of New York, 2014); Lai Huang-wen, "Traveling Abroad, Writing Nationalism, and Performing in Disguise: People on the Japanese Colonial Boundaries, 1909–1943" (PhD diss., University of Pennsylvania, 2016).

12. This is comparable to Tessa Morris-Suzuki's exploration of Japanese history at the northern frontier of Hokkaido. See Tessa Morris-Suzuki, *Henkyō kara nagameru: Ainu ga keiken suru kindai* (Tokyo: Misuzu shobō, 2000).

13. See, for example, Glen D. Hook and Richard Siddle, eds., *Japan and Okinawa: Structure and Subjectivity*, repr. (London: Routledge, 2014); Gavan McCormack and Satoko Oka Norimatsu, *Resistant Islands: Okinawa Confronts Japan and the United States* (Lan-

ham, MD: Rowman & Littlefield, 2012); Michael Weiner, ed., *Japan's Minorities: The Illusion of Homogeneity*, 2nd ed. (London: Routledge, 2009).

14. Alexander C. Diener and Joshua Hagen, *Borders: A Very Short Introduction* (Oxford: Oxford University Press, 2012), 13–17.

15. Michiel Baud and Willem van Schendel, "Toward a Comparative History of Borderlands," *Journal of World History* 8, no. 2 (1997): 211–242.

16. There are myriad studies on people at the borderlands. Relevant books published in recent years include Tone Bringa and Hege Toje, eds., *Eurasian Borderlands: Spatializing Borders in the Aftermath of State Collapse* (New York: Palgrave Macmillan, 2016); David N. Gellner, ed., *Borderland Lives in Northern South Asia: Non-State Perspectives* (Durham, NC: Duke University Press, 2013); Sarah Turner, Christine Bonnin, and Jean Michaud, *Frontier Livelihoods: Hmong in the Sino-Vietnamese Borderlands* (Seattle: University of Washington Press, 2015).

17. See, for example, Bruce Loyd Batten, *To the Ends of Japan: Premodern Frontiers, Boundaries, and Interactions* (Honolulu: University of Hawai'i Press, 2003); Murai Shōsuke, *Kyōkai wo matagu hitobito* (Tokyo: Yamakawa shuppansha, 2006); Murai Shōsuke, Satō Makoto, and Yoshida Nobuyuki, *Kyōkai no Nihonshi* (Tokyo: Yamakawa shuppansha, 1997); Tessa Morris-Suzuki, "Lines in the Snow: Imagining the Russo-Japanese Frontier," *Pacific Affairs* 72, no. 1 (1999): 57–77.

18. Hokkaido University's Slavic Research Center was funded by the Japan Society for the Promotion of Science from 2009 to 2014, and it promoted the Global COE (Center of Excellence) program Reshaping Japan's Border Studies. The program organized conferences and workshops on issues related to borderlands. It also published books, such as Iwashita Akihiro, ed., *Nihon no kokkyō: Ika ni kono "jubaku" wo tokuka* (Hokkaidō: Hokkaidō Daigaku shuppankai, 2010). Additionally, the Japan International Border Studies Network was founded in 2011. Its members include university-based scholars, local government officers, and nongovernmental organizations (NGOs) promoting community development in the borderlands.

19. See, for example, Oguma Makoto, ed., *"Kyōkai" wo koeru Okinawa: Hito, bunka, minzoku* (Tokyo: Shinwasha, 2016); Ryūkyū Shinpō and San'in Chūō Shinpō, *Meguri no umi: Takeshima to Senkaku, kokkyō chiiki kara no toi* (Tokyo: Iwanami shoten, 2015).

20. See, for example, Koike Yasuhito, *Ryūkyū rettō no "mitsubōeki" to kyōkaisen: 1949–1951* (Tokyo: Shinwasha, 2015); Matsuda Yoshitaka, *Yonaguni Taiwan ōraiki: "Kokkyō" ni kurasu hitobito* (Ishigaki: Nanzansha, 2013); Okuno Shūji, *Natsuko: Okinawa mitsubōeki no joō* (Tokyo: Bungei shunjū, 2007).

21. Edward Said, *Orientalism* (London: Routledge and Kegan Paul, 1978).

22. See, for example, Harald Fischer-Tiné and Susanne Gehrmann, *Empires and Boundaries: Rethinking Race, Class, and Gender in Colonial Settings* (New York: Routledge, 2009); and Thomas M. Wilson and Hastings Donnan, eds., *A Companion to Border Studies* (Chichester, UK: Wiley Blackwell, 2012), part 2.

23. Hannah Arendt, *The Origins of Totalitarianism,* 3rd ed. (London: Allen & Unwin, 1967).

24. Oguma Eiji, *"Nihonjin" no kyōkai: Okinawa, Ainu, Taiwan, Chōsen, shokuminchi shihai kara fukki undō made* (Tokyo: Shin'yosha, 1998).

25. Baud and Schendel, "Toward a Comparative History," 212.

26. Kevin Kenny, ed., *Ireland and the British Empire* (Oxford: Oxford University Press, 2004).

27. Alvin Jackson, "Ireland, the Union, and the Empire, 1800–1960," in *Ireland and the British Empire,* ed. Kevin Kenny (Oxford: Oxford University Press, 2004), 136.

28. Steve Rabson, *The Okinawan Diaspora in Japan: Crossing the Borders Within* (Honolulu: University of Hawai'i Press, 2011), 1–2.

29. In addition to Rabson, *Okinawan Diaspora in Japan,* see, for example, Ishikawa Tomonori, *Nihon imin no chirigakuteki kenkyū: Okinawa, Hiroshima, Yamaguchi* (Okinawa: Yōju shorin, 1997); Ronald Y. Nakasone, *Okinawan Diaspora* (Honolulu: University of Hawai'i Press, 2002); Tomiyama Ichirō, *Kindai Nihon shakai to "Okinawajin"* (Tokyo: Nihon hyōronsha, 1990).

30. Fukuzawa Yukichi, "Kikō to sanshoku," 1895, reprinted in *Fukuzawa Yukichi zenshū,* vol. 15, 2nd ed. (Tokyo: Iwanami shoten, 1970), 266–268.

31. Lorenzo Veracini, *Settler Colonialism: A Theoretical Overview* (Basingstoke, UK: Palgrave Macmillan, 2010), 8.

32. Caroline Elkins and Susan Pedersen, *Settler Colonialism in the Twentieth Century* (London: Routledge, 2005), 2.

33. Veracini, *Settler Colonialism,* 3.

34. It should be noted that there has been a debate in Hawai'i—another island group where settler colonialism took place—as to whether Japanese and other Asians were "colonial settlers" who had obtained more privileges than native Hawaiians. For detailed discussions, see Candace Fujikane and Jonathan Y. Okamura, eds., *Asian Settler Colonialism: From Local Governance to the Habits of Everyday Life in Hawaii* (Honolulu: University of Hawai'i Press, 2008).

35. Although settler colonialism in Taiwan has not been sufficiently studied and published in the English language, settler colonialism in Manchuria and colonial Korea has been well studied and published internationally. See, for example, Louise Young, *Japan's Total Empire: Manchuria and the Culture of Wartime Imperialism* (Berkeley: University of California Press, 1998); Emer O'Dwyer, *Significant Soil: Settler Colonialism and Japan's Urban Empire in Manchuria* (Cambridge, MA: Harvard University Asia Center, 2015); Uchida, *Brokers of Empire.*

36. From 2000 onward, both Japanese- and Chinese-language books and articles have discussed the circumstances of these Japanese civilians. See, for example, Andō Nobuhiro, "Shokuminchiki Taiwan no dōka kyōiku ni okeru kyōshi no yakuwari: Kōgakkō ni okeru Nihonjin kyōshi to Taiwanjin kyōshi no kankei wo chūshin ni" (PhD diss., Hiroshima University, 2010); Gan Kyōju (Yan Xinru), "Shokuminchi toshi Taihoku ni okeru Nihonjin no seikatsu bunka: 'Kūkan' to 'jikan' ni okeru ishoku, hen'yō" (PhD diss., University of Tokyo, 2010); Huang Chia-chi, "Nihon tōchi jidai ni okeru 'naitai kyōkon' no kōzō to tenkai," *Hikaku kazokushi kenkyū* 27 (2012):128–155; Lin Yu-ru, "Zhimindi de chanye zhili yu mosuo: Mingzhi mounian Taiwan de guanying Ribenren yuye yimin," *Xin Shixue* 24, no. 3 (2013): 95–133; Okamoto Makiko, *Shokuminchi kanryō no seijishi: Chōsen, Taiwan sōtokufu to teikokunihon* (Tokyo: Sangensha, 2008); Okamoto Makiko, "Shokuminchi zaijūsha no seiji sanka wo meguru sōkoku: 'Taiwan dōkakai' wo chūshin to shite," *Shakai kagaku* 89 (2010): 95–131; Okamoto Makiko "Shokuminchi tōchi shoki Taiwan ni okeru naichijin no seiji, genron katsudō: 6–3 hō taisei wo meguru sōkoku," *Shakai kagaku* 86 (2010): 91–123; Shiode Hiroyuki, *Ekkyōsha no seijishi: Ajia Taiheiyō ni okeru Nihonjin no imin to shokumin* (Aichi: Nagoya Daigaku shuppankai, 2015), chap. 5; Zhang Su-fen, *Taiwan de riben nongye yimin (1905–1945): Yi guanying yimin wei zhongxin* (Xindian: Guoshiguan, 2009).

37. Elkins and Pedersen, *Settler Colonialism;* Uchida, *Brokers of Empire.*

38. Okinawa-ken heiwa kinen shiryōkan, "Heiwa gakushū," Okinawa-ken: n.d. http://www.peace-museum.pref.okinawa.jp/heiwagakusyu/kyozai/qa/q2.html (accessed March 20, 2017).

39. American Consulate in Taipei (Taihoku), "10,132 Okinawans Soon to Enter the Jurisdiction of United States Forces," correspondence to J. Leighton Stuart, American Ambassador, Nanking, China, October 2, 1946, S100584H, 06-A-14–03, Okinawa Prefectural Archives, Okinawa Prefecture.

40. Matayoshi Seikiyo, *Nihon shokuminchika no Taiwan to Okinawa* (Okinawa: Akishobō, 1990).

41. These works include Mizuta Kenji, "Okinawa-ken kara Taiwan e no ijū: Dainiji sekai taisen mae ni okeru Yaeyama-gun shusshinsha wo chūshin to shite," in *Chirigaku no shosō: "Jisshō" no chihei,* ed. Kansai Daigaku Bungakubu Chirigaku Kyōshitsu (Tokyo: Taimeidō, 1998), 380–397; Mizuta Kenji, "Nihon shokuminchika no Taihoku ni okeru Okinawa shusshin 'jochū,'" *Shisen* 98 (2003): 36–55; Kaneto Sachiko, "'Kyōkai' kara toraeru shokuminchi Taiwan no josei rōdō to esunikku kankei: Yaeyama josei no shokuminchi Taiwan eno idō to 'jochū rōdō to no kanren kara," *Rekishi hyōron,* 722 (2010): 19–33; Shu Keisoku (Zhu Huizu), "Teikokuteki idō to 'kindai' no enkinhō: Yaeyama shotō to shokuminchi Taiwan wo yukiki suru hitobito," *Ryūkyū Okinawa kenkyū* 3 (2010): 30–54; Pien Feng-kwei, "Rizhi shiqi zai Taibei de Chongshengren (1937–1943): Juji xiwang de chengshi," in *Haigang, hainan, haitou: Haiyang wenhua lunji,* ed. Chong Ying-chang (Taipei: Liren shuju, 2012), 85–117; Shu Tokulan (Zhu De-lan), "Kiryū Sharyōtō no Okinawa-jin shūraku (1895–1945)," in *Higashi Ajia no bunka to Ryūkyū, Okinawa: Ryūkyū/Okinawa, Nihon, Chūgoku, Etsunan,* ed. Uesato Ken'ichi et al. (Tokyo: Sairyūsha, 2010), 49–77.

42. Virginia Yans-McLaughlin, "Metaphors of Self in History: Subjectivity, Oral Narratives, and Immigration Studies," in *Immigration Reconsidered: History, Sociology, and Politics,* ed. Virginia Yans-McLaughlin (New York: Oxford University Press, 1990), 254–292.

43. Ibid., 272–283.

44. For reviews of the intellectual development of oral history, see Donald A. Ritchie, "Introduction: The Evolution of Oral History," in *The Oxford Handbook of Oral History,* ed. Donald A. Ritchie (Oxford: Oxford University Press, 2010), 3–21; and Alistair Thomson, "Memory and Remembering in Oral History," in *The Oxford Handbook of Oral History,* ed. Donald A. Ritchie (Oxford: Oxford University Press, 2010), 3–22, 77–95.

45. Alessandro Portelli, "What Makes Oral History Different," in *The Oral History Reader,* ed. Robert Perks and Alistair Thomson, 2nd ed. (London: Routledge, 2006), 32–42.

46. Ibid.

47. Popular Memory Group, "Popular Memory: Theory, Politics, Method," in *The Oral History Reader,* ed. Robert Perks and Alistair Thomson, 2nd ed. (London: Routledge, 2006), 43–53.

48. The literature on Japan's war-related memory is extensive. For recent English-language works on this subject, see Akiko Hashimoto, *The Long Defeat: Cultural Trauma, Memory, and Identity in Japan* (Oxford: Oxford University Press, 2015); Kamila Szczepanska, *The Politics of War Memory in Japan: Progressive Civil Society Groups and Contestation of Memory of the Asia-Pacific War* (Abingdon, UK: Routledge, 2014); Ran Zwigenberg, *Hiroshima: The Origins of Global Memory Culture* (Cambridge: Cambridge University Press, 2014).

49. Ronald Y. Nakasone, "An Impossible Possibility," in *Okinawan Diaspora,* ed. Ronald Y. Nakasone (Honolulu: University of Hawai'i Press, 2002), 8.

50. There is abundant Japanese-language literature on Okinawan war memories. For

English-language works on this subject, see Kyle Ikeda, *Okinawan War Memory: Transgenerational Trauma and the War Fiction of Medoruma Shun* (Abingdon, UK: Routledge, 2014); and Christopher T. Nelson, *Dancing with the Dead: Memory, Performance, and Everyday Life in Postwar Okinawa* (Durham, NC: Duke University Press, 2008).

51. Wendy Matsumura, *The Limits of Okinawa: Japanese Capitalism, Living Labor, and Theorizations of Community* (Durham, NC: Duke University Press, 2015).

52. Takushokumushō Nanbukyoku, *Taiwan keisei ippan* (Tokyo: Takushokumushō Nanbukyoku Dainika, 1897), 13–14.

53. Before the Japanese arrived, Taiwan was populated by two different racial groups: Han Taiwanese and Taiwanese aborigines. Han Taiwanese, whose ancestors had been migrating from mainland China since the seventeenth century, comprised two different ethnic groups—Hoklo (Hokkien) and Hakka. Taiwanese aborigines are Austronesian peoples and first settled in Taiwan before the arrival of the Han Chinese. Some of the aborigine groups had assimilated into the Han Chinese and were called *pingpu,* or "plains tribes"; others, who had refused to assimilate, were called "raw/wild tribes," under Qing rule.

54. Ng Chao-tng (Huang Chao-tang), *Taiwan minshukoku no kenkyū: Taiwan dokuritsu undōshi no ichidanshō* (Tokyo: Tokyo Daigaku shuppankai, 1970), 107–114.

55. Ibid., 47–61; Kō Sekai (Xu Shikai), *Nihon tōchika no Taiwan: Teikō* to dan'atsu (Tokyo: Tokyo Daigaku shuppankai, 1971), 31–35.

56. Kō, *Nihon tōchika no Taiwan,* 48–49; *TSKE,* vol. 2, 50–69.

57. Kō, *Nihon tōchika no Taiwan,* chap. 1; *TSKE,* vol. 2, chap. 2.

58. Ide Kiwata, *Taiwan chisekishi* (Taihoku-shi: Taiwan nichinichi Shinpōsha, 1937; repr. Tokyo: Seishisha, 1988), 226.

59. *TSKE,* vol. 2, 267.

60. Kō, *Nihon tōchika no Taiwan,* 80–81.

61. *TSKE,* vol. 2, 204–126.

62. Oguma, "Nihonjin" no kyōkai, 83–86.

63. Ibid., 123–126.

64. Ide, *Taiwan chisekishi,* 314–319.

65. Ibid., 318.

66. Ibid., 193.

67. Ann Laura Stoler, "Sexual Affronts and Racial Frontiers: European Identities and the Cultural Politics of Exclusion in Colonial Southeast Asia," in *Tensions of Empire: Colonial Cultures in a Bourgeois World,* ed. Frederick Cooper and Ann Laura Stoler (Berkeley: University of California Press, 1997), 198–237.

68. See, for example, Ann Laura Stoler, *Carnal Knowledge and Imperial Power: Race and the Intimate in Colonial Rule* (Berkeley: University of California Press, 2002); and Fischer-Tiné and Gehrmann, *Empires and Boundaries.*

69. Taiwanese assimilation in Japan is another well-examined subject in Japanese colonial studies. See, for example, Leo T. S. Ching, *Becoming "Japanese": Colonial Taiwan and the Politics of Identity Formation* (Berkeley: University of California Press, 2001), and Komagome Takeshi, *Shokuminchi teikoku Nihon no bunka tōgō* (Tokyo: Iwanami shoten, 1996).

70. Stress and threats received by the locals in Okinawa were the underlying causes of these "mass suicides," so much so that some scholars have called these "forced mass suicides." Numerous Japanese-language books and articles have investigated the "mass suicides" committed in the Battle of Okinawa. The most representative work is Hayashi Hiroshi, *Okinawasen: Kyōsei sareta shūdan jiketsu* (Tokyo: Yoshikawa kōbunkan, 2009). For more on the debate over "mass suicides" in contemporary Okinawa and Japan, see Iwanami Shoten, *Kiroku,*

Okinawa "Shūdan jiketsu" saiban (Tokyo: Iwanami shoten, 2012). For a brief English-language introduction to the issue, see McCormack and Norimatsu, *Resistant Islands.*

71. Alan S. Christy, "The Making of Imperial Subjects in Okinawa," in *Formations of Colonial Modernity in East Asia,* ed. Tani E. Barlow (Durham, NC: Duke University Press, 1997), 141–169; Nakasone, *Okinawan Diaspora;* Rabson, *Okinawan Diaspora in Japan;* Tomiyama, *Kindai Nihon shakai.*

Chapter 1: Migration in the Age of Modern Colonialism

Epigraph. Robert K. Arakaki, "Theorizing on the Okinawan Diaspora," in *Okinawan Diaspora,* ed. Ronald Y. Nakasone (Honolulu: University of Hawai'i Press, 2002), 26.

1. *Okinawa taimusu,* October 13, 2016, http://www.okinawatimes.co.jp/articles/-/66205 (accessed March 15, 2017).

2. Besides *Okinawan Diaspora,* edited by Ronald Y. Nakasone, see also Hawai'i United Okinawa Association, ed., *Uchinanchu: A History of Okinawans in Hawaii* (Honolulu: Center for Oral History Social Science Research Institute, College of Social Sciences, University of Hawai'i at Mānoa, 1981); Ronald Y. Nakasone, ed., *Reflections on the Okinawan Experience: Essays Commemorating 100 years of Okinawan Immigration* (Fremont, CA: Dharma Cloud Publishers, 1996); Okinawa Club of America, ed., *History of the Okinawans in North America* (Los Angeles: Asian American Studies Center, University of California, Los Angeles, and Okinawa Club of America, 1988). Additionally, numerous oral history collections have been published by Okinawan associations overseas and the local governments of Okinawa Prefecture.

3. Nakasone, *Okinawan Diaspora.*

4. Arakaki, "Theorizing," 37.

5. Ibid., 39.

6. Takaesu Masaya, "Chihō seido no seibi: 'Naichi' no naka no 'ihō iki,'" in *OKK,* 172.

7. The inaugural election of the House of Representatives in Mainland Japan was held in 1890. Okinawa Prefecture, Ogasawara, and Hokkaido were excluded from the inaugural national election.

8. Wakukawa Seiei, *Jidai no senkusha Tōyama Kyūzō: Okinawa gendaishi no issetsu* (Honolulu: Toyama-Kyuzo Memorial Committee, 1953), 26–75.

9. Ōkurashō Kanrikyoku, "Sōron no ichi," in *Nihonjin no kaigai katsudō ni kansuru rekishiteki chōsa,* vol. 1 (Tokyo: Ōkurashō Kanrikyoku, 1949; repr., Tokyo: Yumani shobō, 2000), 185–190. Citations refer to the Yumani shobō ed.

10. Wakukawa, *Jidai no senkusha,* 121–126.

11. Kimura Yukiko, "Social-Historical Background of the Okinawans in Hawaii," in *Uchinanchu,* ed. Hawai'i United Okinawa Association, 53.

12. Wakukawa, *Jidai no senkusha,* 126–128.

13. Ibid., 134–138.

14. Ibid., 146–151.

15. Ishikawa Tomonori, "A Study of the Historical Geography of Early Okinawan Immigrants to the Hawaiian Islands," in *Uchinanchu,* ed. Hawai'i United Okinawa Association, 81.

16. Hokubei Okinawajinshi Henshū Īnkai, *Hokubei Okinawajinshi* (Los Angeles: Okinawa Club of America, 1981), 44–46.

17. Kinjō Isao, "Okinawa imin no keii," in *OKK,* 346.

18. Ishikawa Tomonori, "Kaigai imin no tenkai," in *Okinawa-kenshi,* vol. 7, *Imin,* ed.

Okinawa-ken Kyōiku Īnkai (Okinawa: Okinawa-ken Kyōiku Īnkai, 1974), 252–259; Yabiku Mosei, *Burajiru Okinawa iminshi* (São Paulo: Zaihaku Okinawa Kenjinkai, 1987), 9.

19. Ishikawa, "Kaigai imin no tenkai," 257–276.

20. Ibid., 14, 257–276.

21. Shimabukuro Shinzō, "Nanbei imin no gaiyō," in *OKK*, 375–379.

22. Ishikawa, "Kaigai imin no tenkai," 292–304; Shimabukuro, "Nanbei imin no gaiyō," 379–381.

23. Wakukawa, *Jidai no senkusha*, 179–180.

24. Hayase Shinzō, *"Benketto imin" no kyozō to jitsuzō* (Tokyo: Dōbunkan, 1989), 41–80.

25. Ibid., 80–101.

26. Wakukawa, *Jidai no senkusha*, 179–180.

27. Hayase Shinzō, "Tribes on the Davao Frontier, 1899–1941," *Philippine Studies* 33, no. 2 (1985): 139–150.

28. Kabahara Kōji, *Dabao hōjin kaitakushi* (Davao, Philippines: Nippi shinbunsha, 1938), 57–60.

29. Ibid., 81–85.

30. Ibid., 179.

31. Mark R. Peattie, *Nan'yō: The Rise and Fall of the Japanese in Micronesia, 1885–1945* (Honolulu: University of Hawai'i Press, 1988), 124.

32. Ishikawa, "Kaigai imin no tenkai," 392.

33. Peattie, *Nan'yō*, 123–132; David Hanlon, *Making Micronesia: A Political Biography of Tosiwo Nakayama* (Honolulu: University of Hawai'i Press, 2014), chap. 2.

34. Ishikawa, "Kaigai imin no tenkai," 392–393; Peattie, *Nan'yō*, 127.

35. Imaizumi Yumiko, "Okinawa imin shakai: Sec. 1 Nan'yō," in *OKK*, 348–350.

36. Yabiku, *Burajiru Okinawa iminshi*, 252–275.

37. Edith M. Kaneshiro, "'The Other Japanese': Okinawan Immigrants to the Philippines, 1903–1941," in Nakasone, *Okinawan Diaspora*, 71–89.

38. *Ryūkyū shinpō*, July 22, 1916.

39. Ibid., July 23, 1916.

40. Ibid., February 10, 1917.

41. Murayama Meitoku, *Filipin gaiyō to Okinawa kenjin*, "Appendix" (Davao, Philippines: Davao jihōsha, 1929), 16.

42. Ibid., 16–17.

43. Ibid., 17.

44. Ibid., 22–23.

45. Ibid., 15–28.

46. Imaizumi, "Okinawa imin shakai: Sec. 1 Nan'yō," in *OKK*, 363–365.

47. Chen Junyu and Kuo Haiming, "Taibeishi shigao, no. 10, Zelu," in *Taibeishishi*, vol. 12 (Taipei: Chengwen chubanshe, 1983), 4830–4831.

48. *TSKE*, vol. 2, 238.

49. Taiwan Sōtokufu Minseibu Bunshoka, *Taiwan sōtokufu daiichi tōkeisho* (Taihoku-ken: Taiwan Sōtoku Kanbō Tōkeika, 1899), 54.

50. *Taiwan nichinichi shinpō*, November 22, 1899.

51. *Okinawa mainichi shinbun*, August 11, 1910.

52. Ibid., August 12, 1910.

53. I borrowed the term from Oguma Eiji, *"Nihonjin" no kyōkai: Okinawa, Ainu, Taiwan, Chōsen, shokuminchi shihai kara fukki undō made* (Tokyo: Shin'yōsha, 1998), chap. 5.

54. Okamoto Makiko, *Shokuminchi kanryō no seijishi: Chōsen, Taiwan sōtokufu to teikokunihon* (Tokyo: Sangensha, 2008), 51.

55. Ibid., 51–55.

56. Agar was used not only for various food products but also in paint, medicine, and glue.

57. Chen Shiyi, *Jilong yuyeshi* (Jilong-shi: Jilong shizhengfu, 2001), 96.

58. *Taiwan nichinichi shinpō,* June 13, 1901.

59. Ibid., September 8, 1904.

60. *Taiwan nichinichi shinpō,* August 8, 1907.

61. Chen Shiyi, *Jilong yuyeshi,* 34.

62. Taiwan Sōtokufu Kanbō Rinji Kokusei Chōsabu, *Kokusei chōsa kekkahyō Showa 5-nen, Zentō-hen* (Taihoku-shi: Taiwan Sōtoku Kanbō Rinji Kokusei Chōsa-bu, 1934), 456.

63. Fukumura Yoshiko, "Sharyō-tō (gen Waheijima) no omoide," in *Ryūkyū Uminchu no Zō konryō kinenshū,* ed. Ryūkyū Uminchu no Zō Konryū Kiseikai (Okinawa: Ryūkyū Uminchu no Zō Konryū Kiseikai, 2011), 10.

64. Asato Tsumichiyo, *Hitotsubu no mugi: Beigun shiseika no shihanseiki* (Okinawa: Minshatō Okinawa-ken Rengōkai, 1983), 104–108; *Sakishima asahi shinbun,* July 3, 1935.

Chapter 2: Crossing the National/Imperial Border

1. Okinawa Gaichi Hikiagesha Kyōkai, Ishigakishibu, *Zaigai shisan hoshō kakutoku undō no kiroku: 1956–1996* (Okinawa: Okinawa Gaichi Hikiagesha Kyōkai, Ishigakishibu, 1997), 19.

2. As of 2015, twelve Yaeyama Islands are inhabited: Ishigaki, Taketomi, Iriomote, Hatoma, Yufu, Kohama, Kayama, Kuroshima, Aragusuku-kamiji, Aragusuku-Shimoji, Hateruma, and Yonaguni.

3. Okinawa-ken, "Yaeyama ken'iki no ichi, kikō, menseki, jinkō," Okinawa Prefectural Government, http://www.pref.okinawa.jp/site/somu/yaeyama/shinko/positionetc.html (accessed March 25, 2017).

4. Ishigaki Shishi Henshū Īnkai, ed., *Ishigaki-shishi, Kakuron-hen, Minzoku,* vol. 1 (Okinawa: Ishigaki-shi, 1995), 941–957. Learning from the Tokugawa Shogunate, which established a system of beacon fires to report sudden arrivals of foreign ships, the Shimazu introduced the same system in the Ryukyu Kingdom in 1644. The fire beacon system was also implemented in the Yaeyama Islands to announce the arrival of foreigners.

5. Hara Tomoaki, *Minzoku bunka no gendai: Okinawa, Yonaguni-jima no "minzoku" eno manazashi* (Tokyo: Dōseisha, 2000).

6. For details, see Arano Yasunori, *Kinsei Nihon to Higashi Ajia* (Tokyo: Tokyo Daigaku shuppankai, 1988); Arano Yasunori, Ishii Masatoshi, and Murai Shōsuke, eds., *Jiishiki to sōgo rikai* (Tokyo: Tokyo Daigaku shuppankai, 1993).

7. The Matsumae Domain ruled the territory at the northern end of Honshu Island and monopolized trade with the Ainu.

8. Fukaya Katsumi, "Sōron: Bakuhansei kokka to iiki, ikoku," in *Bakuhansei kokka to iiki, ikoku,* ed. Katō Eiichi et al. (Tokyo: Azekura shobō, 1989); Kikuchi Isao, "Kyōkai to etonosu," in *Ajia no naka no Nihonshi: Chiiki to etonosu,* ed. Arano Yasunori, Ishii Masatoshi, and Murai Shōsuke (Tokyo: Tokyo Daigaku shuppankai, 1992).

9. Arano, *Kinsei Nihon.*

10. For the transformation of the East Asian international system in the nineteenth century, see Takeshi Hamashita, "The Intra-regional System in East Asia in Modern

Times," in *Network Power: Japan and Asia,* ed. Peter J. Katzenstein and Takashi Shiraishi (Ithaca, NY: Cornell University Press, 1997).

11. The status of the northern "foreign zone" of Yezochi had been a contentious issue for the Tokugawa Shogunate even before the 1850s, due to Russia's attempt to extend its control there. Ainu revolts as well as conflicts between Russians and Japanese exacerbated the shogunate's anxiety over the northern border at Yezochi. For details on defining the northern border, see Morris-Suzuki, "Lines in the Snow.

12. Maehira Fusa'aki, "Bakumatsu ishinki ni okeru Ryūkyū no ichi," in *Meiji Ishin to Ajia,* ed. Meiji Ishin Gakkai (Tokyo: Yoshikawa kōbunkan, 2001).

13. Kokaze Hidemasa, "Kai chitsujo to Nihon gaikō: Ryūkyū, Chōsen wo me-gutte," in *Meiji Ishin to Ajia,* ed. Meiji Ishin Gakkai (Tokyo: Yoshikawa kōbunkan, 2001), 5–7.

14. Ishii Takashi, *Meiji shoki no Nihon to Higashi Ajia* (Tokyo: Yūrindō, 1982), chap. 1.

15. The Taiwan expedition, often interpreted as modern Japan's first imperialistic act, has been intensively studied by Japanese scholars. See, for example, Ishii, *Meiji shoki no Nihon;* Mōri Toshihiko, *Taiwan shuppei: Dainihon teikoku no kaimakugeki* (Tokyo: Chūkō shinsho, 1996); Namihira Tsuneo, "'Ryūkyū shobun' saikō: Ryūkyū han'ō sappō to Taiwan shuppei mondai," *Seisakukagaku, kokusaikankei ronshū* 11 (2009): 1–78. For English-language works on the subject, see Robert Eskildsen, "Of Civilization and Savages: The Mimetic Imperialism of Japan's 1874 Expedition to Taiwan," *American Historical Review* 107, no. 2 (2002): 388–418; Mizuno Norihito, "Early Meiji Politics towards the Ryukyus and the Taiwanese Aboriginal Territories," *Modern Asian Studies* 43, no. 3 (2009): 683–739.

16. Mōri, *Taiwan shuppei.*

17. Numerous documents reveal the discussions and negotiations between Japan and the Qing over the division of the Ryukyu Islands. The most significant documents are compiled in Ryūkyū Seifu, *Okinawa kenshi,* vol. 15, *Zassan, no. 2, shiryō-hen, no. 5* (Ryukyu: Ryūkyū Seifu, 1969).

18. Hattori Kazuma, "Kindaiteki seitōgyō no seiritsuki ni okeru hutari no kigyōka: Suzuki Tōsaburō to Nakagawa Toranosuke," in *Kindai kigyōka no hassei: Shihonshugi keizai seiritsu katei no ichimen,* ed. Shakai Keizaishi Gakkai (Tokyo: Yūhikaku, 1963), 18–19.

19. Ibid., 126–127.

20. Ichiki Kitokurō, "Ichiki shokikan torishirabesho," in *Okinawa kenshi, vol. 14, Shiryō-hen 4, Zassan no. 1,* ed. Ryūkyū Seifu (Ryukyu: Ryūkyū Seifu, 1965), 599; Yaeyama Rekishi Henshū Īnkai, ed., *Yaeyama rekishi* (Yaeyama, Ryukyu: Yaeyama Rekishi Henshū Īnkai, 1954), 401.

21. Shibusawa Seien Kinen Zaidan Ryūmonsha, *Shibusawa Eiichi denkishiryō,* vol. 11 (Tokyo: Shibusawa Eiichi Denki Shiryō Kankōkai, 1956), 202–215.

22. Ibid., 219.

23. Ichiki, "Ichiki shokikan torishirabesho," 599.

24. Shibusawa Seien, *Shibusawa Eiichi denkishiryō,* 234–242.

25. Hattori, "Kindaiteki seitōgyō," 132.

26. Shibusawa Seien, *Shibusawa Eiichi denkishiryō,* 251–254.

27. Hattori, "Kindaiteki seitōgyō," 143. Nakagawa's factory in Taiwan was established in 1902 and closed within three years.

28. Makino Kiyoshi, *Shin Yaeyama rekishi* (Okinawa: privately printed, 1972), 281–286; Miki Takeshi, "Iriomote tankō gaishi: Sono shihon to rōdō no hensen," *Yaeyama Bunka* 3 (1975): 4–63. In addition to developers attracted to the coal industry's potential in the late nineteenth century, many migrants worked as coal miners on Iriomote Island. The coal mining companies were funded by investments from the Japanese mainlanders. After

Mitsui Corporation began coal mining in 1885, several other companies followed suit. Despite several attempts to mine coal after the war, all projects were discontinued in 1968. As the coal mining companies employed mostly laborers from outside Yaeyama, the Iriomote mines were isolated from the local islander communities.

29. Dōmae Ryōhei, "Kindaiki, Ishigakijima Shika no shōgyō kūkan ni kansuru jakkan no kōsatsu," in *Ishigakijima chōsa hōkokusho,* vol. 1 (Okinawa: Okinawa Kokusai Daigaku Nantō Bunka Kenkyūjo, 2003), 115–132.

30. The scientific name for *tengusa* is Gelidiaceae. It is used to make agar.

31. While most Okinawa Islanders were primarily farmers under the Ryukyu Kingdom's pro-agrarian policies, Itoman villagers dominated fishery across the Ryukyu Islands. During the rule of the Ryukyu Kingdom, Itoman fish products such as shark fins and dried cuttlefish were exported to China. Thus, the abolishment of the Ryukyus' tributary trade with China was a vital blow to the Itoman fishing industry. In a bid to overcome the crisis, Itoman fishers adopted new fishing techniques and began to fish around Mainland Japan as well as in waters south of the Ryukyu Islands. For details on the history of the Itoman fishery, see Ueda Fujio, "Itoman gyomin to Tōnan Ajia," in *Ajia no umi to Nihonjin,* ed. Omoto Keiichi et al. (Tokyo: Iwanami shoten, 2001).

32. Katō Hisako, *Umi no kariudo Okinawa gyomin: Itoman uminchu no rekishi to seikatsushi* (Tokyo: Gendai shokan, 2012), 129–133; Mochizuki Masahiro, "Koga Tatsushirō to Osaka Koga Shōten," *Nantō shigaku* 35 (1990): 1–21.

33. Miki Takeshi, "Yaeyama gasshūkoku wo ikiru," in *Yaima nasake ni sasaerare,* ed. Miki Takeshi (Okinawa: privately printed, 2002), 195–198.

34. *Sakishima asahi shinbun,* August 25, 1917; *Yaeyama shinpō,* December 1, 1923.

35. The Yaeyama newspaper industry was one of the enterprises dominated by new settlers. It was also closely associated with other commercial businesses in Yaeyama. After the first newspaper, *Sakishima News* (*Sakishima shinbun*) (1917–1926), was published, others appeared one after another—*Yaeyama News* (*Yaeyama shinpō*) (1921–1934), *Sakishima Asahi News* (*Sakishima asahi shinbun*) (1927–1940), *Yaeyama People's News* (*Yaeyama minpō*) (1932–936), and *Kainan Times* (*Kainan jihō*) (1935–1945). The first three papers were published by newcomers. They tended to be patriotic and frequently critical of Yaeyama traditional culture. Like the other newspapers in Okinawa Prefecture, none of these papers enjoyed wide circulation, and only about three hundred copies were sold at a time. Circulation was approximately 6 percent of the total number of households. Added to the fact that primary school education was not widespread until the beginning of the twentieth century, this meant that only a limited number of residents had easy access to newspapers. For details on Yaeyama's local newspapers in the early twentieth century, see Haebaru Eiiku, *Minami no shima no shinbunjin: Shiryō ni miru sono hensen* (Okinawa: Hirugi-sha, 1988).

36. *Sakishima shinbun,* January 3, 1932.

37. *Yaeyama minpō,* January 11, 1932. Moji, which is at the northernmost tip of Fukuoka Prefecture, was one of Japan's largest international ports in the early twentieth century.

38. *Yaeyama shinpō,* March 15, 1929.

39. Ikema Nae, *Yonaguni Yūbinkyoku to chichi no shōgai: Yonaguni Yūbinkyoku sōritsu nanajūsshūnen* (Okinawa: privately printed, 1996).

40. Yaeyama Rekishi Henshū Īnkai, *Yaeyama rekishi,* 401.

41. Ishigaki Shishi Henshū Īnkai, *Ishigaki-shishi,* 598–599.

42. Yaeyama Rekishi Henshū Īnkai, *Yaeyama rekishi,* 374–375.

43. Kinjō Isao, "Yaeyama no tōgyō ni tsuite," *Okinawa rekishi kenkyū* 10 (1973): 40–60.

44. Iba Nantetsu, *Yaeyama jinji kōshinroku* (Yaeyama, Ryukyu: Yaeyama Jinji Kōshinroku Henshūsho, 1951), 46.

45. Ibid., 4.

46. Okinawa-ken Naimu-bu, Chōsa-ka, *Taishō 10-nen Okinawa-ken tōkeisho,* vol. 1, *Naimu no bu* (Okinawa: Okinawa-ken, 1922), 41.

47. Okinawa-ken Naimu-bu, Chōsa-ka, *Taishō 11-nen Okinawa-ken tōkeisho,* vol. 1, *Naimu no bu* (Okinawa: Okinawa-ken, 1924), 41.

48. Tsuji Hiroshi, *Taketomijima ima mukashi* (Okinawa: privately printed, 1985), 365.

49. Kuroshima Nae (pseudonym), interview by author, audio recorded, Okinawa Prefecture, Japan, April 16, 2005.

50. Tsuji Hiroshi, *Watashi no ayunda 88-nen: Tōkachi iwai ni yosete* (Okinawa: privately printed, 2002), 37.

51. Kinjō Isao, "Imin no shakaiteki haikei," in *Okinawa-kenshi,* vol. 7, *Imin,* ed. Okinawa-ken Kyōiku Īnkai (Okinawa: Okinawa-ken Kyōiku Īnkai, 1974), 92.

52. Mizuta Kenji, "Okinawa-ken kara Taiwan e no ijū."

53. Tsuji, *Taketomijima,* 364–365.

54. Yamamoto Kiyoko (pseudonym), interview by author, audio recorded, Okinawa Prefecture, Japan, June 30, 2003.

55. Makino, *Shin Yaeyama rekishi,* 348–350.

56. Indica rice is native to Taiwan. In 1918, the Japanese succeeded in modifying Japonica rice to suit Taiwan's natural environment. The modified rice was later named "Hōrai-mai" and was widely cultivated in Taiwan for export to Japan.

57. Ishigaki Shishi Henshū Īnkai, *Ishigaki-shishi,* chap. 3.

58. Bill Mihalopoulos, *Sex in Japan's Globalization, 1870–1930: Prostitutes, Emigration and Nation Building* (London: Ouckering & Chatto, 2011).

Chapter 3: Making Distinctions in the Extension of Japan

1. Wakabayashi Masahiro argues that the Gradual Extension of the Inner Territory policy aimed to control the nationalism of the colonized subjects, as nationalistic opposition against imperialism developed worldwide after World War I. Haruyama Meitetsu points out that the Korean nationalistic resistance of the March 1 Movement, which occurred in 1919, greatly influenced Japanese colonial policies. While the Japanese government attempted to strengthen unity between the Inner Territory and colonial Taiwan, the residents of Taiwan were denied suffrage—which might develop into Taiwanese nationalism—under the Gradual Extension policy. For details, see Haruyama Meitetsu and Wakabayashi Masahiro, eds., *Nihon shokuminchishugi no seijiteki tenkai: Sono tōchi taisei to Taiwan no minzoku undo, 1895–1934-nen* (Tokyo: Ajia Seikei Gakkai, 1980); Wakabayashi Masahiro, *Taiwan kōnichi undōshi kenkyū,* 2nd ed. (Tokyo: Kenbun shuppan, 2001).

2. Numerous scholars have discussed the assimilation policies and actual practices of assimilation during the period. See, for example, Chin, *"Dōka" no dōshō imu: Nihon tōchika Taiwan no kokugo kyōikushi saikō* (Tokyo: Sangensha, 2001); Ching, *Becoming "Japanese";* Oguma, *"Nihonjin" no kyōkai.*

3. Law No. 63 was followed by Law No. 31 of Meiji 39 (Meiji 39-nen Hōritsu Dai 31 gō). As Law No. 63 expired, Law No. 3 (Hōritsu Dai 3 gō) was enacted in 1921. Law No. 3 also maintained the authority of the governor-general of Taiwan. Because this was a permanent law, the autonomy of the governor-general was secured until the end of Japanese colonial rule. The colonial government denied the Taiwanese equal rights and obligations

as well as cultural autonomy and applied several policies in order to "extend Japanese systems and institutions."

4. Mary Louise Pratt, *Imperial Eyes: Travel Writing and Transculturation,* 2nd ed. (London: Routledge, 2008), 7.

5. Takemoto Seigi, *Ari no uta: Takemoto Seigi jiden* (Okinawa: Miru shuppan, 1995), 34.

6. Higa Takeshi (pseudonym), interview by author, audio recorded, Okinawa Prefecture, Japan, April 12, 2005.

7. Ishigaki Shincho, interview by author, audio recorded, Okinawa Prefecture, Japan, June 25, 2004.

8. Maruyama Kandō and Imamura Nanshi, "Decchi seido no kenkyū," reprinted in *Decchi seido no kenkyū: Kyōto-shi ni okeru Jochū ni kansuru chōsa,* vol. 4, *Decchi to totei no yōsei,* ed. Kimura Hajime (1912; repr., Tokyo: Kyūzansha, 1998), 3.

9. Ishigaki, interview, June 25, 2004.

10. Tsuji, *Watashi no ayunda,* 38.

11. Ibid.

12. Ibid.

13. Taiwan Sōtokufu Kanbō Rinji Kokusei Chōsabu, *Kokusei chōsa kekkahyō, Showa 5-nen, Shūchō-hen, Taihoku-shū* (Taihoku-shi: Taiwan Sōtoku Kanbō Rinji Kokusei Chōsa-bu, 1934), 2.

14. Ibid., 80–81.

15. Taihoku-shi Shokugyō Shōkaijo, "Shokugyō shōkaijo jigyō gaiyō," reprinted in *Shokuminchi shakai jigyō kankei shiryōshū: Keizai hogo jigyō: Shokugyō shōkai to rōdō jigyō,* ed. Kingendai Shiryō Kankōkai (Taihoku-shi: Taihoku-shi Shokugyō Shōkaijo, 1935; repr., Tokyo: Kiongendai Shiryō Kankōkai, 2001), 29–30. Citations refer to the Kiongendai Shiryō Kankōkai ed.

16. Ibid., 37.

17. Yamamoto Kiyoko (pseudonym), interview by author, audio recorded, Okinawa Prefecture, Japan, June 17, 2004.

18. Ibid.

19. According to the *Taiwan Daily News,* rent in the Taishō District was the most expensive in Taipei City in 1925 (*Taiwan nichinichi shinpō,* December 10, 1925).

20. Yamamoto Kiyoko, interview, June 17, 2004.

21. Ibid.

22. Ibid.

23. Iwashita Kiyoko, "Daiichiji Taisengo ni okeru 'shokugyō fujin,'" *Shakaigaku hyōron* 76 (1969): 41–53.

24. Murakami Nobuhiko, *Taishōki no shokugyō fujin* (Tokyo: Domesu shuppan, 1983).

25. Yamashita Etsuko, *Nihon josei kaihō shisō no kigen* (Tokyo: Kaimeisha, 1988), 163–182.

26. Ōhara Yayoi (pseudonym), interview by author, audio recorded, Okinawa Prefecture, Japan, May 26, 2011.

27. There is a paucity of studies on the Miyako Islanders' migration to colonial Taiwan. For a study of schoolteachers migrating from Miyako Island to colonial Taiwan, see Motomura Ikue, "Nihon tōchika no Taiwan to Miyako shusshin kyōin: Totai kyōin no kibo to sono haikei ni tsuite," *Ryūkyū shigaku* 17 (2015): 29–39.

28. Ōhara Yayoi, interview, May 26, 2011.

29. Gangshan District Office, "Lishi yange," Gangshan District Office, http://www.gsto.gov.tw/main.php?mode=content&act=history&content_id=E01 (accessed April 20, 2017).

30. Ōhara Yayoi, interview, May 26, 2011.

31. Taiwan Sōtokufu Kanbō Rinji Kokusei Chōsa-bu, *Kokusei chōsa kekkahyō, Showa 5-nen, Zentō-hen* (Taihoku-shi: Taiwan Sōtoku Kanbō Rinji Kokusei Chōsa-bu, 1934), 127.

32. Ibid., 458.

33. *Yaeyama shinpō,* October 21, 1924.

34. Oku Takenori, "Kokumin kokka no naka no josei: Meijiki wo chūshin ni," in *On'na to otoko no jikū: Nihon joseishi saikō,* vol. 5, *Semegiau on'na to otoko: Kindai,* ed. Tsurumi Kazuko and Kōno Nobuko (Tokyo: Fujiwara shoten, 1995), 434–440.

35. Okuda Akiko, "Jochū no rekishi," in *On'na to otoko no jikū: Nihon joseishi saikō,* vol. 5, *Semegiau on'na to otoko: Kindai (jō),* ed. Tsurumi Kazuko and Kōno Nobuko (Tokyo: Fujiwara shoten, 1995), 379.

36. Naikaku Tōkeikyoku, *Kokusei chōsa hōkoku, Shōwa 5-nen,* vol. 2 (Tokyo: Tokyo Tōkei Kyōkai, 1939), 160.

37. Okuda, "Jochū no rekishi," 381.

38. *Taiwan nichinichi shinpō,* July 13, 1923.

39. Ibid., *yūkan,* June 25, 1924.

40. One tatami mat is about 1.62 square meters.

41. Kuroshima Nae (pseudonym), interview by the author, audio recorded, Okinawa prefecture, Japan, June 16, 2004.

42. Ibid.

43. Murakami, *Taishōki no shokugyō fujin,* 120–121.

44. Ōhama Eishō, *Ōhama Eishō shishi: Yaeyama "Hama no Yu" no Shōwa* (Okinawa: Sakishima Bunka Kenkyūjo, 1992), 27.

45. Kuroshima Nae, interview, June 16, 2004.

46. Kondō Ken'ichirō, "Kindai Okinawa ni okeru hōgenfuda (1): Yaeyama chiiki no gakkō kinenshi wo shiryō to shite," *Aichi kenritsu daigaku bungakubu ronshū* 47 (1998): 29–49.

47. Kondō Ken'ichirō, "Okinawa ni okeru imin/dekasegisha kyōiku: Okinawaken shotō kyōiku kenkyūkai 'Shima no Kyōiku (1928)' wo chūshin ni," *Kyōikugaku kenkyū* 62, no. 2 (1995): 116–124.

48. Taiwan Kyōikukai, *Taiwan kyōiku enkakushi* (Taihoku-shi: Taiwan Kyōikukai, 1939; repr., Tokyo: Seishinsha, 1982). Citations refer to the Seishinsha ed.

49. Ōyama Masao, *Shōwa no Taketomi: Tareka kokyō wo omowazaru* (Okinawa: privately printed, 1985), 111.

50. Ibid., 123.

51. Yanaihara Tadao, "Teikokushugika no Taiwan," reprinted in *Yanaihara Tadao "Teikoku shugika no Taiwan" seidoku,* ed. Wakabayashi Masahiro (1929; repr., Tokyo: Iwanami shoten, 2001), 173–174.

52. Kamei Tōru (pseudonym), interview by author, audio recorded, Okinawa Prefecture, Japan, April 5, 2005.

53. Pierre Bourdieu, *Distinction: A Social Critique of the Judgement of Taste,* trans. Richard Nice (London: Routledge & Kegan Paul, 2010), 479.

54. Kondō Masami, *Sōryokusen to Taiwan: Nihon shokuminchi hōkai no kenkyū* (Tokyo: Tōsui shobō, 1996), 37.

Chapter 4: Imperial Schooling across the Border

1. Ming-Cheng M. Lo, *Doctors within Borders: Profession, Ethnicity, and Modernity in Colonial Taiwan* (Berkeley: University of California Press, 2002).

2. Yanaihara Tadao, "Teikokushugika no Taiwan," in *Yanaihara Tadao "Teikoku shugika no Taiwan" seidoku,* ed. Wakabayashi Masahiro (1929; repr., Tokyo: Iwanami shoten, 2001), 249–274.

3. See, for example, Chin Baihō, *"Dōka" no dōshō imu;* Kitamura Kae, *Nihon shokuminchika no Taiwan senjūmin kyōikushi* (Hokkaido: Hokkaidō Daigaku tosho kankōkai, 2008); Li Yuan-hui, *Riju shiqi Taiwan shifan jiaoyu jidu* (Taipei: Nantian shuju, 1997); Patricia Tsurumi, *Japanese Colonial Education in Taiwan, 1895–1945* (Cambridge, MA: Harvard University Press, 1977); Yamamoto Kazuyuki, *Jiyū, byōdō, shokuminchisei: Taiwan ni okeru shokuminchi kyōiku seido no keisei* (Taipei: National Taiwan University Press, 2015).

4. The most recent studies include Īijima Wataru, *Mararia to teikoku: Shokuminchi igaku to Higashi Ajia no kōiki chitsujo* (Tokyo: Tokyo Daigaku shuppankai, 2005); Sakai Tetsuya and Matsuda Toshihiko, eds., *Teikoku Nihon to shokuminchi daigaku* (Tokyo: Yumani shobō, 2014).

5. Existing studies include Paula Harrell, *Sowing the Seeds of Change: Chinese Students, Japanese Teachers, 1895–1905* (Stanford, CA: Stanford University Press, 1992); Park Sunmi, *Chōsen josei no chi no kaiyū: Shokuminchi bunka shihai to Nihon ryūgaku* (Tokyo: Yamakawa shuppansha, 2005); Sakaguchi Naoki, *Senzen Dōshisha no Taiwan ryūgakusei: Kirisutokyō kokusaishugi no genryū wo tadoru* (Tokyo: Hakuteisha, 2002).

6. Inafuku Moriteru, *Okinawa igakushi: Kinsei, kindai-hen* (Okinawa: Wakanatsusha, 1998), 37.

7. Ibid., 73.

8. Ibid., 71–72.

9. Ibid., 140–141.

10. Kōseishō Imukyoku, ed., *Isei hyakunenshi (kijutsu-hen)* (Tokyo: Gyōsei, 1976), 61–67.

11. Ibid., 64–65.

12. Ibid., 77.

13. Inafuku, *Okinawa igakushi,* 145.

14. Hamamatsu Tetsuo, *Okinawa isei kyōshūjo kinenshi* (Okinawa: Okinawa-ken Ishi Dōsōkai, 1929), 26.

15. Ibid., 12.

16. Kinjō Kiyomatsu, *Insui shigen: Kinjō Kiyomatsu ikōshū* (Okinawa: privately printed, 1977), 168.

17. Inafuku, *Okinawa igakushi,* 126; Hamamatsu, *Okinawa isei kyōshūjo kinenshi,* 18–26.

18. Higashion'na Kanjun, "Jo ni kaete," quoted in Hamamatsu, *Okinawa isei kyōshūjo kinenshi,* 7.

19. Ibid.

20. Hamamatsu, *Okinawa isei kyōshūjo kinenshi,* 44.

21. Inafuku, *Okinawa igakushi,* 124; Hamamatsu, *Okinawa isei kyōshūjo kinenshi,* 20.

22. Hamamatsu, *Okinawa isei kyōshūjo kinenshi,* 43–46.

23. Ibid.

24. Kōseishō Imukyoku, *Isei hyakunenshi,* 199.

25. Hamamatsu, *Okinawa isei kyōshūjo kinenshi,* 40–41.

26. Saika Yajin, "Yamaguchi Hidetaka no shōgai (sono 14)," *Jikken ganka zasshi* 13, no. 111 (1930): 63–64.

27. Saika Yajin, "Yamaguchi Hidetaka no shōgai (sono 13)," *Jikken ganka zasshi* 13, no. 110 (1930): 60–64.

28. Hamamatsu, *Okinawa isei,* 14–15.

29. Oda Toshirō, *Taiwan igaku gojūnen* (Tokyo: Igaku shoin, 1974), 48–49.

30. Saika Yajin, "Yamaguchi Hidetaka no shōgai (sono 15)," *Jikken ganka zasshi* 14, no. 115 (1931): 56–58.

31. Taiwan Kyōikukai, *Taiwan kyōiku enkakushi,* 918; Oda, *Taiwan igaku gojūnen,* 65–67.

32. Oda, *Taiwan igaku gojūnen,* 65–67; Taiwan Kyōikukai, *Taiwan kyōiku enkakushi,* 918.

33. Oda, *Taiwan igaku gojūnen,* 67–68; Taiwan Sōtokufu Igaku Senmon Gakkō, *Taiwan sōtokufu igaku senmon gakkō ichiran* (Taihoku-shi: Taiwan Sōtokufu Igaku Senmon Gakkō, 1922), 3–4.

34. Oda, *Taiwan igaku gojūnen,* 80–81.

35. Chin, *"Dōka" no dōshō imu,* chap. 5.

36. Ibid.

37. Oda, *Taiwan igaku gojūnen,* 112–115.

38. Taiwan Kyōikukai, *Taiwan kyōiku enkakushi,* 929–936.

39. Ibid., 936–939.

40. Taiwan Sōtokufu Taihoku Igaku Senmon Gakkō, ed., *Taiwan Sōtokufu Taihoku Igaku Senmon Gakkō ichiran, 1931–1933* (Taihoku-shi: Taiwan Sōtokufu Taihoku Igakku Senmon Gakkō, 1933), 124–127.

41. Ibid., 109.

42. Taihoku Teikoku Daigaku, ed., *Taihoku Teikoku Daigaku ichiran Shōwa 18-nen* (Taihoku-shi: Taihoku Teikoku Daigaku, 1944).

43. Taiwan Sōtokufu Taihoku Igaku Senmon Gakkō, *Taiwan Sōtokufu Taihoku Igaku,* 86–97.

44. Taihoku Teikoku Daigaku, *Taihoku Teikoku Daigaku ichiran Shōwa 18-nen,* 347–358.

45. Ibid., 319–324.

46. Kan'no Hisao, *Nanmeikai kaiin meibo* (Taihoku-shi: Nanmei-kai, 1941).

47. Yoshino Kōzen, *Furusato to tomoni* (Okinawa: privately printed, 1967), 23–80.

48. Inafuku Zenshi, "Waga seishun no koro," *Naha-shi ishikai hō,* June 1977, 25.

49. Genga Chōyō, "Yomitan shusshin hatsu no igaku hakase Genga Chōkō," in *Yomitan no senjintachi,* ed. Yomitan Sonshi Henshū Īnkai (Okinawa: Yomitan Sonshi Henshū Īnkai, 2005), 248–250.

50. Tanaka Kōei, "Waga seishun no koro," *Naha-shi ishikai hō,* July 1981, 43.

51. Tanaka Kōei, interview by author, audio recorded, Okinawa Prefecture, Japan, September 4, 2012; Tanaka Kōei, letter to author, August 25, 2013.

52. Okinawa-ken Miyakojima Iryōshi Hensan Īnkai, ed., *Okinawa-ken Miyajijima iryōshi* (Okinawa: Okinawa-ken Miyakojima Ishikai, 2011).

53. Ishimine Genki, interview by author, audio recorded, Okinawa Prefecture, Japan, October 8, 2011.

54. Okinawa-ken Miyakojima, *Okinawa-ken Miyajijima iryōshi,* 275–276.

55. Ishimine Genki, interview by author, October 8, 2011.

56. Shōwa Igaku Senmon Gakkō, ed., *Shōwa igaku senmon gakkōyōran Shōwa 7-nen genzai* (Tokyo: Shōwa Igaku Senmon Gakkō, 1934), 34–35.

57. Kanazawa Ika Daigaku, ed., *Kanazawa Ika Daigaku ichiran Shōwa 7-nen* (Kanazawa: Kanazawa Ika Daigaku, 1935), 57.

58. Taiwan Sōtokufu Taihoku Igaku Senmon Gakkō, *Taiwan Sōtokufu Taihoku Igaku*, 30–31, 57.

59. Yoshino, *Furusato to tomoni*, 105–130.

60. Genga, "Yomitan shusshin," 252.

61. Tanaka Kōei, interview by author, September 4, 2012; Tanaka Kōei, letter, August 25, 2013.

62. Shinzato Kōtoku, "Gun'i to shite Okinawasen ni," in *Okinawa-ken Ishikaishi: Shūsen kara sokoku fukki made*, ed. Okinawa-ken Ishikai Kaishi Henshū Īnkai (1987; repr., Okinawa: Okinawa-ken Ishikai, 2000), 22–23.

Chapter 5: Between Japanese and Okinawan

1. Ben Kobashigawa, "Okinawan Issei Identity: Pride and Shame among the Early Immigrants," in *Reflections on the Okinawan Experience: Essays Commemorating 100 Years of Okinawan Immigration*, ed. Ronald Y. Nakasone (Fremont, CA: Dharma Cloud Publishers, 1996), 29–44.

2. Tomiyama, *Kindai Nihon shakai*.

3. Christy, "Making of Imperial Subjects," 152.

4. Taiwan Sōtokufu Kanbō Rinji Kokusei Chōsa-bu, *Kokusei chōsa kekkahyō, Showa 5-nen, Zentō-hen*, 446, 452.

5. Noda Yoshiko (pseudonym), interview by author, audio recorded, Okinawa Prefecture, Japan, May 19, 2011.

6. In the Ryukyu Islands, numerous local leaders had competed with one another, but three dominant figures gained power and came to the fore in the fourteenth century. The time when the islands were ruled by these three figures is commonly known as the Age of the Three Kingdoms (Sanzan Jidai).

7. Dana Masayu ki, "Koryūkyū no Kumemura," in *Kumemura: Rekishi to jinbutsu*, ed. Ikemiya Masaharu, Kowatari Kiyotaka, and Dana Masayuki (Okinawa: Hirugisha, 1993), 9–15; Tomishima Sōei, "Shinnyū tōeijin," in *Kumemura: Rekishi to jinbutsu*, ed. Ikemiya Masaharu, Kowatari Kiyotaka, and Dana Masayuki (Okinawa: Hirugisha, 1993), 16–22.

8. Noda Yoshiko, interview, May 19, 2011.

9. Ibid.

10. *TZZ* (accessed November 3, 2014).

11. Noda Yoshiko, interview, May 19, 2011.

12. Ibid.

13. Ibid.

14. This testimony is corroborated by the personnel list of the Taiwan Colonial Government (Taiwan Sōtokufu shokuinroku).

15. Noda Yoshiko, interview, May 19, 2011.

16. Gan, "Shokuminchi toshi," 89–93.

17. Ibid., 93–105.

18. Noda Yoshiko, interview, May 19, 2011.

19. Taiwan Sōtokufu Keimukyoku, *Taiwan no keisatsu* (Taihoku-shi: Taiwan Sōtokufu Keimukyoku, 1932), 121.

20. Shimoji Yasuo, *Junsa hitosuji: Shimoji Keikō no shōgai* (Okinawa: privately printed, 2001), 34.

21. Taiwan Sōtokufu Keimukyoku, *Taiwan no keisatsu,* 43–46.

22. Ibid., 61–63.

23. Ibid., 66–67.

24. See, for example, Chen Tian-shou, *Taiwan zhianshi yanjiu: Jincha yu zhengjing tizhi guanxi de yanbian* (Taipei: Lantai chubanshe, 2012); Ō Tetsugun (Wang Tiejun), "Gaichi tōchi to keisatsu kanri: Taiwan tōchi ni okeru Taiwan sōtokufu keisatsukan," *Chūkyō hōgaku* 45, nos. 3–4 (2011), 425–572.

25. The Seediq were officially recognized as the fourteenth indigenous group of Taiwan on April 23, 2008. Until this formal recognition, the Seediq were classified as Atayal.

26. Taiwan Sōtokufu Keimukyoku, ed., "Musha jikenshi," in *Taiwan Musha Hōki Jiken: Kenkyū to shiryō,* ed. Tai Kuo Hui (n.d.; repr., Tokyo: Shakai shisōsha, 1981), 353–520.

27. Tai Kuo Hui, "Musha Hōki jiken no gaiyō to kenkyū no kon'nichiteki imi," in *Taiwan Musha Hōki Jiken: Kenkyū to shiryō,* ed. Tai Kuo Hui (n.d.; repr., Tokyo: Shakai shisōsha, 1981), 20.

28. Taiwan Sōtokufu Keimukyoku, "Musha jikenshi," 403–415.

29. Ibid., 424–438.

30. Ibid., 465–469.

31. Taiwan Sōtokufu Keimukyoku, *Taiwan no keisatsu,* 32–34.

32. Shimoji Yasuo, interview by author, audio recorded, Okinawa Prefecture, Japan, May 25, 2011.

33. Ibid.

34. Ibid.

35. Ibid.

36. Ibid.

37. Ibid.

38. Sakiyama Masa, interview by author, audio recorded, Okinawa Prefecture, Japan, January 21, 2008.

39. Taiwan Kyōikukai, "Taiwan gakuji hōki, kan, vol. 1," in *Nihon shokuminchi kyōiku seisaku shiryō shūsei, Taiwan-hen,* vol. 12, ed. Abe Hiroshi (1929; repr., Tokyo: Ryūkei shosha, 2007), 97–98.

40. Ibid., 139–140.

41. Sakiyama Toshi, "Ōkina ai ni tsutsumarete," in *CNT,* 54.

42. Kōnan Shinbunsha, ed., *Taiwan jinshikan* (Taihoku-shi: Kōnan shinbunsha, 1943), 177.

43. Sakiyama Masa, interview by author, audio recorded, Okinawa Prefecture, Japan, June 23, 2004.

44. Taihoku-shū Giran Kōgakko, *Taihokushū Giran Kōgakkō sōritsu yonjusshūnen kinenshi* (Taihoku-shū: Taihoku-shū Giran Kōgakkō, 1939), 51.

45. Taiwan Sōtokufu, *Shōwa 8-nen 7-gatsu tsutachi genzai Taiwan Sōtokufu oyobi shozoku kansho shokuinroku* (Taihoku-shi: Taiwan Sōtokufu, 1933), 363.

46. Furushō Hiroyuki, ed., *Sōritsu yonjusshūnen kinenshi* (Taihoku-shū: Giran Jinjō Kōtō Shōgakkō, 1941), 25–30, 62–66.

47. Sakiyama Toshi, "Ōkina ai ni tsutsumarete," in *CNT,* 56.

48. Sakiyama Masa, interview, June 23, 2004.

49. Ibid.

50. Arakawa Kiku (pseudonym), interview by author, audio recorded, Okinawa Prefecture, Japan, July 3, 2004.

51. Sakiyama Masa, interview, June 23, 2004.

52. Yamamoto Reiko, *Shokuminchi Taiwan no kōtō jogakkō kenkyū* (Tokyo: Taga shuppan, 1999), 72.

53. In 1940, there were 342 Han Taiwanese teachers in Taiwan. Of these, only 13 taught in advanced girls' schools. Although the number of Han Taiwanese teachers in elementary schools was growing, secondary education was dominated by Japanese migrant teachers. For details, see Yamamoto, *Shokuminchi Taiwan,* 64–65.

54. Sakiyama Masa, interview by author, audio recorded, Okinawa Prefecture, Japan, April 13, 2005.

55. Ibid.

56. Passing for Japanese was not unique to Okinawans in Taiwan; Okinawan migrants in many destinations also did the same. For examples of Okinawans passing in Japan proper, see, Rabson, *Okinawan Diaspora in Japan.*

57. Gan, "Shokuminchi toshi," 80–83.

58. *Taiwan nichinichi shinpō,* July 30, 1925.

59. Gan, "Shokuminchi toshi," 80–83.

60. Rabson, *Okinawan Diaspora in Japan;* Tomiyama, *Kindai nihon shakai.*

61. Kabira Chōshin, "Watashi no sengoshi," in *Watashi no sengoshi,* vol. 6, ed. Okinawa Taimususha (Okinawa: Okinawa Taimususha, 1982), 175–179.

62. Kabira Chōsei, interview by author, audio recorded, Okinawa Prefecture, Japan, February 15, 2012; Kabira Chōshin, *Rirekisho* [curriculum vitae], n.d., Kabirake Shiryō, 10000287, box 10-029, Naha City Museum of History, Okinawa Prefecture.

63. Kabira, *Rirekisho;* Kabira Chōshin, "Watashi no sengoshi," 181–182.

64. Kabira Chōshin, "Waga hansei no ki, no. 4: Rekishi to minzoku to hito," *Okinawa shunjū,* January 1974, 50.

65. Ibid.

66. Utsushikawa Nenozō (1884–1947) was born in Fukushima Prefecture and obtained his doctoral degree from Harvard University. After teaching in several schools, including Taihoku High School, he took a position as a professor at Taihoku Imperial University in 1928.

67. Kabira Chōshin, "Taiwan no omoide: Taiwan ni okeru kyōdoshi kenkyū," *Shin Okinawa bungaku,* October 1968.

68. Yanagita expressed his thoughts on Okinawa in articles, books, and lecture notes. The most representative is Yanagita Kunio, *Kaijō no michi* (1962; repr., Tokyo: Chikuma shobō, 1967).

69. Sudō Riichi, "Henshū kōki," *Nantō,* no. 1 (August 28, 1940):104-107.

70. See *Nantō,* no. 1 (August 28, 1940).

71. Kabira, "Taiwan no omoide." Higa worked for the colonial government, and Miyara was employed at Taihoku County Kyūfun Public School. For details, see "Taiwan zongdufu ziyuan xitong" (Taiwan sōtokufu shokuinroku keitō), Institute of Taiwan History, Academia Sinica. http://who.ith.sinica.edu.tw/mpView.action (accessed November 3, 2014) (*TZZ*).

72. See *Nantō,* no. 1 (August 28, 1940).

73. See *Nantō,* no. 2 (May 19, 1942).

74. Nantō Hakkōjo, *Nantō kaiin meibo,* 1941, Kabirake Shiryō, 10001540, box 10-092, Naha City Museum of History, Okinawa Prefecture.

75. Kabira, "Waga hansei no ki," 48.

76. Kobata Atsushi et al., "Okinawa no bunka wo kataru," *Nantō,* May 19, 1942, 124.

77. Kabira, "Waga hansei no ki," 48.

78. Nakamura Tadayuki, "Henshū kōki," *Nantō,* no. 3 (September 30, 1944): 230.

79. Kabira, "Watashi no sengoshi," 54.

80. *TZZ.*

81. Kabira, "Waga hansei no ki," 46.

82. For details on the dialect debate, see Hugh Clarke, "The Great Dialect Debate: The State and Language Policy in Okinawa," in *Society and the State in Interwar Japan,* ed. Elise K. Tipton (London and New York: Routledge, 1997), 193–217.

83. *Yaeyama shinpō,* January 25, 1933.

84. Ibid.

85. For details on historical relationships between Yaeyama and Okinawa, see Hiroko Matsuda, "Yaeyama: From Periphery of the Ryukyus to Frontier of Japan," *Japanese Studies* 28, no. 2 (2008): 149–164.

Chapter 6: Going Home?

1. Kōseishō Engokyoku, *Hikiage to engo 30-nen no ayumi* (Tokyo: Gyōsei, 1978), 689. While the majority of Japanese repatriates returned to Mainland Japan between 1945 and 1950, Japan continued to receive small numbers of repatriates annually until the mid-1970s. Many of the delayed returnees had been detained as laborers in Siberia; others had been ordered by the KMT, People's Republic of China (PRC), or North Korean governments to work as internees for each newly established administration. Also, a small number of former Japanese soldiers were unaware that the war had come to an end and remained in hiding near former battlefields. See Beatrice Trefalt, *Japanese Army Stragglers and Memories of the War in Japan, 1950–1975* (London: Routledge, 2003); Yoshikuni Igarashi, *Homecomings: The Belated Return of Japan's Lost Soldiers* (New York: Columbia University Press, 2016).

2. Recent publications on the subject include Lori Watt, *When Empire Comes Home: Repatriation and Reintegration in Postwar Japan* (Cambridge, MA: Harvard University Press, 2010); Araragi Shinzō, *Teikoku igo no hito no idō: Posuto koroniarizumu to gurōbarizumu no kōsakuten* (Tokyo: Bensei shuppan, 2013); Imaizumi Yumiko, Yanagisawa Asobu, and Kimura Kenji, eds., *Nihon teikoku hōkaiki "hikiage" no hikaku kenkyū* (Tokyo: Nihon Keizai Hyōronsha, 2016); Masuda Hiroshi, *Dainippon teikoku no hōkai to hikiage, fukuin* (Tokyo: Keiō Daigaku shuppankai, 2012).

3. See, for example, Yō Shishin (Yang Zi-cheng), "Teikoku kaitai no naka no jinteki idō: Sengo shoki Taiwan ni okeru Nihonjin no hikiage oyobi ryūyō wo chūshin ni," *Higashi Ajia Chiiki Kenkyū* 13 (2006): 25–47.

4. See Nakamura Haruna, "Sengo Taiwan ni okeru Okinawa sekimin no hikiage no yōsō: 'Ryūkyū kanpei' no keisei katei to sono yakuwari," *Okinawa bunka* 49, no. 2 (2015): 18–41; Onga Takashi, "Sengo Okinawa ni okeru hikiage no rekishiteki haikei to sono igi," *Higashi Ajia kindaishi* 10 (2007): 10–30; Sensui Hidekazu, "Zai Taiwan Okinawajin hikiage ni kansuru oboegaki," *Project Paper* 25 (2012): 1–25.

5. Sōmushō Tōkeikyoku, "1950-nen kokusei chōsa kekka gaiyō," in *1950-nen kokusei chōsa hōkoku (fukkokuban), dai 1-pen sōkatsu oyobi Okinawa guntō, sono 1,* ed. Sōmushō Tōkeikyoku (Okinawa: Okinawa-ken Kikaku Kaihatsu-bu Tōkei-ka, 1998), 35.

6. See, for example, James Clifford, *Returns: Becoming Indigenous in the Twenty-First Century* (Cambridge, MA: Harvard University Press, 2013); Takeyuki Tsuda, *Strangers in*

the Ethnic Homeland: Japanese Brazilian Return Migration in Transnational Perspective (New York: Columbia University Press, 2003); Xiang Biao, Brenda S. A. Yeo, and Mika Toyota, eds., *Returns: Nationalizing Transnational Mobility in Asia* (Durham, NC: Duke University Press, 2013).

7. Watt, *When Empire Comes Home.*

8. Although many Taiwanese were not recruited as combatants, they participated in the war effort, mostly as laborers. At the end of World War II, nearly 207,000 Taiwanese were involved in the Japanese military as either combatants or laborers. Approximately 41,900 military personnel and civilians in Taiwan—regardless of ethnicity and country of origin—became victims of war. See Kōseishō Engokyoku, *Hikiage to engo 30-nen*, 74, 311.

9. Takemoto, *Ari no uta,* 99–108.

10. Higa Takeshi (pseudonym), interview by author, audio recorded, Okinawa Prefecture, Japan, July 3, 2004.

11. Tsuji, *Watashi no ayunda,* 46–47.

12. War-related evacuation from Okinawa to Taiwan consisted of the "evacuation of people who relied on personal networks" (*yūenko sokai*) and the "evacuation of people who depended on the government because they had no connections in Taiwan" (*muenko sokai*). Matsuda Yoshitaka estimates that the latter group accounted for nearly 65 percent of total war evacuees between July 1944 and August 1945. See Matsuda Yoshitaka, *Taiwan sokai: "Ryūkyū nanmin" no ichinen jūikkagetsu* (Okinawa: Nanzansha, 2010), 49–53.

13. Matsushita Hitoshi, *Ishihara Yatarōden* (Okinawa: Ishihara Yatarō-shi Kenshōkai, 1963), 181–184.

14. Bōeichō Bōei Kenshūjo Senshi-bu, *Okinawa hōmen rikugun sakusen* (Tokyo: Asagumo shinbunsha, 1968), 614–616.

15. Ibid. The exact number of Okinawans who evacuated to Taiwan after the government issued its instructions is unknown, as several documents note different numbers. For detailed examinations of relevant archival documents, see Matsuda Yoshitaka, *Taiwan sokai,* 49–53.

16. Kōseishō, ed., "III-7 Nan'yō guntō zaijū hōjin no naichi hikiage oyobi sono zaigai zaisan nit suite," in *Hikiage engo no kiroku, zoku zoku,* vol. 3 (Tokyo: Kōseishō, 2000), 379–384.

17. Matsushita, *Ishihara Yatarōden,* 185–186; Matsuda Yoshitaka, *Taiwan sokai,* 55–166.

18. By the end of 1976, 479,544 Japanese military personnel and civilians had been repatriated, but the number presumably excludes those who repatriated to Okinawa Prefecture. Kōseishō Engokyoku, *Hikiage to engo 30-nen*, 89, 689.

19. Gaimushō Kanrikyoku Sōmu-bu Nanpō-ka, "Taiwan no genkyō," in *Kaigai hikiage kankei shiryō shūsei,* vol. 31, ed. Katō Kiyofumi (Tokyo: Yumani shobō, 2002), 35.

20. Ibid., 35–36.

21. For a detailed report and analysis of the violence and crimes committed during the immediate postwar period, see Douglas L. Fix, "Reading the Numbers: Ethnicity, Violence and Wartime Mobilization in Colonial Taiwan," in *Taiwan under Japanese Colonial Rule, 1895–1945: History, Culture, Memory,* ed. Liao Ping-hui and David Der-wei Wang (New York: Columbia University Press, 2006), 327–357.

22. Shiomi Shunji, *Hiroku, Shūsen chokugo no Taiwan: Watashi no shūsen nikki* (Kōchi: Kōchi shinbunsha, 1979), 44–50.

23. Taiwan Sōtokufu Zanmu Seiri Jimusho, "Taiwan tōchi shūmatsu hōkokusho," in

Kaigai hikiage shiryō shūsei (kokugai-hen), vol. 31, ed. Katō Kiyofumi (Tokyo: Yumiani shobō, 2002), 19–22.

24. Ōkurashō Kanrikyoku, "Yoroku Nikkyō no tsuioku," reprinted in *Nihonjin no kaigai katsudō ni kansuru rekishiteki chōsa,* vol. 9, ed. Kobayashi Hideo (1950; repr., Tokyo: Yumani shobō, 2000), 91.

25. Shiomi, *Hiroku, Shūsen chokugo,* 91–92.

26. Taiwan Sōtokufu Zanmu Seiri Jimusho, "Jimu hikitsugi hōkokusho," in *Kaigai hikiage kankei shiryō shūsei,* vol. 31, ed. Katō Kiyofumi (Tokyo: Yumani shobō, 2002), 146–149; Ōkurashō, "Yoroku Nikkyō no tsuioku," 94–95.

27. Ōkurashō, "Yoroku Nikkyō no tsuioku," 94–95. For instance, Iso Eikichi (1886–1972), one of the most famous and admired Japanese scientists, was a long-term resident of Taiwan. He migrated to Taiwan in 1912 and worked on improving rice breeds under the Taiwan Colonial Government. He later worked for the ROC Ministry of Agriculture and Forestry as a technical adviser until his repatriation to Japan in 1957.

28. Ishihara Masaie, *Kūhaku no Okinawa shakaishi: Senka to mitsubōeki no jidai* (Okinawa: Banseisha, 2000), 30–54.

29. Matsuda Yoshitaka, *Taiwan sokai,* 188–206.

30. Tsuji Hiroshi, "Taiwan de tsuma ya ko wo nakushite," in *Ishigaki Shishi Henshūshitsu, shimin no senji, sengo taiken kiroku: Ano koro watashi wa,* vol. 1, ed. Ishigaki Shishi Henshūshitsu (Okinawa: Ishigaki Shiyakusho, 1983), 29.

31. Okinawa-ken Kyōiku Īnkai, *Okinawa kenshi,* vol. 10, *Okinawasen kiroku, no. 2* (Okinawa: Okinawa-ken, 1974), 403–409.

32. Asato Tsumichiyo, *Hitotsubu no mugi,* 86.

33. Matsuda Yoshitaka, *Taiwan sokai,* 276.

34. Kabira Chōshin, "Waga hansei no ki, no. 7," *Okinawa shunjū,* August 1974, 82–84.

35. Ibid., 84.

36. Yogi Kisen, "Muenko sokai seru Okinawa tōmin no sōkan ni kanshi tangan no ken," in "Taiwan ni okeru Ryūkyū kankei shiryō chōsa hōkoku: Taiwan Sōtokufu bunsho, Taiwanshō gyōsei chōkan kōsho shiryō wo chūshin ni," special issue, *Shiryō henshūshitsu kiyō* 31 (2006): , 98–99.

37. Matsuda Yoshitaka, *Taiwan sokai,* 284–285.

38. Ibid., 288–290; "Note by Gan Yanjia Sending to Chen Yi, February 5, 1946," in special issue, "Taiwan ni okeru Ryūkyū kankei shiryō chōsa hōkoku: Taiwan Sōtokufu bunsho, Taiwanshō gyōsei chōkan kōsho shiryō wo chūshin ni," *Shiryō Henshūshitsu kiyō* 31 (2006): 101.

39. "Repatriation," in *Papers of James Watkins IV,* vol. 38, ed. Committee Members for the Watkins Papers Publication (Okinawa: Ryokuindō shoten, 1994), 140.

40. Arnold G. Fisch, Jr., *Military Government in the Ryukyu Islands, 1945–1950* (Washington, DC: Center for Military History, United States Army, 1988), 69–89.

41. Deputy Commander for Military Government, "Land and Population on Okinawa—A Staff Study," in *Papers of James T. Watkins IV,* vol. 38 (Okinawa: Ryokuindō shoten, 1994), 144.

42. Kabira, "Waga hansei no ki, no. 7," 85.

43. Ibid.

44. Ibid., 85–86.

45. Higa Atsuo, "Nikkyō gojūman wo okuru: Kiryū jōsenchi shireibu heitanhan roeichi kinmu taichō wo meizerarete," in *RKT,* 95–96.

46. Ibid., 97.

47. See *RKT,* 3–7.

48. Ibid.

49. Ōshiro Yoshimitsu, "Kyōmintai no zakkan," in *RKT,* 259–260; "Shiryō 1, Okinawa sekimin chōsasho," in *RKT,* 312–316.

50. "Shiryō 1, Okinawa sekimin chōsasho," in *RKT,* 312–316; Tasato Isei, "Yonjūnen mae no Taihoku shūchūei no omoide," in *RKT,* 264–265.

51. "Shiryō 1," 316–318.

52. Inafuku Zenshi, "Kyōdo no rikugun butai to kōdō wo tomo ni shite," in *RKT,* 21–36.

53. *Previous Documents of Successive Generations* (Rekidai hōan) is the compilation of nearly 5,700 diplomatic documents issued between 1424 and 1867. The original held by the Okinawa Prefectural Library was destroyed by fire during the ground battle in Okinawa. After World War II, the copy in Taiwan was microfilmed and kept at the Institute of History and Philology, Academia Sinica. The microfilm has been reproduced and distributed to several distinguished research institutes, including the University of the Ryukyus and others in Tokyo, the United Kingdom, and the United States. Some sections have been translated into English and published under the title *Ryukyuan Relations with Korean and South Sea Countries: An Annotated Translation of Documents in the "Rekidai Hoan."* The copy that Kabira brought back was initially located in the Okinawa Central Library (Okinawa Chūō Toshokan) and has been held by the Naha City Museum of History since 2011. For a detailed history of the transcriptions, reproductions, and relocations of *Previous Documents of Successive Generations* in modern times, see Kawashima Jun, "Nahashi Rekishi Hakubutsukan shozō 'Rekidai hōan' ni kansuru shiryōteki kōsatsu: Seisei, raireki, mokuroku kijutsu ni shōten wo atete," *Tsuboya Yakimono Hakubutsukan kiyō* 13 (2012): 7–31; and Kobata Atsushi, "'Rekidai hōan' ni tsuite no omoide: Watashi no Ryūkyūshi kenkyū," *Okinawa bunka kenkyū* 16 (1990): 1–12.

54. Kabira Chōshin, *Shūsengo no Okinawa bunka gyōseishi* (Okinawa: Okinawasha, 1997), 30–33, 56–65.

55. *Uruma shinpo,* August 23, 1946; Headquarters Ryukyu Command Military Government, "Repatriation to and from the Ryukyus during Period 1 July 1946 to 31 December 1946," January 9, 1947, S100584H, 06-A-14-03, Okinawa Prefectural Archives, Okinawa Prefecture.

56. Headquarters Ryukyu Command Military Government, "Repatriation."

57. "Shiryō 1," in *RKT,* 335–338.

58. Headquarters Ryukyu Command Military Government, "Repatriation."

59. Ibid.

60. Higa Takeshi (pseudonym), interview, July 3, 2004.

61. Noda Yoshiko, interview, May 19, 2011.

62. Nakamura Tameo (pseudonym), interview by author, audio recorded, May 18, 2011.

63. Itosu Masa, "Sakiyama-ke to chichi," in *Chichi no nukumori toki wo koete,* ed. Itosu Masa (Okinawa: privately published, 1994), 103.

64. Sakiyama Masa, interview by author, notes taken by hand, March 10, 2006.

65. Itosu, "Sakiyama-ke to chichi," in *CNT,* 102–104.

66. Kabira Chōshin, "Waga hansei no ki, no. 11," *Okinawa shunjū,* June 1975, 80.

67. Kabira, *Shūsengo no Okinawa,* 49–50.

68. Ibid., 106.

69. For the relationship between historiographies, Okinawan war memories, and

records of Okinawan migration to colonial Taiwan, see Noiri Naomi, "Okinawa ni okeru Taiwan hikiagesha no tokuchō: Hikiagesha zaigai jijitsu chōsahyō to ken, shichōson no taiken kiroku wo chūshin ni," in *Teikoku igo no hito no idō: Posuto koroniarizumu to gurōbarizumu no kōsakuten,* ed. Araragi Shinzō (Tokyo: Bensei shuppan, 2013), 305–350.

70. Yakabi Osamu, *Okinawasen, beigun senryōshi wo manabinaosu: Kioku wo ikani keishō suruka* (Kanagawa: Seori shobō, 2009), 5–54.

71. Due to the development of migration studies and Taiwan history studies, there has been growing interest in Okinawan migration to colonial Taiwan. For instance, in 2015, the Okinawa Prefectural Memorial Museum held a special exhibition, *Uchinanchu Perspectives on Colonial Taiwan and the Philippines before and during World War II.* Although this exhibition presented images of Okinawans in colonial Taiwan, its emphasis was on war rather than colonialism.

72. Okinawa-ken Taiwan-kai, *Heisei 14-nen (dai 10 kai) Okinawa-ken Taiwan-kai, sōkai, konshinkai* (Okinawa: privately printed, 2002), 6.

73. Imaizumi Yumiko, "Nan'yō guntō hikiagesha no dantai keisei to sono katsudō: Nihon no haisen chokugo wo chūshin to shite," *Shiryō Henshūshitsu kiyō* 30 (2005): 30.

74. Īјima Mariko, "Firipin Nikkei diasupora no sengo no 'kikan' keiken to kokyō ninshiki," *Bunka jinruigaku* 81 (2016): 80–84.

75. Okinawa Gaichi Hikiagesha Kyōkai Ishigakishibu, *Zaigai shisan hoshō kakutoku undō no kiroku* (Okinawa: Okinawa Gaichi Hikiagesha Kyōkai Ishigakishibu, 1997), 129.

76. Ibid. For the details of the Taiwan repatriates' movement for government compensation, see Kawarabayashi Naoto, "Hikiagego no hōjin 'Nanpō' keiken no yukue," in *Nan'yō guntō to teikoku, kokusai chitsujo,* ed. Asano Toyomi (Tokyo: Jigakusha shuppan, 2007).

77. Tsubota-Nakanishi Miki, "Okinawa e no hikiagesha ni yoru sengo Okinawa shakai e no setsuzoku: Taiwan deno kōmu keikensha to sono shijo wo chūshin ni," *Imin kenkyū* 9 (2013): 163–165.

78. Okinawa Taimususha, *Gendai Okinawa jimbutsu sanzennin* (Okinawa: Okinawa Taimususha, 1966), 640; Okinawa Ishikai Kaishi Hensan Īnkai, *Okinawa ishikai-shi: Shūsen kara sokoku fukki made* (Okinawa: Okinawa-ken Ishikai, 2000), 48.

79. Kabira, *Shūsengo no Okinawa,* 383.

80. Shimoji, *Junsa hitosuji,* 19–20.

81. Shimoji Yasuo, interview, May 25, 2011.

82. Tsubota-Nakanishi, "Okinawa e no hikiagesha," 153–157.

83. Tomioka Mieko (pseudonym), interview by author, audio recorded, May 22, 2011.

84. Ibid.

85. Ibid.

86. Tsubota-Nakanishi, "Okinawa e no hikiagesha," 159–163.

87. Abe Yasunari and Katō Kiyofumi, "'Hikiage' to iu rekishi no toikata (jō)," *Hikone ronsō* 349 (2004): 139.

Epilogue

1. Okinawa Taimususha, *Gendai Okinawa,* 702.

2. Hazama Rihō, "Letter from Dr. Hazama," in *Papers of James T. Watkins IV,* vol. 38, ed. Committee Members for the Watkins Papers Publication (Okinawa: Ryokuindō shoten, 1994), 155.

3. Ibid.

4. Ishihara, *Kūhaku no Okinawa,* 30.

5. Ibid., 44–47.

6. Ishigaki Shincho, interview, June 25, 2004; Nanzansha, ed., *Yaeyamapitu no shōzo* (Okinawa: Nanzansha, 2004), 30–31.

7. "Report on Okinawans in Taiwan," in *Papers of James T. Watkins IV*, vol. 38, ed. Committee Members for the Watkins Papers Publication (Okinawa: Ryokuindō shoten, 1994), 213.

8. Kawahara Isao, *Taiwan hikiage, ryūyō kiroku*, vol. 8 (Tokyo: Yumani shobō, 1998), 129–156.

9. Nishimura Kazuyuki, "Taiwan higashi kaigan ni okeru Kanjin, Ami gyomin to Okinawa gyomin no sesshoku: Shokumin tōchi makki kara sengo shoki wo chūshin ni," in *Shokuminchi no Chōsen to Taiwan: Rekishi, bunka jinruigakuteki kenkyū*, ed. Choi Kilsong and Harada Tamaki (Tokyo: Daiichi shobō, 2007), 47–82.

10. Kudaka Takao (pseudonym), interview by author, audio recorded, Okinawa Prefecture, Japan, September 3, 2011.

11. Taipei 228 Memorial Museum, "Tansuo 228," Taipei 228 Memorial Museum, http://228memorialmuseum.gov.taipei/ct.asp?xItem=1938462&ctNode=41711&mp=119 00A (accessed January 31, 2017).

12. Matayoshi Seikiyo, "Taiwan 2.28 jiken to Okinawa," *Shokuminchi bunka kenkyū* 6 (2007): 155–157.

13. Kiyuna Tsugumasa, "Koritsu muen de attemo: Isshi kōha no ben," *Shin Okinawa bungaku* 55 (1983): 128.

14. Tominaga Yūsuke, "Kiyuna Tsugumasa ga mita 'Nihon': Ryūkyū dokuritsu undō to 'Taiwanshō Ryūkyū Jinmin Kyōkai'no katsudō kara," *Ōsaka Daigaku Nihon gakuhō* 31 (2012): 100.

15. Books and articles discussing the production of colonial memory in postwar Taiwan are abundant. Among the most recent books are Min-Chin Chiang, *Memory Contested, Locality Transformed: Representing Japanese Colonial "Heritage" in Taiwan* (Leiden: Leiden University Press, 2014); Shozawa Jun and Lin Shobai (Chu-mei), eds., *Taiwan no naka no Nihon kioku: Sengo no saikai ni yoru arata na imēji no kōchiku* (Tokyo: Sangensha, 2016); Mio Yūko, Endō Hisashi, and Ueno Hiroko, eds., *Teikoku Nihon no kioku: Taiwan, Kyū-nan'yō guntō ni okeru gairai seiken no jūsōka to datsushokuminchika* (Tokyo: Keiō Daigaku shuppankai, 2016).

16. Kuroshima Nae (pseudonym), interview by author, June 16, 2004.

17. Morita Shin'ya, "Kankōkyaku ni totte no sairei, chiiki ni totteno sairei: Okinawa Taketomijima no Tanedorisai kara," in Kioku, ed. Iwamoto Michiya (Tokyo: Asakura shoten, 2003), 186–187.

18. Rin Patsu, *Okinawa pain sangyōshi* (Okinawa: Okinawa pain sangyōshi kankōkai, 1984), 38–39.

19. For historical and ethnographical studies of Taiwanese in Okinawa Prefecture, see Kuninaga Michiko, Noiri Naomi, and Matsuda Hiroko et al., *Ishigakijima de Taiwan wo aruku: Mo hitotsu no Okinawa gaido* (Okinawa: Okinawa Taimushsha, 2012); Matsuda Yoshitaka, *Yaeyama no Taiwanjin* (Okinawa: Nanzansha, 2005); Wu Li-jun, "Sengo Okinawa hontō ni okeru Taiwankei kakyō wo chūshin ni" (PhD diss., University of the Ryukyus, 2012).

Bibliography

Journals and Newspapers

Nantō, no. 1, August 28, 1940.
Nantō, no. 2, May 19, 1942.
Okinawa mainichi shinbun
Ryūkyū shinpō
Sakishima asahi shinbun
Sakishima shinbun
Taiwan nichinichi shinpō
Taiwan xinsheng bao
Uruma shinpō
Yaeyama minpō
Yaeyama shinpō

References

Abe Yasunari and Katō Kiyofumi. "'Hikiage' to iu rekishi no toikata (jō)." *Hikone ronsō* 349 (2004): 129–154.

American Consulate in Taipei (Taihoku). "10,132 Okinawans Soon to Enter the Jurisdiction of United States Forces." Correspondence to J. Leighton Stuart, American Ambassador, Nanking, China, October 2, 1946. S100584H, 06-A-14-03. Okinawa Prefectural Archives, Okinawa Prefecture.

Anderson, Benedict. *Imagined Communities: Reflections on the Origin and Spread of Nationalism*. 2nd ed. London: Verso, 2006.

Andō Nobuhiro. "Shokuminchiki Taiwan no dōka kyōiku ni okeru kyōshi no yakuwari: Kōgakkō ni okeru Nihonjin kyōshi to Taiwanjin kyōshi no kankei wo chūshin ni." PhD diss., Hiroshima University, 2010.

Arakaki, Robert K. "Theorizing on the Okinawan Diaspora." In *Okinawan Diaspora*, edited by Ronald Y. Nakasone, 26–43. Honolulu: University of Hawai'i Press, 2002.

Arano Yasunori. *Kinsei Nihon to Higashi Ajia*. Tokyo: Tokyo Daigaku shuppankai, 1988.

Arano Yasunori, Ishii Masatoshi, and Murai Shōsuke, eds. *Jiishiki to sōgo rikai*. Tokyo: Tokyo Daigaku shuppankai, 1993.

Araragi Shinzō, ed. *Teikoku igo no hito no idō: Posuto koroniarizumu to gurōbarizumu no kōsakuten*. Tokyo: Bensei shuppan, 2013.

Arashiro Hajime, ed. *Shōwa 17nen-ban Taihokushimin jūshoroku, Naichijin no bu*. Taihokushi: Jūsho Geppōsha, 1942.

Arendt, Hannah. *The Origins of Totalitarianism.* 3rd ed. London: Allen & Unwin, 1967.
Asato Tsumichiyo. *Hitotsubu no mugi: Beigun shiseika no shihanseiki.* Okinawa: Minshatō Okinawa-ken Rengōkai, 1983.
Batten, Bruce Loyd. *To the Ends of Japan: Premodern Frontiers, Boundaries, and Interactions.* Honolulu: University of Hawai'i Press, 2003.
Baud, Michiel, and Willem van Schendel. "Toward a Comparative History of Borderlands." *Journal of World History* 8, no. 2 (1997): 211–242.
Bōeichō Bōei Kenshūjo Senshi-bu. *Okinawa hōmen rikugun sakusen.* Tokyo: Asagumo shimbunsha, 1968.
Bourdieu, Pierre. *Distinction: A Social Critique of the Judgement of Taste.* Translated by Richard Nice. London: Routledge & Kegan Paul, 2010.
Bringa, Tone, and Hege Toje, eds. *Eurasian Borderlands: Spatializing Borders in the Aftermath of State Collapse.* New York: Palgrave Macmillan, 2016.
Chen Junyu and Kuo Haiming. "Taibeishi shigao, no. 10, Zelu." In *Taibeishishi,* vol. 12, 4830–4831. Taipei: Chengwen chubanshe, 1983.
Chen Shiyi. *Jilong yuyeshi.* Jilong-shi: Jilong Shizhengfu, 2001.
Chen Tian-shou. *Taiwan zhianshi yanjiu: Jincha yu zhengjing tizhi guanxi de yanbian.* Taipei: Lantai chubanshe, 2012.
Chiang, Min-Chin. *Memory Contested, Locality Transformed: Representing Japanese Colonial "Heritage" in Taiwan.* Leiden: Leiden University Press, 2014.
Chin Baihō (Cheng Peifong). *"Dōka" no dōshō imu: Nihon tōchika Taiwan no kokugo kyōikushi saikō.* Tokyo: Sangensha, 2001.
Ching, Leo T. S. *Becoming "Japanese": Colonial Taiwan and the Politics of Identity Formation.* Berkeley: University of California Press, 2001.
Christy, Alan S. "The Making of Imperial Subjects in Okinawa." In *Formations of Colonial Modernity in East Asia,* edited by Tani E. Barlow, 141–169. Durham, NC: Duke University Press, 1997.
Clarke, Hugh. "The Great Dialect Debate: The State and Language Policy in Okinawa." In *Society and the State in Interwar Japan,* edited by Elise K. Tipton, 193–217. London: Routledge, 1997.
Clifford, James. *Returns: Becoming Indigenous in the Twenty-First Century.* Cambridge, MA: Harvard University Press, 2013.
Cooper, Frederick, and Ann Laura Stoler, eds. *Tensions of Empire: Colonial Cultures in a Bourgeois World.* Berkeley: University of California Press, 1997.
Dana Masayuki. "Koryūkyū no Kumemura." In *Kumemura: Rekishi to jinbutsu,* edited by Ikemiya Masaharu, Kowatari Kiyotaka, and Dana Masayuki, 9–15. Okinawa: Hirugisha, 1993.
Deputy Commander for Military Government. "Land and Population on Okinawa—A Staff Study." In *Papers of James Watkins IV,* vol. 38, edited by Committee Members for the Watkins Papers Publication, 141–145. Okinawa: Ryokuindō shoten, 1994.
Diener, Alexander C., and Joshua Hagen. *Borders: A Very Short Introduction.* Oxford: Oxford University Press, 2012.
Dōmae Ryōhei. "Kindaiki, Ishigakijima Shika no shōgyō kūkan ni kansuru jakkan no kōsatsu." In *Ishigakijima chōsa hōkokusho,* vol. 1, 115–132. Okinawa: Okinawa Kokusai Daigaku Nantō Bunka Kenkyūjo, 2003.
Elkins, Caroline, and Susan Pedersen. *Settler Colonialism in the Twentieth Century.* London: Routledge, 2005.

Eskildsen, Robert. "Of Civilization and Savages: The Mimetic Imperialism of Japan's 1874 Expedition to Taiwan." *American Historical Review* 107, no. 2 (2002): 388–418.
Fisch, Arnold G., Jr. *Military Government in the Ryukyu Islands, 1945–1950.* Washington, DC: Center for Military History, United States Army, 1988.
Fischer-Tiné, Harald, and Susanne Gehrmann. *Empires and Boundaries: Rethinking Race, Class, and Gender in Colonial Settings.* New York: Routledge, 2009.
Fitzpatrick, Matthew P. "The Threat of 'Woolly-Haired Grandchildren': Race, the Colonial Family and German Nationalism." *History of the Family* 14, no. 4 (2009): 356–368.
Fix, Douglas L. "Reading the Numbers: Ethnicity, Violence and Wartime Mobilization in Colonial Taiwan." In *Taiwan under Japanese Colonial Rule, 1895–1945: History, Culture, Memory,* edited by Liao Ping-hui and David Der-wei Wang, 327–357. New York: Columbia University Press, 2006.
Forest, Timothy S. "Defenders of Empire or Agents of Ruin? Hebridean Scot Colonies in British Columbia in the 1920s." *Canadian Historical Review* 96, no. 2 (2015): 194–222.
Fujikane, Candace, and Jonathan Y. Okamura, eds. *Asian Settler Colonialism: From Local Governance to the Habits of Everyday Life in Hawaii.* Honolulu: University of Hawai'i Press, 2008.
Fukaya Katsumi. "Sōron: Bakuhansei kokka to iiki, ikoku." In *Bakuhansei kokka to iiki, ikoku,* edited by Katō Eiichi, Kitajima Manji, and Fukaya Katsumi, 9–44. Tokyo: Azekura shobō, 1989.
Fukumura Yoshiko. "Sharyō-tō (gen Waheijima) no omoide." In *Ryūkyū Uminchu no* Zō *konryō kinenshi,* edited by Ryūkyū Uminchu no Zō Konryū Kiseikai, 10. Okinawa: Ryūkyū Uminchu no Zō Konryū Kiseikai, 2011.
Fukuzawa Yukichi. "Kikō to sanshoku." 1895. Reprinted in *Fukuzawa Yukichi zenshū,* vol. 15, 255–268. 2nd ed. Tokyo: Iwanami shoten, 1970.
Furushō Hiroyuki, ed. *Sōritsu yonjusshūnen kinenshi.* Taihoku-shū: Giran Jinjō Kōtō Shōgakkō, 1941.
Gaimushō Kanrikyoku Sōmu-bu Nanpō-ka. "Taiwan no genkyō." In *Kaigai hikiage kankei shiryō shūsei,* vol. 31, edited by Katō Kiyofumi, 31–67. Tokyo: Yumani shobō, 2002.
Gaimushō Tsūshōkyoku. *Kaigai kakuchi zairyū honpōjin shokugyōbetsu jinkōhyō.* Tokyo: Gaimushō Tsūshōkyoku, 1928.
Gan Kyōju (Yan Xinru). "Shokuminchi toshi Taihoku ni okeru Nihonjin no seikatsu bunka: 'Kūkan' to 'jikan' ni okeru ishoku, hen'yō." PhD diss., University of Tokyo, 2009.
Gangshan District Office. "Lishi yange." Gangshan District Office. http://www.gsto.gov.tw/main.php?mode=content&act=history&content_id=E01. Accessed April 23, 2014.
Gellner, David N., ed. *Borderland Lives in Northern South Asia: Non-state Perspectives.* Durham, NC: Duke University Press, 2013.
Genga Chōyō. "Yomitan shusshin hatsu no igaku hakase Genga Chōkō." In *Yomitan no senjintachi,* edited by Yomitan Sonshi Henshū Īnkai, 247–264. Okinawa: Yomitan Sonshi Henshū Īnkai, 2005.
van Gennep, Arnold. *The Rites of Passage.* Chicago: University of Chicago Press, 1960.
Haebaru Eiiku. *Minami no shima no shinbunjin: Shiryō ni miru sono hensen.* Okinawa: Hirugisha, 1988.
Hamamatsu Tetsuo. *Okinawa isei kyōshūjo kinenshi.* Okinawa: Okinawa-ken Ishi Dōsōkai, 1929.

Hamashita Takeshi. "The Intra-regional System in East Asia in Modern Times." In *Network Power: Japan and Asia,* edited by Peter J. Katzenstein and Takashi Shiraishi, 113–135. Ithaca, NY: Cornell University Press, 1997.

Hanlon, David. *Making Micronesia: A Political Biography of Tosiwo Nakayama.* Honolulu: University of Hawai'i Press, 2014.

Hara Tomoaki. *Minzoku bunka no gendai: Okinawa, Yonaguni-jima no "minzoku" eno manazashi.* Tokyo: Dōseisha, 2000.

Harrell, Paula. *Sowing the Seeds of Change: Chinese Students, Japanese Teachers, 1895–1905.* Stanford, CA: Stanford University Press, 1992.

Haruyama Meitetsu and Wakabayashi Masahiro, eds. *Nihon shokuminchishugi no seijiteki tenkai: Sono tōchi taisei to Taiwan no minzoku undo, 1895–1934-nen.* Tokyo: Ajia Seikei Gakkai, 1980.

Hashimoto, Akiko. *The Long Defeat: Cultural Trauma, Memory, and Identity in Japan.* Oxford: Oxford University Press, 2015.

Hattori Kazuma. "Kindaiteki seitōgyō no seiritsuki ni okeru hutari no kigyōka: Suzuki Tōsaburō to Nakagawa Toranosuke." In *Kindai kigyōka no hassei: Shihonshugi keizai seiritsu katei no ichimen,* edited by Shakai Keizaishi Gakkai, 105–144. Tokyo: Yūhikaku, 1963.

Hawai'i United Okinawa Association, ed. *Uchinanchu: A History of Okinawans in Hawaii.* Honolulu: Center for Oral History Social Science Research Institute, College of Social Sciences, University of Hawai'i at Mānoa, 1981.

Hayase Shinzō.*"Benketto imin" no kyozō to jitsuzō.* Tokyo: Dōbunkan, 1989.

———. "Tribes on the Davao Frontier, 1899–1941." *Philippine Studies* 33, no. 2 (1985): 139–150.

Hayashi Hiroshi. *Okinawasen: Kyōsei sareta shūdan jiketsu.* Tokyo: Yoshikawa Kōbunkan, 2009.

Hazama Rihō. "Letter from Dr. Hazama." In *Papers of James Watkins IV,* vol. 38, edited by Committee Members for the Watkins Papers Publication, 155–156. Okinawa: Ryokuindō shoten, 1994.

Headquarters Ryukyu Command Military Government. "Repatriation to and from the Ryukyus during Period 1 July 1946 to 31 December 1946," January 9, 1947. S100584H, 06-A-14-03. Okinawa Prefectural Archives, Okinawa Prefecture.

Higa Atsuo. "Nikkyō gojūman wo okuru: Kiryū jōsenchi shireibu heitanhan roeichi kinmu taichō wo meizerarete." In *Ryūkyū kanpei tenmatsuki,* edited by Taiwan Hikiage Kankō Kiseikai, 95–107. Okinawa: Taiwan Hikiageki Kankō Kiseikai, 1986. [*RKT*]

Hokubei Okinawajinshi Henshū Īnkai. *Hokubei Okinawajinshi.* Los Angeles: Okinawa Club of America Inc., 1981.

Hook, Glen D., and Richard Siddle, eds. *Japan and Okinawa: Structure and Subjectivity.* Reprint. London: Routledge, 2014.

Huang Chia-chi. "Nihon tōchi jidai ni okeru 'naitai kyōkon' no kōzō to tenkai." *Hikaku kazokushi kenkyū* 27 (2012):128–155.

Iba Nantetsu. *Yaeyama jinji kōshinroku.* Yaeyama, Ryukyu: Yaeyama Jinji Kōshinroku Henshūsho, 1951.

Ichiki Kitokurō. "Ichiki shokikan torishirabesho." In *Okinawa kenshi,* vol. 14, *Shiryō-hen 4, Zassan no. 1,* edited by Ryūkyū Seifu, 491–606. Ryukyu: Ryūkyū Seifu, 1965.

Ide Kiwata. *Taiwan chisekishi.* Taiwan nichinichi shinpōsha, 1937. Reprint. Tokyo: Seishisha, 1988.

Igarashi, Yoshikuni. *Homecomings: The Belated Return of Japan's Lost Soldiers.* New York: Columbia University Press, 2016.
Īјima Mariko. "Firipin Nikkei diasupora no sengo no 'kikan' keiken to kokyō ninshiki." *Bunka jinruigaku* 81(2016): 592–614.
Īјima Wataru. *Mararia to teikoku: Shokuminchi igaku to Higashi Ajia no kōiki chitsujo.* Tokyo: Tokyo Daigaku shuppankai, 2005.
Ikeda, Kyle. *Okinawan War Memory: Transgenerational Trauma and the War Fiction of Medoruma Shun.* Abingdon, UK: Routledge, 2014.
Ikema Nae. *Yonaguni Yūbinkyoku to chichi no shōgai: Yonaguni Yūbinkyoku sōritsu nanajūsshūnen.* Okinawa: privately printed, 1996.
Imaizumi Yumiko. "Nan'yō guntō hikiagesha no dantai keisei to sono katsudō: Nihon no haisen chokugo wo chūshin to shite." *Shiryō Henshūshitsu kiyō* 30 (2005): 1–44.
———. "Okinawa imin shakai: Sec. 1 Nan'yō." In *Okinawa-kenshi, Kakuron-hen,* vol. 5, *Kindai,* edited by Zaidan Hōjin Okinawa-ken Bunka Shinkōkai Shiryō Henshūshitsu, 347–369. Okinawa: Okinawa-ken Kyōiku Īnkai, 2011. [*OKK*]
Imaizumi Yumiko, Yanagisawa Asobu, and Kimura Kenji, eds. *Nihon teikoku hōkaiki "hikiage" no hikaku kenkyū.* Tokyo: Nihon Keizai Hyōronsha, 2016.
Inafuku Moriteru. *Okinawa igakushi: Kinsei, kindai-hen.* Okinawa: Wakanatsusha, 1998.
Inafuku Zenshi. "Kyōdo no rikugun butai to kōdō wo tomo ni shite." In *Ryūkyū kanpei tenmatsuki,* edited by Taiwan Hikiage Kankō Kiseikai, 21–36. Okinawa: Taiwan Hikiageki Kankō Kiseikai, 1986. [*RKT*]
———. "Waga seishun no koro." *Naha-shi ishikai hō,* June 1977, 25.
Ishigaki Shishi Henshū Īnkai. *Ishigaki-shishi, Kakuron-hen, Minzoku.* Vol. 1. Okinawa: Ishigaki-shi, 1995.
Ishihara Masaie. *Kūhaku no Okinawa shakaishi: Senka to mitsubōeki no jidai.* Okinawa: Banseisha, 2000.
Ishii Takashi. *Meiji shoki no Nihon to Higashi Ajia.* Tokyo: Yūrindō, 1982.
Ishikawa Tomonori. "Kaigai imin no tenkai." In *Okinawa-kenshi,* vol. 7, *Imin,* edited by Okinawa-ken Kyōiku Īnkai, 205–420. Okinawa: Okinawa-ken Kyōiku Īnkai, 1974.
———. *Nihon imin no chirigakuteki kenkyū: Okinawa, Hiroshima, Yamaguchi.* Okinawa: Yōju Shorin, 1997.
———. "A Study of the Historical Geography of Early Okinawan Immigrants to the Hawaiian Islands." In *Uchinanchu: A History of Okinawans in Hawaii,* edited by Hawai'i United Okinawa Association, 80–104. Honolulu: Center for Oral History Social Science Research Institute, College of Social Sciences, University of Hawai'i at Mānoa, 1981.
Itosu Masa. "Sakiyama-ke to chichi." In *Chichi no nukumori toki wo koete,* edited by Itosu Masa, 87–100. Okinawa: privately printed, 1994. [*CNT*]
Iwashita Akihiro, ed. *Nihon no kokkyō: Ika ni kono "jubaku" wo tokuka.* Hokkaidō: Hokkaidō Daigaku shuppankai, 2010.
Iwashita Kiyoko. "Daiichiji Taisengo ni okeru 'shokugyō fujin' no keisei." *Shakaigaku hyōron* 76 (1969): 41–53.
Jackson, Alvin. "Ireland, the Union, and the Empire, 1800–1960." In *Ireland and the British Empire,* edited by Kevin Kenny, 123–153. Oxford: Oxford University Press, 2004.
Kabahara Kōji. *Dabao hōjin kaitakushi.* Davao, Philippines: Nippi shinbunsha, 1938.
Kabira Chōshin. *Rirekisho* [curriculum vitae], n.d. Kabirake Shiryō, 10000287, box 10-029, Naha City Museum of History, Okinawa Prefecture.
———. *Shūsengo no Okinawa bunka gyōseishi.* Okinawa: Okinawasha, 1997.

———. "Taiwan no omoide: Taiwan ni okeru kyōdoshi kenkyū." *Shin Okinawa bungaku,* October 1968, 162–167.

———. "Waga hansei no ki, no. 4: Rekishi to minzoku to hito." *Okinawa shunjū,* January 1974, 46–57.

———. "Waga hansei no ki, no. 7." *Okinawa shunjū,* August 1974, 78–89.

———. "Waga hansei no ki, no. 11." *Okinawa shunjū,* June 1975, 78–89.

———. *Watashi no sengoshi.* Vol. 6, edited by Okinawa Taimususha. Okinawa: Okinawa Taimususha, 1982.

Kanazawa Ika Daigaku, ed. *Kanazawa Ika Daigaku ichiran Shōwa 7-nen.* Ishikawa: Kanazawa Ika Daigaku, 1935.

Kaneshiro, Edith M. "'The Other Japanese': Okinawan Immigrants to the Philippines, 1903–1941." In *Okinawan Diaspora,* edited by Ronald Y. Nakasone, 71–89. Honolulu: University of Hawai'i Press, 2002.

Kaneto Sachiko. "'Kyōkai' kara toraeru shokuminchi Taiwan no josei rōdō to esunikku kankei: Yaeyama josei no shokuminchi Taiwan eno idō to 'jochū rōdō to no kanren kara." *Rekishi hyōron,* 722 (2010): 19–33.

Kanna Keiko, Ryō Jinushien, and Tomomi Negawa. Special issue, "Taiwan ni okeru Ryūkyū kankei shiryō chōsa hōkoku: Taiwan Sōtokufu bunsho, Taiwanshō gyōsei chōkan kōsho shiryō wo chūshin ni." *Shiryō Henshūshitsu kiyō* 31 (2006): 77–112.

Kan'no Hisao. *Nanmeikai kaiin meibo.* Taihoku-shi: Nanmei-kai, 1941.

Katō Hisako. *Umi no kariudo Okinawa gyomin: Itoman uminchu no rekishi to seikatsushi.* Tokyo: Gendai shokan, 2012.

Kawahara Isao. *Taiwan hikiage, ryūyō kiroku.* Vol. 8. Tokyo: Yumani shobō, 1998.

Kawarabayashi Naoto. "Hikiagego no hōjin 'Nanpō' keiken no yukue." In *Nan'yō guntō to teikoku, kokusai chitsujo,* edited by Asano Toyomi, 97–138. Tokyo: Jigakusha shuppan, 2007.

Kawashima Jun. "Nahashi Rekishi Hakubutsukan shozō 'Rekidai hōan' ni kansuru shiryōteki kōsatsu: Seisei, raireki, mokuroku kijutsu ni shōten wo atete." *Tsuboya Yakimono Hakubutsukan kiyō* 13 (2012): 7–31.

Kenny, Kevin, ed. *Ireland and the British Empire.* Oxford: Oxford University Press, 2004.

Kikuchi Isao. "Kyōkai to etonosu." In *Ajia no naka no Nihonshi: Chiiki to etonosu,* edited by Arano Yasunori, Ishii Masatoshi, and Murai Shōsuke, 55–80. Tokyo: Tokyo Daigaku shuppankai, 1992.

Kimura, Yukiko. "Social-Historical Background of the Okinawans in Hawaii." In *Uchinanchu: A History of Okinawans in Hawaii,* edited by Hawai'i United Okinawa Association, 51–71. Honolulu: Center for Oral History Social Science Research Institute, College of Social Sciences, University of Hawai'i at Mānoa, 1981.

Kinjō Isao. "Imin no shakaiteki haikei." In *Okinawa-kenshi,* vol. 7, *Imin,* edited by Okinawa-ken Kyōiku Īnkai, 89–204. Okinawa: Okinawa-ken Kyōiku Īnkai, 1974.

———. "Okinawa imin no keii." In *Okinawa-kenshi,* vol. 7, *Imin,* edited by Okinawa-ken Kyōiku Īnkai, 89–204. Okinawa: Okinawa-ken Kyōiku Īnkai, 1974.

———. "Yaeyama no tōgyō ni tsuite." *Okinawa rekishi kenkyū* 10 (1973): 40–60.

Kinjō Kiyomatsu. *Insui shigen: Kinjō Kiyomatsu ikōshū.* Okinawa: privately printed, 1977.

Kitamura Kae. *Nihon shokuminchika no Taiwan senjūmin kyōikushi.* Hokkaido: Hokkaidō Daigaku tosho kankōkai, 2008.

Kiyuna Tsugumasa. "Koritsu muen de attemo: Isshi kōha no ben." *Shin Okinawa bungaku* 55 (1983): 122–131.

Kō Sekai (Xu Shikai). *Nihon tōchika no Taiwan: Teikō to dan'atsu.* Tokyo: Tōkyo Daigaku shuppankai, 1971.

Kobashigawa, Ben. "Okinawan Issei Identity: Pride and Shame among the Early Immigrants." In *Reflections on the Okinawan Experience: Essays Commemorating 100 Years of Okinawan Immigration,* ed. Ronald Y. Nakasone, 29–44. Fremont, CA: Dharma Cloud Publishers, 1996.

Kobata Atsushi. "'Rekidai hōan' ni tsuite no omoide: Watashi no Ryūkyūshi kenkyū." *Okinawa bunka kenkyū* 16 (1990): 1–12.

Kobata Atsushi et al. "Okinawa no bunka wo kataru." *Nantō,* no. 2 (May 19, 1942): 118–125.

Koike Yasuhito. *Ryūkyū rettō no "mitsubōeki" to kyōkaisen: 1949–1951.* Tokyo: Shinwasha, 2015.

Kokaze Hidemasa. "Kai chitsujo to Nihon gaikō: Ryūkyū, Chōsen wo megutte." In *Meiji Ishin to Ajia,* edited by Meiji Ishin Gakkai, 3–29. Tokyo: Yoshikawa Kōbunkan, 2001.

Komagome Takeshi. *Shokuminchi teikoku Nihon no bunka tōgō.* Tokyo: Iwanami shoten, 1996.

Kōnan Shinbunsha, ed. *Taiwan jinshikan.* Taihoku-shi: Kōnan Shinbunsha, 1943.

Kondō Ken'ichirō. "Kindai Okinawa ni okeru hōgenfuda (1): Yaeyama chiiki no gakkō kinenshi wo shiryō to shite." *Aichi kenritsu daigaku bungakubu ronshū* 47 (1998): 29–49.

———. "Okinawa ni okeru imin / dekasegisha kyōiku: Okinawa-ken shotō kyōiku kenkyūkai 'Shima no Kyōiku (1928)' wo chūshin ni." *Kyōikugaku kenkyū* 62, no. 2 (1995): 116–124.

Kondō Masami. *Sōryokusen to Taiwan: Nihon shokuminchi hōkai no kenkyū.* Tokyo: Tōsui shobō, 1996.

Kōseishō, ed. "III-7 Nan'yō guntō zaijū hōjin no naichi hikiage oyobi sono zaigai zaisan nit suite." In *Hikiage engo no kiroku, zoku zoku,* vol. 3, edited by Kōseishō, 379–384. Tokyo: Kōseishō, 2000.

Kōseishō Engokyoku. *Hikiage to engo 30-nen no ayumi.* Tokyo: Gyōsei, 1978.

Kōseishō Imukyoku, ed. *Isei hyakunenshi (kijutsu-hen).* Tokyo: Gyōsei, 1976.

Kuninaga Michiko, Noiri Naomi, Matsuda Hiroko, Matsuda Yoshitaka, and Mizuta Kenji, eds. *Ishigakijima de Taiwan wo aruku: Mō hitotsu no Okinawa gaido.* Okinawa: Okinawa Taimususha, 2012.

Lai Huang-wen. "Traveling Abroad, Writing Nationalism, and Performing in Disguise: People on the Japanese Colonial Boundaries, 1909–1943." PhD diss., University of Pennsylvania, 2016.

Li Yuan-hui. *Riju shiqi Taiwan shifan jiaoyu jidu.* Taipei: Nantian shuju, 1997.

Lin Yu-ru. "Zhimindi de chanye zhili yu mosuo: Mingzhi mounian Taiwan de guanying Ribenren yuye yimin." *Xin shixue* 24, no. 3 (2013): 95–133.

Lo, Ming-Cheng M. *Doctors within Borders: Profession, Ethnicity, and Modernity in Colonial Taiwan.* Berkeley: University of California Press, 2002.

Maehira Fusa'aki. "Bakumatsu ishinki ni okeru Ryūkyū no ichi." In *Meiji Ishin to Ajia,* edited by Meiji Ishin Gakkai, 181–205. Tokyo: Yoshikawa Kōbunkan, 2001.

Makino Kiyoshi. *Shin Yaeyama rekishi.* Okinawa: privately printed, 1972.

Maruyama Kandō and Imamura Nanshi. "Decchi seido no kenkyū." 1912. Reprinted in *Ningen keisei to shakai: Gakkō, chīki, shokugyō,* vol. 4, *Decchi to totei no yōsei,* edited by Kimura Hajime, 1–18. Tokyo: Kuresu shuppan, 1998.

Masuda Hiroshi. *Dainippon teikoku no hōkai to hikiage, fukuin.* Tokyo: Keiō Daigaku shuppankai, 2012.

Matayoshi Seikiyo. *Nihon shokuminchika no Taiwan to Okinawa.* Okinawa: Aki-shobō, 1990.

———. "Taiwan 2.28 jiken to Okinawa." *Shokuminchi bunka kenkyū* 6 (2007): 155–157.

Matsuda, Hiroko. "Yaeyama: From Periphery of the Ryukyus to Frontier of Japan." *Japanese Studies* 28, no. 2 (2008): 149–164.

Matsuda Yoshitaka. *Taiwan sokai: "Ryūkyū nanmin" no ichinen jūikkagetsu.* Okinawa: Nanzansha, 2010.

———. *Yaeyama no Taiwanjin.* Okinawa: Nanzansha, 2005.

———. *Yonaguni Taiwan ōraiki: "Kokkyō" ni kurasu hitobito.* Okinawa: Nanzansha, 2013.

Matsumura, Wendy. *The Limits of Okinawa: Japanese Capitalism, Living Labor, and Theorizations of Community.* Durham, NC: Duke University Press, 2015.

Matsushita Hitoshi. *Ishihara Yatarōden.* Okinawa: Ishihara Yatarō-shi Kenshōkai, 1963.

McCormack, Gavan, and Satoko Oka Norimatsu. *Resistant Islands: Okinawa Confronts Japan and the United States.* Lanham, MD: Rowman & Littlefield, 2012.

Mihalopoulos, Bill. *Sex in Japan's Globalization, 1870–1930: Prostitutes, Emigration and Nation Building.* London: Ouckering & Chatto, 2011.

Miki Takeshi. "Iriomote tankō gaishi: Sono shihon to rōdō no hensen." *Yaeyama bunka* 3 (1975): 4–63.

———. "Yaeyama gasshūkoku wo ikiru." In *Yaima nasake ni sasaerare,* edited by Miki Takeshi, 171–273. Okinawa: privately printed, 2002.

Mio Yūko, Endō Hisashi, and Ueno Hiroko, eds. *Teikoku Nihon no kioku: Taiwan, Kyūnan'yō guntō ni okeru gairai seiken no jūsōka to datsushokuminchika.* Tokyo: Keiō Daigaku shuppankai, 2016.

Mizuno Norihito. "Early Meiji Politics towards the Ryukyus and the Taiwanese Aboriginal Territories." *Modern Asian Studies* 43, no. 3 (2009): 683–739.

Mizuta Kenji. "Nihon shokuminchika no Taihoku ni okeru Okinawa shusshin 'jochū.'" *Shisen* 98 (2003): 36–55.

———. "Okinawa-ken kara Taiwan e no ijū: Dainiji sekai taisen mae ni okeru Yaeyama-gun shusshinsha wo chūshin to shite." In *Chirigaku no shosō: "Jisshō" no chihei,* edited by Kansai Daigaku Bungakubu Chirigaku Kyōshitsu, 380–397. Tokyo: Taimeidō, 1998.

Mochizuki Masahiro. "Koga Tatsushirō to Osaka Koga Shōten." *Nantō shigaku* 35 (1990): 1–21.

Mōri Toshihiko. *Taiwan shuppei: Dainihon teikoku no kaimakugeki.* Tokyo: Chūkō Shinsho, 1996.

Morita Shin'ya. "Kankōkyaku ni totte no sairei, chiiki ni totteno sairei: Okinawa Taketomijima no Tanedorisai kara." In *Kioku,* edited by Iwamoto Michiya, 178–203. Tokyo: Asakura shoten, 2003.

Morris-Suzuki, Tessa. *Henkyō kara nagameru: Ainu ga keiken suru kindai.* Tokyo: Misuzu shobō, 2000.

———. "Lines in the Snow: Imagining the Russo-Japanese Frontier." *Pacific Affairs* 72, no. 1 (1999): 57–77.

Motomura Ikue. "Nihon tōchika no Taiwan to Miyako shusshin kyōin: Totai kyōin no kibo to sono haikei ni tsuite." *Ryūkyū shigaku* 17 (2015): 29–39.

Murai Shōsuke. *Kyōkai wo matagu hitobito.* Tokyo: Yamakawa shuppansha, 2006.

Murai Shōsuke, Satō Makoto, and Yoshida Nobuyuki. *Kyōkai no Nihonshi.* Tokyo: Yamakawa shuppansha, 1997.

Murakami Nobuhiko. *Taishōki no shokugyō fujin*. Tokyo: Domesu shuppan, 1983.
Murayama Meitoku. *Filipin gaiyō to Okinawa kenjin*. Davao, Philippines: Davao jihōsha, 1929.
Naikaku Tōkeikyoku. *Kokusei chōsa hōkoku*. Vol. 4, *Okinawa-ken*. Tokyo: Naikaku Tōkeikyoku, 1935.
———. *Kokusei chōsa hōkoku, Shōwa 5-nen*. Vol. 2. Tokyo: Tokyo Tōkei Kyōkai, 1939.
Nakamura Haruna. "Sengo Taiwan ni okeru Okinawa sekimin no hikiage no yōsō: 'Ryūkyū kanpei' no keisei katei to sono yakuwari." *Okinawa bunka* 49, no. 2 (2015): 18–41.
Nakamura Tadayuki. "Henshū kōki." *Nantō*, no. 3 (September 30, 1944): 230.
Nakasone, Ronald Y. "An Impossible Possibility." In *Okinawan Diaspora*, edited by Ronald Y. Nakasone, 3–25. Honolulu: University of Hawai'i Press, 2002.
———. *Okinawan Diaspora*. Honolulu: University of Hawai'i Press, 2002.
———. *Reflections on the Okinawan Experience: Essays Commemorating 100 Years of Okinawan Immigration*. Fremont, CA: Dharma Cloud Publishers, 1996.
Namihira Tsuneo. "'Ryūkyū shobun' saikō: Ryūkyū han'ō sappō to Taiwan shuppei mondai." *Seisakukagaku, Kokusaikankei ronshū* 11 (2009): 1–78.
Nantō Hakkōjo. *Nantō kaiin meibo*. 1941. Kabirake Shiryō, 10001540, box 10-092, Naha City Museum of History, Okinawa Prefecture.
Nan'yōchō. *Nan'yō guntō tōsei chōsa hōkoku, Taishō 14-nen*. Koror: Nan'yōchō, 1927.
———. *Nan'yō guntō tōsei chōsasho, Shōwa 5-nen*. Vol. 3. Koror: Nan'yōchō, 1932.
Nan'yōchō Chōkan Kanbō Bunshoka, ed. *Nan'yō guntō tōsei chōsasho Shōwa 10-nen*. Vol. 1. Tokyo: Nan'yōchō Chōkan Kanbō Bunshoka, 1937.
Nanzansha, ed. *Yaeyamapitu no shōzo*. Okinawa: Nanzansha, 2004.
Nelson, Christopher T. *Dancing with the Dead: Memory, Performance, and Everyday Life in Postwar Okinawa*. Durham, NC: Duke University Press, 2008.
Ng Chao-tng (Huang Chao-tang). *Taiwan minshukoku no kenkyū: Taiwan dokuritsu undōshi no ichidanshō*. Tokyo: Tōkyo Daigaku shuppankai, 1970.
Nishimura Kazuyuki. "Taiwan higashi kaigan ni okeru Kanjin, Ami gyomin to Okinawa gyomin no sesshoku: Shokumin tōchi makki kara sengo shoki wo chūshin ni." In *Shokuminchi no Chōsen to Taiwan: Rekishi, bunka jinruigakuteki kenkyū*, edited by Choi Kilsong and Harada Tamaki, 47–82. Tokyo: Daiichi shobō, 2007.
Noiri Naomi. "Okinawa ni okeru Taiwan hikiagesha no tokuchō: Hikiagesha zaigai jijitsu chōsahyō to ken, shichōson no taiken kiroku wo chūshin ni." In *Teikoku igo no hito no idō: Posuto koroniarizumu to gurōbarizumu no kōsakuten*, edited by Araragi Shinzō, 305–350. Tokyo: Bensei shuppan, 2013.
"Note by Gan Yanjia sending to Chen Yi, February 5, 1946." Special issue, "Taiwan ni okeru Ryūkyū kankei shiryō chōsa hōkoku: Taiwan Sōtokufu bunsho, Taiwanshō gyōsei chōkan kōsho shiryō wo chūshin ni," edited by Kanna Keiko, Ryo Jinushien, and Tomomi Negawa, *Shiryō Henshūshitsu kiyō* 31 (2006): 101.
Ō Tetsugun (Wang Tiejun). "Gaichi tōchi to keisatsu kanri: Taiwan tōchi ni okeru Taiwan sōtokufu keisatsukan." *Chūkyō hōgaku* 45, nos. 3–4 (2011): 425–572.
Oda Toshirō. *Taiwan igaku gojūnen*. Tokyo: Igaku shoin, 1974.
O'Dwyer, Emer. *Significant Soil: Settler Colonialism and Japan's Urban Empire in Manchuria*. Cambridge, MA: Harvard University Asia Center, 2015.
Oguma Eiji. *"Nihonjin" no kyōkai: Okinawa, Ainu, Taiwan, Chōsen, shokuminchi shihai kara fukki undō made*. Tokyo: Shin'yōsha, 1998.
Oguma Makoto, ed. *"Kyōkai" wo koeru Okinawa: Hito, bunka, minzoku*. Tokyo: Shinwasha, 2016.

Ōhama Eishō. *Ōhama Eishō shishi: Yaeyama "Hama no yu" no Shōwa*. Okinawa: Sakishima Bunka Kenkyūsho, 1992.

Okamoto Makiko. *Shokuminchi kanryō no seijishi: Chōsen, Taiwan sōtokufu to teikokunihon*. Tokyo: Sangensha, 2008.

———. "Shokuminchi tōchi shoki Taiwan ni okeru Naichijin no seiji, genron katsudō 6-3 hō taisei wo chūshin to shite." *Shakai kagaku* 86 (2010): 91–123.

———. "Shokuminchi zaijūsha no seiji sanka wo meguru sōkoku: 'Taiwan dōkakai' wo chūshin to shite." *Shakai kagaku* 89 (2010): 95–131.

Okinawa Club of America, ed. *History of the Okinawans in North America*. Los Angeles: Asian American Studies Center, University of California, Los Angeles, and Okinawa Club of America, 1988.

Okinawa Gaichi Hikiagesha Kyōkai, Ishigakishibu. *Zaigai shisan hoshō kakutoku undō no kiroku: 1956–1996*. Okinawa: Okinawa Gaichi Hikiagesha Kyōkai, Ishigakishibu, 1997.

Okinawa Ishikai Kaishi Hensan Īnkai. *Okinawa ishikai-shi: Shūsen kara sokoku fukki made*. Okinawa: Okinawa-ken Ishikai, 2000.

Okinawa Taimususha. *Gendai Okinawa jimbutsu sanzennin*. Okinawa: Okinawa Taimususha, 1966.

Okinawa-ken, ed. *Okinawa-ken tōkeisho, Shōwa 2-nen*. Vol. 2. Okinawa: Okinawa-ken, 1933.

———. *Okinawa-ken tōkeisho, Taishō 12-nen*. Vol. 2. Okinawa: Okinawa-ken, 1926.

———. "Yaeyama ken'iki no ichi, kikō, menseki, jinkō." Okinawa Prefectural Government. http://www.pref.okinawa.jp/site/somu/yaeyama/shinko/positionetc.html. Accessed October 20, 2016.

Okinawa-ken Chiji Kanbō, ed. *Okinawa-ken tōkeisho, Shōwa 7-nen*. Vol. 2. Okinawa: Okinawa-ken, 1939.

Okinawa-ken Kyōiku Īnkai, ed. *Okinawa-kenshi*. Vol. 7, *Imin*. Okinawa: Okinawa-ken Kyōiku Īnkai, 1974.

———. *Okinawa kenshi*. Vol. 10, *Okinawasen kiroku, no. 2*. Okinawa: Okinawa-ken, 1974.

Okinawa-ken Miyakojima Iryōshi Hensan Īnkai, ed. *Okinawa-ken Miyajijima iryōshi*. Okinawa: Okinawa-ken Miyakojima Ishikai, 2011.

Okinawa-ken Naimu-bu, Chōsa-ka. *Taishō 10-nen Okinawa-ken tōkeisho*. Vol. 1, *Naimu no bu*. Okinawa: Okinawa-ken, 1922.

———. *Taishō 11-nen Okinawa-ken tōkeisho*. Vol. 1, *Naimu no bu*. Okinawa: Okinawa-ken, 1924.

Okinawa-ken Sōmu-bu Tōkei-ka, ed. *Okinawa-ken tōkeisho, Shōwa 11-nen*. Vol. 2. Okinawa: Okinawa-ken, 1939.

Okinawa-ken Taiwan-kai. *Heisei 14-nen (dai 10 kai) Okinawa-ken Taiwan-kai, sōkai, konshinkai*. Okinawa: privately printed, 2002.

Oku Takenori. "Kokumin kokka no naka no josei: Meijiki wo chūshin ni." In *On'na to otoko no jikū: Nihon joseishi saikō*, vol. 5, *Semegiau on'na to otoko: Kindai*, edited by Tsurumi Kazuko and Kōno Nobuko, 415–450. Tokyo: Fujiwara shoten, 1995.

Okuda Akiko. "Jochū no rekishi." In *On'na to otoko no jikū: Nihon joseishi saikō*, vol. 5, *Semegiau on'na to otoko: Kindai (jō)*, edited by Tsurumi Kazuko and Kōno Nobuko, 376–410. Tokyo: Fujiwara shoten, 1995.

Okuno Shūji. *Natsuko: Okinawa mitsubōeki no joō*. Tokyo: Bungei Shunjū, 2007.

Ōkurashō Kanrikyoku. "Sōron no ichi." In *Nihonjin no kaigai katsudō ni kansuru rekishiteki chōsa,* vol. 1, edited by Kobayashi Hideo. Tokyo: Ōkurashō Kanrikyoku, 1949. Reprint, Tokyo: Yumani Shobō, 2000.

———. "Yoroku Nikkyō no tsuioku." In *Nihonjin no kaigai katsudō ni kansuru rekishiteki chōsa,* vol. 9, edited by Kobayashi Hideo, 75–168. Tokyo: Ōkurashō Kanrikyoku, 1950. Reprint, Tokyo: Yumani Shobō, 2000.

Onga Takashi. "Sengo Okinawa ni okeru hikiage no rekishiteki haikei to sono igi." *Higashi Ajia kindaishi* 10 (2007): 10–30.

Ōshiro Yoshimitsu. "Kyōmintai no zakkan." In *Ryūkyū kanpei tenmatsuki,* edited by Taiwan Hikiage Kankō Kiseikai, 259–262. Okinawa: Taiwan Hikiageki Kankō Kiseikai, 1986. [*RKT*]

Ōyama Masao. *Shōwa no Taketomi: Tareka kokyō wo omowazaru.* Okinawa: privately printed, 1985.

Park Sunmi. *Chōsen josei no chi no kaiyū: Shokuminchi bunka shihai to Nihon ryūgaku.* Tokyo: Yamakawa shuppansha, 2005.

Peattie, Mark R. *Nan'yō: The Rise and Fall of the Japanese in Micronesia, 1885–1945.* Honolulu: University of Hawai'i Press, 1988.

Pien Feng-kwei. "Rizhi shiqi zai Taibei de Chongshengren (1937–1943): Juji xiwang de chengshi." In *Haigang, hainan, haitou: Haiyang wenhua lunji,* edited by Chong Yingchang, 85–117. Taipei: Liren shuju, 2012.

Popular Memory Group. "Popular Memory: Theory, Politics, Method." In *The Oral History Reader,* 2nd ed., edited by Robert Perks and Alistair Thomson, 43–53. London: Routledge, 2006.

Portelli, Alessandro. "What Makes Oral History Different." In *The Oral History Reader,* edited by Robert Perks and Alistair Thomson, 32–42. 2nd ed. London: Routledge, 2006.

Prasenjit, Duara. *Sovereignty and Authenticity: Manchukuo and the East Asian Modern.* Lanham, MD: Rowman & Littlefield, 2003.

Pratt, Mary Louise. *Imperial Eyes: Travel Writing and Transculturation.* 2nd ed. London and New York: Routledge, 2008.

Rabson, Steve. *The Okinawan Diaspora in Japan: Crossing the Borders Within.* Honolulu: University of Hawai'i Press, 2011.

"Repatriation." In *Papers of James Watkins IV,* vol. 38, edited by Committee Members for the Watkins Papers Publication, 138–140. Okinawa: Ryokuindō shoten, 1994.

"Report on Okinawans in Taiwan." In *Papers of James Watkins IV,* vol. 38, edited by Committee Members for the Watkins Papers Publication, 148–154. Okinawa: Ryokuindō shoten, 1994.

Rin Patsu. *Okinawa pain sangyōshi.* Okinawa: Okinawa pain sangyōshi kankōkai, 1984.

Ritchie, Donald A. "Introduction: The Evolution of Oral History." In *The Oxford Handbook of Oral History,* edited by Donald A. Ritchie, 3–21. Oxford: Oxford University Press, 2010.

Ryūkyū Shinpō and San'in Chūō Shinpō. *Meguri no umi: Takeshima to Senkaku, kokkyō chiiki kara no toi.* Tokyo: Iwanami shoten, 2015.

Said, Edward. *Orientalism.* London: Routledge and Kegan Paul, 1978.

Saika Yajin. "Yamaguchi Hidetaka no shōgai (sono 13)." *Jikken ganka zasshi* 13, no. 110 (1930): 60–68.

———. "Yamaguchi Hidetaka no shōgai (sono 14)." *Jikken ganka zasshi* 13, no. 111 (1930): 58–66.

———. "Yamaguchi Hidetaka no shōgai (sono 15)." *Jikken ganka zasshi* 14, no. 115 (1931): 55–64.

Sakaguchi Naoki. *Senzen Dōshisha no Taiwan ryūgakusei: Kirisutokyō kokusaishugi no genryū wo tadoru.* Tokyo: Hakuteisha, 2002.

Sakai Tetsuya and Matsuda Toshihiko, eds. *Teikoku Nihon to shokuminchi daigaku.* Tokyo: Yumani shobō, 2014.

Sakiyama Toshi. "Ōkina ai ni tsutsumarete." In *Chichi no nukumori toki wo koete,* edited by Itosu Masa, 49–60. Okinawa: privately printed, 1994. [*CNT*]

Sensui Hidekazu. "Zai Taiwan Okinawajin hikiage ni kansuru oboegaki." *Project Paper* 25 (2012): 1–25.

Shibusawa Seien Kinen Zaidan Ryūmonsha. *Shibusawa Eiichi denkishiryō.* Vol. 11. Tokyo: Shibusawa Eiichi Denki Shiryō Kankōkai, 1956.

Shimabukuro Shinzō. "Nanbei imin no gaiyō." In *Okinawa-kenshi, Kakuron-hen,* vol. 5, *Kindai,* edited by Zaidan Hōjin Okinawa-ken Bunka Shinkōkai Shiryō Henshūshitsu, 370–385. Okinawa: Okinawa-ken Kyōiku Īnkai, 2011. [*OKK*]

Shimoji Yasuo. *Junsa hitosuji: Shimoji Keikō no shōgai.* Okinawa: privately printed, 2001.

Shinzato Kōtoku. "Gun'i to shite Okinawasen ni." In *Okinawa-ken Ishikaishi: Shūsen kara sokoku fukki made,* edited by Okinawa-ken Ishikai Kaishi Henshū Īnkai, 22–23. Okinawa: Okinawa-ken Ishikai Kaishi Henshū Īnkaim, 1987. Reprint, Okinawa: Okinawa-ken Ishikai, 2000.

Shiode Hiroyuki. *Ekkyōsha no seijishi: Ajia Taiheiyō ni okeru Nihonjin no imin to shokumin.* Aichi: Nagoya Daigaku shuppankai, 2015.

Shiomi Shunji. Hiroku, *Shūsen chokugo no Taiwan: Watashi no shūsen nikki.* Kōchi: Kōchi shinbunsha, 1979.

"Shiryō 1, Okinawa sekimin chōsasho." In *Ryūkyū kanpei tenmatsuki,* edited by Taiwan Hikiage Kankō Kiseikai, 305–362. Okinawa: Taiwan Hikiageki Kankō Kiseikai, 1986. [*RKT*]

Shōwa Igaku Senmon Gakkō, ed. *Shōwa igaku senmon gakkōyōran Shōwa 7-nen genzai.* Tokyo: Shōwa Igaku Senmon Gakkō, 1934.

Shozawa Jun and Lin Shobai (Lin Chu-mei), eds. *Taiwan no naka no Nihon kioku: Sengo no saikai ni yoru arata na imēji no kōchiku.* Tokyo: Sangensha, 2016.

Shu Keisoku (Zhu Huizu). "Teikokuteki idō to 'kindai' no enkinhō: Yaeyama shotō to shokuminchi Taiwan wo yukiki suru hitobito." *Ryūkyū Okinawa kenkyū* 3 (2010): 30–54.

Shu Tokulan (Zhu De-lan). "Kiryū Sharyōtō no Okinawajin shūraku (1895–1945)." In *Higashi Ajia no bunka to Ryūkyū, Okinawa: Ryūkyū/Okinawa, Nihon, Chūgoku, Etsunan,* edited by Uesato Ken'ichi et al., 49–77. Tokyo: Sairyūsha, 2010.

Sōmushō Tōkeikyoku. "1950-nen kokusei chōsa kekka gaiyō." In *1950-nen kokusei chōsa hōkoku (fukkokuban), dai 1-pen sōkatsu oyobi Okinawa guntō, sono 1,* edited by Sōmushō Tōkeikyoku, 33–46. Okinawa: Okinawa-ken Kikaku Kaihatsu-bu Tōkei-ka, 1998.

Stoler, Ann Laura. *Carnal Knowledge and Imperial Power: Race and the Intimate in Colonial Rule.* Berkeley: University of California Press, 2002.

———. "Sexual Affronts and Racial Frontiers: European Identities and the Cultural Politics of Exclusion in Colonial Southeast Asia." In *Tensions of Empire: Colonial Cultures in a Bourgeois World,* edited by Frederick Cooper and Ann Laura, 198–237. Berkeley: University of California Press, 1997.

Sudō Riichi. "Henshū kōki." *Nantō,* no.1 (August 28, 1940): 104–107.

Szczepanska, Kamila. *The Politics of War Memory in Japan: Progressive Civil Society Groups and Contestation of Memory of the Asia-Pacific War.* Abingdon, UK: Routledge, 2014.

Tai Kuo Hui. "Musha Hōki jiken no gaiyō to kenkyū no kon'nichiteki imi." In *Taiwan Musha Hōki Jiken: Kenkyū to shiryō,* edited by Tai Kuo Hui, 13–46. Tokyo: Shakai shisōsha, 1981.

Taihoku-shi Shokugyō Shōkaijo. "Shokugyō shōkaijo jigyō gaiyō." In *Shokuminchi shakai jigyō kankei shiryōshū: Keizai hogo jigyō: Shokugyō shōkai to rōdō jigyō,* edited by Kingendai Shiryō Kankōkai, 17–47. Taihoku-shi: Taihoku-shi Shokugyō Shōkaijo. 1935. Reprint, Tokyo: Kingendai Shiryō Kankōkai, 2001.

Taihoku-shū Giran Kōgakko. *Taihokushū Giran Kōgakkō sōritsu yonjusshūnen kinenshi.* Taihoku-shū: Taihoku-shū Giran Kōgakkō, 1939.

Taihoku Teikoku Daigaku, ed. *Taihoku Teikoku Daigaku ichiran Showa 18-nen.* Taihoku-shi: Taihoku Teikoku Daigaku, 1944.

Taipei 228 Memorial Museum. "Tansuo 228." Taipei 228 Memorial Museum. http://228memorialmuseum.gov.taipei/ct.asp?xItem=1938462&ctNode=41711&mp=11900A. Accessed January 31, 2017.

Taiwan Kyōikukai. "Taiwan gakuji hōki, kan, vol. 1." In *Nihon shokuminchi kyōiku seisaku shiryō shūsei, Taiwan-hen,* vol. 12, edited by Abe Hiroshi. 1929. Reprint, Tokyo: Ryūkei shosha, 2007.

———. *Taiwan kyōiku enkakushi.* Taihoku-shi: Taiwan Kyōikukai. 1939. Reprint, Tokyo: Seishinsha, 1982.

Taiwan Sōtokufu. *Shōwa 8-nen 7-gatsu 1-nichi genzai Taiwan Sōtokufu oyobi shozoku kansho shokuinroku.* Taihoku-shi: Taiwan Sōtokufu, 1933.

———. *Taiwan tōsei yōran, Shōwa 20-nen ban.* Taihoku-shi: Taiwan Sōtokufu, 1945. Reprint, Taipei: Chengwen chubanshe, 1985.

Taiwan Sōtokufu Igaku Senmon Gakkō. *Taiwan sōtokufu igaku senmon gakkō ichiran.* Taihoku-shi: Taiwan Sōtokufu Igaku Senmon Gakkō, 1922.

Taiwan Sōtokufu Kanbō Rinji Kokusei Chōsabu. *Kokusei chōsa kekkahyō, Showa 5-nen, Shūchō-hen, Taihoku-shū.* Taihoku-shi: Taiwan Sōtoku Kanbō Rinji Kokusei Chōsa-bu, 1934.

———. *Kokusei chōsa kekkahyō, Showa 5-nen, Zentō-hen.* Taihoku-shi: Taiwan Sōtokufu Kanbō Rinji Kokusei Chōsa-bu, 1934.

———. *Kokusei chōsa kekkahyō, Taishō 14-nen.* Taihoku-shi: Taiwan Sōtokufu Kanbō Rinji Kokusei Chōsabu, 1932.

———. *Taiwan kokusei chōsa shūkei genpyō.* Vol. 1, *Zentō no bu.* Taihoku-shi: Taiwan Sōtoku Kanbō Rinji Kokusei Chōsabu, 1924.

Taiwan Sōtokufu Keimukyoku, ed. "Musha jikenshi." N.d. Reprinted in *Taiwan Musha Hōki Jiken: Kenkyū to shiryō,* edited by Tai Kuo Hui, 353–520. Tokyo: Shakai shisōsha, 1981.

———. *Taiwan no keisatsu.* Taihoku-shi: Taiwan Sōtokufu Keimukyoku, 1932.

———. *Taiwan sōtokufu keisatsu enkakushi.* Vol. 2. Taihoku-shi: Taiwan Sōtokufu Keimukyoku, 1938. Reprint, Tokyo: Ryokuin Shobō, 1986. [*TSKE*]

Taiwan Sōtokufu Minseibu Bunshoka. *Taiwan sōtokufu daiichi tōkeisho.* Taihoku-ken: Taiwan Sōtoku Kanbō Tōkeika, 1899.

Taiwan Sōtokufu Taihoku Igaku Senmon Gakkō, ed. *Taiwan Sōtokufu Taihoku Igaku Senmon Gakkō ichiran, 1931–1933.* Taihoku-shi: Taiwan Sōtokufu Taihoku Igakku Senmon Gakkō, 1933.

Taiwan Sōtokufu Zanmu Seiri Jimusho. "Jimu hikitsugi hōkokusho." In *Kaigai hikiage kankei shiryō shūsei,* vol. 31, edited by Katō Kiyofumi, 132–175. Tokyo: Yumani shobō, 2002.

———. "Taiwan tōchi shūmatsu hōkokusho." In *Kaigai hikiage shiryō shūsei (kokugai-hen),* vol. 31, edited by Katō Kiyofumi, 7–29. Tokyo: Yumiani shobō, 2002.

"Taiwan zongdufu ziyuan xitong" (Taiwan sōtokufu shokuinroku keitō). Institute of Taiwan History, Academia Sinica. http://who.ith.sinica.edu.tw/mpView.action. Accessed November 3, 2014. [*TZZ*]

Takaesu Masaya. "Chihō seido no seibi: 'Naichi' no naka no 'ihō iki.'" In *Okinawa-kenshi, Kakuron-hen,* vol. 5, *Kindai,* edited by Zaidan Hōjin Okinawa-ken Bunka Shinkōkai Shiryō Henshūshitsu, 169–188. Okinawa: Okinawa-ken Kyōiku Īnkai, 2011. [*OKK*]

Takemoto Seigi. *Ari no uta: Takemoto Seigi jiden.* Okinawa: Miru shuppan, 1995.

Takushokumushō Nanbukyoku. *Taiwan keisei ippan.* Tokyo: Takushokumushō Nanbukyoku Dainika, 1897.

Tanaka Kōei. "Waga seishun no koro." *Naha-shi ishikai hō,* July 1981, 43.

Tasato Isei. "Yonjūnen mae no Taihoku shūchūei no omoide." In *Ryūkyū kanpei tenmatsuki,* edited by Taiwan Hikiage Kankō Kiseikai, 263–269. Okinawa: Taiwan Hikiageki Kankō Kiseikai, 1986. [*RKT*]

Thomassen, Bjørn. *Liminality and the Modern: Living through the In-Between.* London and New York: Routledge, 2014.

Thomson, Alistair. "Memory and Remembering in Oral History." In *The Oxford Handbook of Oral History,* edited by Donald A. Ritchie, 77–95. Oxford: Oxford University Press, 2010.

Tokushima Kenritsu Hakubutsukan. *Tokushima Kenritsu Hakubutsukan nyūsu,* no. 60 (September 5, 2005).

Tominaga Yūsuke. "Kiyuna Tsugumasa ga mita 'Nihon': Ryūkyū dokuritsu undō to 'Taiwanshō Ryūkyū Jinmin Kyōkai'no katsudō kara." Ōsaka Daigaku Nihon gakuhō 31 (2012): 87–109.

Tomishima Sōei. "Shinnyū tōeijin." In *Kumemura: Rekishi to jinbutsu,* edited by Ikemiya Masaharu, Kowatari Kiyotaka, and Dana Masayuki, 16–22. Okinawa: Hirugisha, 1993.

Tomiyama Ichirō. *Kindai Nihon shakai to "Okinawajin."* Tokyo: Nihon Hyōronsha, 1990.

Trefalt, Beatrice. *Japanese Army Stragglers and Memories of the War in Japan, 1950–1975.* London: Routledge, 2003.

Tseng Lin-yi. "A Cross-Boundary People: The Commercial Activities, Social Networks, and Travel Writings of Japanese and Taiwanese Sekimin in the Shantou Treaty Port (1895–1937) ."PhD diss., City University of New York, 2014.

Tsubota-Nakanishi Miki. "Okinawa e no hikiagesha ni yoru sengo Okinawa shakai e no setsuzoku: Taiwan deno kōmu keikensha to sono shijo wo chūshin ni." *Imin kenkyū* 9 (2013): 151–168.

Tsuda, Takeyuki. *Strangers in the Ethnic Homeland: Japanese Brazilian Return Migration in Transnational Perspective.* New York: Columbia University Press, 2003.

Tsuji Hiroshi. "Taiwan de tsuma ya ko wo nakushite." In *Ishigaki Shishi Henshūshitsu, shimin no senji, sengo taiken kiroku: Ano koro watashi wa,* vol. 1, edited by Ishigaki Shishi Henshūshitsu, 25–29. Okinawa: Ishigaki Shiyakusho, 1983.

———. *Taketomijima ima mukashi.* Okinawa: privately printed, 1985.

———. *Watashi no ayunda 88-nen: Tōkachi iwai ni yosete.* Okinawa: privately published, 2002.

Tsurumi, E. Patricia. *Japanese Colonial Education in Taiwan, 1895–1945*. Cambridge, MA: Harvard University Press, 1977.

Turner, Sarah, Christine Bonnin, and Jean Michaud. *Frontier Livelihoods: Hmong in the Sino-Vietnamese Borderlands*. Seattle: University of Washington Press, 2015.

Turner, Victor W. *The Ritual Process: Structure and Anti-Structure*. Chicago: Aldine Publishing Company, 1969.

Uchida, Jun. *Brokers of Empire: Japanese Settler Colonialism in Korea, 1876–1945*. Cambridge, MA: Harvard University Press, 2011.

Ueda Fujio. "Itoman gyomin to Tōnan Ajia." In *Ajia no umi to Nihonjin*, edited by Omoto Keiichi et al., 163–182. Tokyo: Iwanami shoten, 2001.

Veracini, Lorenzo. *Settler Colonialism: A Theoretical Overview*. Basingstoke, UK: Palgrave Macmillan, 2010.

Wakabayashi Masahiro. *Taiwan kōnichi undōshi kenkyū*. 2nd ed. Tokyo: Kenbun shuppan, 2001.

Wakukawa Seiei. *Jidai no senkusha Tōyama Kyūzō: Okinawa gendaishi no issetsu*. Honolulu: Toyama-Kyuzo Memorial Committee, 1953.

Watt, Lori. *When Empire Comes Home: Repatriation and Reintegration in Postwar Japan*. Cambridge, MA: Harvard University Press, 2010.

Weiner, Michael, ed. *Japan's Minorities: The Illusion of Homogeneity*. 2nd ed. London: Routledge, 2009.

Wilson, Thomas M., and Hastings Donnan, eds. *A Companion to Border Studies*. Chichester, UK: Wiley Blackwell, 2012.

Wu Li-jun. "Sengo Okinawa hontō ni okeru Taiwankei kakyō wo chūshin ni." PhD diss., University of the Ryukyus, 2012.

van Wyk Smith, Malvern. "Misfits in the Margins: Transgression and Transformation on the (South) African Frontier." *English in Africa* 43, no. 1 (2016): 9–30.

Xiang Biao, Brenda S. A. Yeo, and Mika Toyota, eds. *Returns: Nationalizing Transnational Mobility in Asia*. Durham, NC: Duke University Press, 2013.

Yabiku Mosei. *Burajiru Okinawa iminshi*. São Paulo: Zaihaku Okinawa Kenjinkai, 1987.

Yaeyama Rekishi Henshū Īnkai, ed. *Yaeyama rekishi*. Yaeyama, Ryukyu: Yaeyama Rekishi Henshū Īnkai, 1954.

Yakabi Osamu. *Okinawasen, beigun senryōshi wo manabinaosu: Kioku wo ikani keishō suruka*. Kanagawa: Seori shobō, 2009.

Yamamoto Kazuyuki. *Jiyū, byōdō, shokuminchisei: Taiwan ni okeru shokuminchi kyōiku seido no keisei*. Taipei: National Taiwan University Press, 2015.

Yamamoto Reiko. *Shokuminchi Taiwan no kōtō jogakkō kenkyū*. Tokyo: Taga shuppan, 1999.

Yamashita Etsuko. *Nihon josei kaihō shisō no kigen*. Tokyo: Kaimeisha, 1988.

Yanagita Kunio. *Kaijō no michi*. Tokyo: Chikuma shobō, 1962. Reprint, Tokyo: Chikuma shobō, 1967.

Yanaihara Tadao. "Teikokushugika no Taiwan." In *Yanaihara Tadao "Teikoku shugika no Taiwan" seidoku*, edited by Wakabayashi Masahiro. 1929. Reprint, Tokyo: Iwanami shoten, 2001.

Yans-McLaughlin, Virginia. "Metaphors of Self in History: Subjectivity, Oral Narratives, and Immigration Studies." In *Immigration Reconsidered: History, Sociology, and Politics*, edited by Virginia Yans-McLaughlin, 254–292. New York: Oxford University Press, 1990.

Yō Shishin (Yang Zi-cheng). "Teikoku kaitai no naka no jinteki idō: Sengo shoki Taiwan ni

okeru Nihonjin no hikiage oyobi ryūyō wo chūshin ni." *Higashi Ajia Chiiki Kenkyū* 13 (2006): 25–47.
Yogi Kisen. "Muenko sokai seru Okinawatōmin no sōkan ni kanshi tangan no ken." Special issue, "Taiwan ni okeru Ryūkyū kankei shiryō chōsa hōkoku: Taiwan Sōtokufu bunsho, Taiwanshō gyōsei chōkan kōsho shiryō wo chūshin ni," edited by Kanna Keiko, Ryo Jinushien, and Tomomi Negawa, *Shiryō Henshūshitsu kiyō* 31 (2006): 98–100.
Yonaguni Chōshi Hensan Īnkai. *Chinmoku no dotō: Dounan no 100-nen.* Okinawa: Yonaguni-chō, 1997.
Yoshino Kōzen. *Furusato to tomoni.* Okinawa: privately printed, 1967.
Young, Louise. *Japan's Total Empire: Manchuria and the Culture of Wartime Imperialism.* Berkeley: University of California Press, 1998.
Zhang Su-fen. *Taiwan de riben nongye yimin (1905–1945): Yi guanying yimin wei zhongxin.* Xindian: Guoshiguan, 2009.
Ziomek, Kristen L. "The Possibility of Liminal Colonial Subjecthood: Yayutz Bleyh and the Search for Subaltern Histories in the Japanese Empire." *Critical Asian Studies* 47, no. 1 (2015): 123–150.
Zwigenberg, Ran. *Hiroshima: The Origins of Global Memory Culture.* Cambridge: Cambridge University Press, 2014.

Index

Page numbers in **boldface** type refer to illustrations. The letter t following a page number denotes a table.

About the Author

Hiroko Matsuda is associate professor at Kobe Gakuin University, Japan. She received her doctoral degree from the Australian National University, and her contributions to journals and multiauthor works have been published in English and Japanese. She is coeditor of *Rethinking Postwar Okinawa: Beyond American Occupation* (Lexington Press, 2017).

 **Perspectives on the Global Past**

Anand A. Yang and Kieko Matteson
SERIES EDITORS

Interactions: Transregional Perspectives on World History
Edited by Jerry H. Bentley, Renate Bridenthal, and Anand A. Yang

Contact and Exchange in the Ancient World
Edited by Victor H. Mair

Seascapes: Maritime Histories, Littoral Cultures, and Transoceanic Exchanges
Edited by Jerry H. Bentley, Renate Bridenthal, and Kären Wigen

Anthropology's Global Histories: The Ethnographic Frontier in German New Guinea, 1870–1935
Rainer F. Buschmann

Creating the New Man: From Enlightenment Ideals to Socialist Realities
Yinghong Cheng

Glamour in the Pacific: Cultural Internationalism and Race Politics in the Women's Pan-Pacific
Fiona Paisley

The Qing Opening to the Ocean: Chinese Maritime Policies, 1684–1757
Gang Zhao

Navigating the Spanish Lake: The Pacific in the Iberian World, 1521–1898
Rainer F. Buschmann, Edward R. Slack Jr., and James B. Tueller

Nomads as Agents of Cultural Change: The Mongols and Their Eurasian Predecessors
Edited by Reuven Amitai and Michal Biran

Sea Rovers, Silver, and Samurai: Maritime East Asia in Global History, 1550–1700
Edited by Tonio Andrade and Xing Hang

Exile in Colonial Asia: Kings, Convicts, Commemoration
Edited by Ronit Ricci

Burnt by the Sun: The Koreans of the Russian Far East
Jon K. Chang

Encounters Old and New in World History: Essays Inspired by Jerry H. Bentley
Edited by Alan Karras and Laura J. Mitchell

Shipped but Not Sold: Material Culture and the Social Protocols of Trade during Yemen's Age of Coffee
Nancy Um

At the Edge of the Nation: The Southern Kurils and the Search for Russia's National Identity
Paul B. Richardson

Liminality of the Japanese Empire: Border Crossings from Okinawa to Colonial Taiwan
Hiroko Matsuda